MAINE CLASSICS

MORE THAN 150 DELICIOUS RECIPES FROM DOWN EAST

MARK GAIER & CLARK FRASIER
with RACHEL FORREST

<table>
<tr><td>AUTHORS OF
THE ARROWS COOKBOOK</td><td></td><td>WINNERS OF THE 2010
JAMES BEARD FOUNDATION
BEST CHEFS: NORTHEAST</td></tr>
</table>

RUNNING PRESS
PHILADELPHIA · LONDON

9 8 7 6 5 4 3 2 1
Digit on the right indicates the number of this printing
Library of Congress Control Number: 2010936975
ISBN 978-0-7624-3870-9

Edited by Geoffrey Stone
Cover and interior design by Amanda Richmond
Typography: Chronicle Text, Archive, and Memoir
Prop Styling by Wendy Gamage

Running Press Book Publishers
2300 Chestnut Street
Philadelphia, PA 19103-4371

Visit us on the web!
www.runningpresscooks.com

TO THE TALENTED PEOPLE WHO WORK WITH US
at Arrows, MC Perkins Cove, and Summer Winter,
their hard work and loyalty helped to
make *Maine Classics* possible

TABLE of CONTENTS

ACKNOWLEDGMENTS

IN THE LATE SEVENTIES, A NUMBER OF MARK'S SIBLINGS MOVED TO THE great state of Maine. They were soon calling him in his home town of Piqua, Ohio, extolling the virtues of the place. They regaled him with stories of the vast Victorian house, which they had named the "Heartbreak Hotel" (no doubt because of all the hippies that were having romps there), and of the great sailing and living in the picturesque town of Blue Hill. Mark soon moved to Maine and fell in love with the beauty of the land and sea so unlike the cornfields and factories of his home town.

A few years later, while we were working together in San Francisco, Mark kept telling me about how great Maine was. As a typical "West Coaster" I had only the foggiest, third-grade-geography notion about this far away place. But in time we vacationed there, and like legions before me, I, too, fell in love with this unique place. Soon after that we had packed our bags to move across country to open a restaurant. Eventually that restaurant, Arrows, became known to food lovers around the country, and the rest, as they say, is history.

This book is a culmination of our long love affair with this wonderful rugged land. As with any book, it involved many creative people working together in a concerted effort. Stacey Glick, our agent, must be thanked for having the vision to see what a special book this could be—and for persevering in finding us just the right editor. Without the right editor no book is possible. Therefore, we must thank Geoffrey Stone for consistently and patiently guiding this book to completion. Our co-author, Rachel Forrest, has been a joy to work with. In addition to putting our thoughts into words, she has spent countless hours contacting people, planning meetings, and organizing photo shoots. While writing the book, we have spent many hours together, and now count her as a friend. We must also thank the talented Ron Manville. His evocative photos capture the spirit of Maine; besides that, he's just a great guy.

Mark and I would like to thank all of the many talented people on our staff at Arrows, MC Perkins Cove, and Summer Winter. Our executive chef, Justin Walker, spent many hours ordering food, organizing dishes, and assisting us in testing each recipe. He is a great chef and we count him as a good friend. We would also like to thank our dedicated core staff, including Danielle Johnson Walker, Janice Blanchard, Norman Dufour, and Lee Frank, who all contributed to making this book a reality.

Finally, we would like to thank the many bakers, cheese makers, oyster people, lobstermen and women, fisher folk, butter makers, and countless others who gave their time to make this a great book about a great and unique land.

A note of thanks from Rachel Forrest

WHEN MARK AND CLARK CALLED TO ASK ME TO CO-AUTHOR THEIR NEW book, I swooned. I'd worked with them before in my role as a food journalist, but this was a chance to learn more about the craft of these renowned chefs, how they create great food, and how they work with all of the wonderful ingredients that come from only a few miles away. I did learn about all of that, but we were also able to deepen our friendship, which is the most precious outcome from our year of working on the book. Thank you, Mark and Clark. Thanks also to the team at Arrows and MC Perkins—Justin, Lee, and Danielle.

Thanks also to my editors and mentors at Seacoast Media Group current and past. You all helped teach me how to be a better writer at a newspaper that is dedicated to creating an environment where food journalism is recognized as important and honored. Thanks to the people in the Seacoast of Maine and New Hampshire for reading and supporting my work and helping me to make all of us more aware of the wonderful artisan food producers, fishermen, and farmers who are a part of this book. I'm honored to be able to help tell their stories.

To my parents, Carol Stinnett and David Forrest, thank you for encouraging my writing from the age of five, when I first learned to write a poem. You always told me I could achieve whatever I wanted in life, and I have, with confidence, many times over. To my Stepdad, James Stinnett, thanks for all of your support and help through good and tough times. To Sonia Aviles, my stepmom, thanks for your inspirational cooking and calm. To my daughter, Avalon, thanks for saying, "I love you Mom," every day and for telling me everything I cook is "sooo good." Finally, for my brother, Alex, if you could be here again, I would grill you up a huge steak, well done.

FOREWORD

COMMITMENT AND INNOVATION AREN'T NECESSARILY TERMS THAT go together. One can be committed to something, but not necessarily change with the times or devise anything new; one can be innovative—changing and moving—but not committed to an ideal. But commitment and innovation blend admirably and completely in the character and skills of Clark Frasier and Mark Gaier.

I've known them for a long time—maybe even at the beginning: they probably cooked for me at Stars in San Francisco without me knowing it. I was much lower on the masthead then to be sure, and they were cooking on the line, working hard, honing their talents, refining the techniques and signature style that would eventually define them back east in Ogunquit, Maine. In 1988 they opened what was to become their landmark Arrows restaurant, followed seventeen years later by the energetic MC Perkins Cove with its mesmerizing seaside view, and then on even further into New England.

Theirs is a commitment not only to their own cherished families, but, of course, to their customers—regulars and first-timers alike—and to their amazing staff. They are committed to the extraordinary farmers and food artisans and other suppliers who contribute to their success, and perhaps most importantly, to their community. They know the importance of encouraging local spirit and fostering relationships to help build and maintain their dream. After all, Maine is their home, and their love for and enjoyment of it infuses everything they do. And their commitment also comes to friendship: "Mark and Clark," as they are known, have become family. To my second family, that is the amazing and dedicated staff at Bon Appétit, they have been welcome and valued contributors many times over; to my first and natural family, they have become true friends, and to me personally, thoughtful confidants. We have spent many wonderful evenings together catching up over a good meal and good wines, laughing and connecting in ways that only time around a dinner table can provide.

That their food is always innovative and delicious goes without saying—but I will. There is never a false note, and for the two of them, the process of creating a new dish is rewarding and fun. They still take time to travel the world to discover new flavors, translating each new ingredient, new taste, and new passion to the plate. And now for you, onto the pages of this book.

You're in for a treat. Consider yourselves lucky to have such committed and innovative friends as Clark Frasier and Mark Gaier in your home kitchen. I know that I do.

Barbara Fairchild
former Editor-in-Chief
Bon Appétit Magazine
Los Angeles

INTRODUCTION

A Life in Maine

WHEN WE FIRST CAME TO MAINE AND OPENED ARROWS IN A RUSTIC colonial farmhouse in 1988, we never thought that two dozen years later we'd have two more restaurants, more than just a few awards, and international acclaim for our gardens and our cuisine. We dreamed about it, of course, but it was tough going at first so it all seemed far away. We also never thought we'd finally feel like "Mainers," but we do. Many New Englanders will say we're still "from away," and we can accept that; after all, there have been true Maine families here for centuries. Through getting to know the hard-working people who helped us find the ingredients we needed to start our first restaurant (and who still help us today) and by relying on the old ways and food traditions of Maine to inspire our cuisine, we feel we've become a part of the life and landscape of this beautiful state and of New England. That's why we wrote this book, as an homage to what Maine has given us. In turn, we're eager to share with anyone who loves Maine or wants to learn about cooking with Maine traditions and the foods that come from here, the wisdom from what we've learned in our almost twenty-five years in this wonderful place.

Our three restaurants reflect our connection to New England. At Arrows, we try to cook in the old ways, making all of our dishes from scratch. We use mushrooms foraged in the dark forest near our house and restaurant and cure hams and prosciutto made from pigs raised just a few miles away. We make our own ice cream from milk from nearby dairies and, of course, our garden holds two hundred seventy different kinds of vegetables and herbs. We love to find centuries-old New England recipes and use our own style and the influences from our travels in Southeast Asia and beyond to create something surprising but still familiar. Everything we do at Arrows is taken from that spirit, an echo of the old ways and those artisan food producers who still honor them today.

MC Perkins Cove is in many ways a reflection of that same spirit, but in a much more down-to-earth and straightforward way. Arrows is off the beaten path. It's an elegant experience and more of a destination restaurant, but MC is smack dab in the middle of the tourist area of Ogunquit, on a rocky shore in gorgeous Perkins Cove. It's a real American restaurant and, more than that, a Maine restaurant with a view of the ocean where the lobsters and oysters are caught the same day our guests crack them open and then slurp them with gusto. It's a lively place and we love that vivacious vibe where the lobstermen can feel comfortable having a beer at the end of the day sitting right near a gathering of ladies celebrating a baby shower. The food is still made from scratch, still from our own land and sea, but the feeling is all about celebration.

An hour and a half drive to Burlington, Massachusetts, seems a world away from Maine. Summer Winter at the Marriott Hotel, our latest restaurant, is right in the heart of Boston's "Silicon Valley," and our challenge was to plant the seed of authenticity in a place that is emblematic of ferocious modernism. The first step was to create a real, onsite, working garden complete with a greenhouse and a full-time gardener. A kitchen garden at a hotel off a highway is a fairly novel idea, but we

had to have it to create the restaurant we wanted, one in which food was valued, made from real ingredients, and grown the right way.

Maine is a beautiful place with mountains to ski and climb, wild rivers still pure enough to drink from, where you can still land a brook trout. The forests are home to deer and quail, ancient apple orchards, and wild onions. And, of course, there's our gorgeous coast that vacationers flock to every summer, where artists and writers find inspiration, and from which many Mainers make their living. As we've explored our awe-inspiring home state over the decades, we've come to know that Maine has many facets, and we've seen much of its complex and delightful character through its bountiful natural food resources. When we began to set up our restaurant, we needed to find local breads, eggs, meats, and more. It was tough going. Good ingredients were hard to find. Even buying a bottle of extra virgin olive oil was an ordeal and forget about cured hams. So, we set out to find what we needed in order to be able to make things like prosciutto ourselves. As the years have gone by, more people see the joys and benefits of eating local foods, growing your own vegetables, and supporting the regional food ways. The term "farm-to-table" wasn't around when we first started, but that was just what we did—brought ingredients from our own farm and from nearby farms right to the Arrows table. Now, we can offer so many of the things we learned through the recipes in this book, in simple dishes made from artisanal and local foods.

The seafood and lobster for our restaurants comes from the chilly, rough seas right nearby, brought to us by the people who caught it—often that very day—and we're dedicated to making sure our sea life stays in those waters for eons to come. Much of our cheese and butter comes from local artisan cheese makers who are constantly improving the selection and flavor of cheese made from grass-grazing Maine cows, preserving and evolving an ancient art. Now we have so many wonderful artisan bakers throughout the state, and there's a new breed of home chef who will trek out into the woods to find fiddleheads, morel mushrooms, and ramps each spring.

More Mainers are setting up root cellars to take advantage of their garden's delicious seasonal harvest even in our harsh and long winter months. Gardens abound now, from small patches beside an apartment building to acres of fertile fields near barns and pens of sheep. Our farmers' markets are simply *the* place to be on the weekends. More people every day are taking advantage of Maine's offerings: the blueberries, milk, mushrooms, and apples. We also have maple syrup, stone fruit, honey, and raspberries. Our oysters and lobsters are legendary. We've been so blessed to be a part of helping people find their way back to the old ways, raising their own food, cooking with simplicity. It all reminds us of the way we both grew up, pickling cucumbers in the summer to save for winter, stopping at the ice cream stand on a hot summer day, making applesauce, and braising the family meal using root vegetables right from the garden. It just tastes so much better when it's fresh from the land or sea.

As we've explored Maine, we've also explored its history. We're absolutely fascinated by how connected Maine has been to the world even centuries ago. Foods that became a part of our everyday supper table came from far away, brought to us on clipper ships that went around the world. Mainers in Bath and Brunswick built those far-reaching ships, and the exotic spices and herbs, the curry and ginger they brought back found their way to our tables. When we cook a good old Maine or New England recipe, we can touch history. When we put a forkful in our mouths, we wonder why it has molasses, how hominy is made, which tribe of indigenous people taught the original Mainers to find oysters and cook them in a pit filled with seaweed in the ground. There's always a story. There's always an adventure, a romance, and sometimes tragedy. These stories infuse our cooking and inspire us to explore our own culinary legacies in a place filled with the beauty of mountains, forests, fields, and rocky shores.

The recipes are classically Maine, and the stories here are all about Maine. The ingredients and combinations come from the history and legacy of Maine. They come from the land and the sea of Maine, and from the people who work on that land and sea. But they also come from the Maine inside us, from the place where we learned how to grow our own food and create dishes from what Maine has given us in the past two decades. We're honored to share what we've learned through these recipes—the simple, fresh, honest, and delicious food from our hearts and from our home.

Tips on Using This Book

THROUGHOUT THIS BOOK, WE'LL GIVE YOU IDEAS ON PUTTING TOGETHER a menu, but they're just a guide. We encourage you to pair dishes you might not usually pair. Don't worry, it will all taste great.

We also talk about eating local foods. We mean it. Eating locally grown or sourced foods not only tastes better but helps keep our farms going. It might cost a little more but the more local the food is, the better. After that, if you feel you can afford organic ingredients, we believe there is a health benefit, so go for it.

A few details will help you use this book. When we say black pepper, we mean freshly ground black pepper. Just use a coffee grinder or pepper grinder to have fresh pepper on the table and in the kitchen at all times. Salt means kosher salt. Panko means the light, crisp Japanese panko breadcrumbs. You can get them in the supermarket nowadays. Sriracha should be a staple. It's a terrific condiment and can also be found in the Asian section of the market. If you don't make your own chicken stock, then use organic or low-sodium broth. We always use unsalted butter. Never use light olive oil. We use fresh herbs at all times. Try to use them as much as possible but if you must use dry, use half the amount. Finally, when we say to use a nonreactive pan, we mean to use one that is stainless steel. Aluminum pans will react to acidic foods and will spoil the flavor of the dish.

Chapter One **THE SHORE**

*W*e left coastal California and the lovely Monterey Peninsula twenty-three years ago and drove across the country arriving at another coastal town, Ogunquit, Maine, right in the middle of a dark and bleak winter. As we shivered in the blustery winds coming off the shore, our first thought was, "What the heck have we done?" But as we watched the surf from the town's magical Marginal Way, a mile-long footpath on craggy rocks high above the sea, our second thought was, "We're home." Mark rediscovered and Clark, who grew up on the West Coast, discovered for the first time the beauty of Maine, and we both felt very much at home on this beach by this beautiful, bountiful ocean.

Maine has thirty-five hundred miles of coastline from rocky cliffs to smooth soft sand beaches, all of it breathtaking. Ogunquit itself was a thriving art colony in the late 1800s, and landscape painters like Andrew Wyeth have been capturing Maine's coastal landscape for centuries, but it's the delicious clams, crabs, and oysters that come from right under the sand and right off shore that we love. Take a drive up the coast to see locals with their pant cuffs turned up, digging into the clam flats in summer and fall for a mess of clams for dinner. Nothing surprised us more than when new friends invited us to an old-fashioned clam feed with newspapers on the table, plenty of melted butter, and, of course, plump, sweet clams.

Oysters abound here, too. They are plump and salty from Spinney Creek, silky and sweet from Cape Neddick, or lemony and briny Glidden Point or Pemaquid Oysters from the Damariscotta River, where three thousand years ago oyster shell "middens"—basically a shell dump used by the Wawenock Abenaki Indians—were once over thirty feet high. Now, only a small portion of the Whaleback Shell Midden remains, and by the late 1800s the oyster population was gone. But thanks to a new wave of oyster farmers like Chris Davis at Pemaquid Oyster Company, who re-introduced oysters to the river over twenty years ago, there are now over a dozen local oyster farms using sustainable practices to keep the delicious oysters in our waters and on our plates. We have a long tradition of barbecuing local oysters right on our grill

in front of Arrows to welcome guests, and they look forward to seeing just what oysters we got our hands on to slurp down raw with some simple sauces.

Believe it or not, our delicate and prized peekytoe crabs used to be considered trash by the local lobsterman until the late eighties. The rock or sand crabs became peekytoe in the early nineties when Rod Mitchell, owner of Browne Trading Company, a seafood wholesaler in Portland, decided to market the crab under its commonly used slang name, "peekytoe." The word comes from "picked toe" with "picked" (the slang term for pointed) spoken in two syllables. We don't love picking these crabs—it's a tedious task—but we do love the sweet taste. If you can't get it fresh, forget it. It's very delicate and breaks down fast so keep it on a container of ice. In all the crab recipes here, you don't want to mask the flavor of the crab, but enhance it. Our Maine crab is a real gift, like poppies or wisteria that bloom briefly but beautifully. It's here for a short time, and that's what makes it special.

CHILLED OYSTERS *on the* HALF SHELL

OYSTERS ON THE HALF SHELL ARE A FESTIVE WAY TO START A SPECIAL DINNER
or party. Some New Englanders still buy them by the bushel! We like to serve them right in the kitchen on large iced platters. Our guests stand around the platter slurping up the briny sweetness of our local oysters, a glass of sparkling wine in hand. It's very important to keep oysters cold; room-temperature oysters are not at all pleasant. Here, we've assembled a collection of our favorite sauces for serving with oysters on the half shell. They're simple, vibrant, and offer some tasty variety to any oyster feast. Each of the sauce recipes is enough for twenty-four oysters and you just need to drizzle a bit of the sauce on each opened oyster.

Classic Mignonette

THIS FRENCH CONDIMENT ALWAYS
accompanies oysters at Parisian brasseries like La Coupole, and we serve it at MC Perkins Cove where diners can sample a variety of oysters right by one of the most gorgeous ocean views in Maine. The vinegar adds zip to the briny oysters and using two different kinds of vinegar adds an intriguing complexity to a simple, old-fashioned dish.

YIELD: 1 CUP

$^1/_2$ **cup dry white wine**
$^1/_4$ **cup red wine vinegar**
$^1/_4$ **cup champagne vinegar**
2 tablespoons finely chopped shallots
$^1/_2$ **tablespoon coarse ground black peppercorns**

Combine the ingredients in a bowl and mix lightly. The sauce can be made ahead of time and kept for a few days in the refrigerator if sealed tightly.

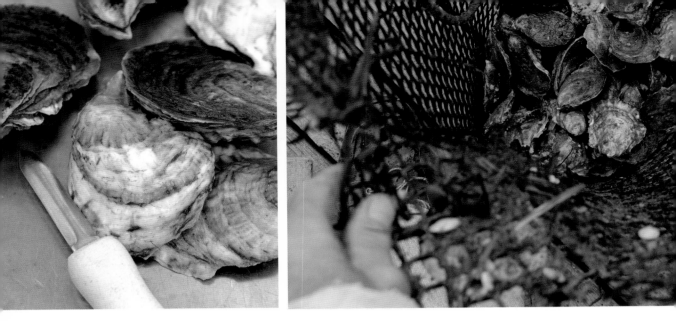

Citrus Vodka Relish with Herbs

AT THE TURN OF THE TWENTIETH CENTURY AND BEFORE THE RUSSIAN REVOLUTION,
all things Russian were fashionable in the culinary world. This relish was inspired by Oysters à la Russe, a dish served on the Titanic and one we like to serve at our annual Titanic dinner at Arrows when we bring the elegant menus from the voyage to life on the table. Guests dress in period clothing and the Moet White Star Champagne flows. Use a citrus vodka for extra zing.

YIELD: 2 CUPS

¹/₂ cup good quality vodka

1 tablespoon red wine vinegar

1 orange, peeled, sectioned, and
  roughly chopped

1 lemon, peeled, sectioned, and
  roughly chopped

1 lime, peeled, sectioned, and
  roughly chopped

1 teaspoon finely chopped chives

1 teaspoon finely chopped chervil

1 teaspoon finely chopped parsley

1 tablespoon finely chopped red onion

1 teaspoon freshly ground black pepper

Combine all the ingredients in a bowl and mix gently. This is best made the day of serving, but it can be made one day in advance if necessary and stored in the refrigerator.

Lemongrass-Chile Dipping Sauce

MOST PEOPLE DON'T THINK OF HOT-AND- *spicy flavors with oysters, but Vietnamese-style dipping sauces transform them into something exotic with a balance of cold and briny, hot and spicy. Having a chilled glass of Champagne or craft beer on hand helps with the heat. For the chile sauce, use the popular Sriracha sauce with the familiar Rooster on the label, now available in most supermarkets.*

YIELD: 1 CUP

2 tablespoons canola or corn oil

3 stalks lemongrass, tough outer layers removed and very finely chopped

1 tablespoon finely chopped shallots

$^1/_4$ cup sugar

$^1/_2$ cup fresh lemon juice

1 serrano chile, finely chopped

1 teaspoon Thai or Vietnamese-style red chile sauce, such as Sriracha

In a small nonreactive saucepan, heat the oil over medium heat until warm and then sauté the lemongrass until soft, 3 to 5 minutes. Add the shallots and cook until soft, 1 to 2 minutes. Add the remaining ingredients and stir to combine. Chill and serve. The sauce can be made up to a week ahead of time and kept covered in the refrigerator.

Herb and Red Wine Sauce

RED WINE WITH OYSTERS? ABSOLUTELY! *In fact, there's nothing like a glass of lightly chilled Pinot Noir with a brace of fresh oysters. Just a little bit of this intense sauce really brings out the briny flavor of oysters.*

YIELD: 1$^1/_2$ CUPS

$^1/_2$ cup medium-bodied red wine, such as a Beaujolais

$^1/_2$ cup red wine vinegar

2 tablespoons finely chopped red onion

1 tablespoon finely chopped fresh tarragon

$^1/_4$ cup sugar

Combine all the ingredients in a small bowl. Mix lightly and chill. This sauce can be made up to three days ahead of time and stored covered in the refrigerator.

Classic Cocktail Sauce

SOME PEOPLE TURN UP THEIR NOSES
at this old-time favorite—and there's no denying cocktail sauce can overwhelm more delicate tasting oysters like West Coast Kumamotos. But with big, meaty, metallic oysters like Bélons or some of the larger Damariscotta oysters from Maine, cocktail sauce is appropriately bold and—well, saucy. Add as much or as little Tabasco or other hot sauce as you like. We know some like it hot!

YIELD: 1¼ CUPS

1 cup ketchup

1 tablespoon fresh lemon juice

2 tablespoons horseradish, preferably freshly grated, but prepared will do

1 teaspoon finely ground black pepper

Tabasco sauce to taste

Combine all the ingredients in a bowl and mix lightly. This sauce can be kept up to a week, tightly sealed, in the refrigerator.

HOW TO OPEN AN OYSTER
(without losing your fingers)

EXPERT OYSTER OPENING BEGINS WITH TWO IMPORTANT ITEMS of equipment, both used before you start sipping your ice cold beer or that glass of Champagne you have waiting for you when the oysters are served. The first is a heavy-duty, sturdy oyster knife. The knife is flat edged and thicker than the common clam knife so it's great for those stubborn, hard shells. The second is a thick, terry cloth kitchen towel to protect your hand. With those two things, you're ready to shuck.

Place the oyster in the cloth towel, draping the towel over your left hand. Completely cover the space between your thumb and index finger. Place the oyster flat top up into that space in your hand to secure the oyster. Take the knife in your right hand and place it at the point of the shell. You'll notice a small indentation and feel it insert. Reverse the procedure if you are left handed.

Twist the oyster knife until the shell pops. Turn the knife so that it runs perpendicular to the oyster and run the knife across the top of the inside of the shell.

It's important to keep the knife away from the meat of the oyster, so keep the knife running inside the top of the shell. Remove the top shell and discard, although some Mainers recycle, using the shells to pave the driveway. Be careful to keep the oyster "liquor" from spilling. At this point, the only thing holding the oyster to the shell is the muscle. Run the knife under that muscle to disengage it. Place the oysters on crushed ice, rock salt, or kosher salt. Sip a cold glass of beer and slurp away.

GRILLED OYSTERS

AT ARROWS IN THE SPRING AND FALL WE LIGHT UP OUR WOOD-FIRED GRILL ON *our front walkway and roast oysters. Our guests really enjoy this, from inhaling the great smells to chatting with the chefs amid the curling smoke. At home, roasting oysters on the grill is a great way to start a party any time of year. Heat reduces and concentrates the oyster liquid and intensifies the flavor. Oysters have a wild, almost "savage" taste that is greatly complemented by the smoke from real wood. The combination of forest and sea is tantalizing, so even if you use a gas grill, be sure to put some wood chips in the smoker tray.*

YIELD: 6 SERVINGS

24 to 36 oysters (4 to 6 per person)
Rock salt

Light the grill, preferably using hardwood lump charcoal, which gets extremely hot. As the coals get going, toss on some hickory or mesquite chips, or some cuttings from fruit trees, such as apple, that have been submerged in water. If using a gas grill, turn it up all the way and use a smoker tray with some hardwood chips. When the fire is quite hot, place the oysters on a grate over the fire. As soon as the oyster shell pops, remove it from the fire. This will take just a few minutes. Using a towel and an oyster knife or screwdriver, open the shell. Place the oyster on a platter of rock salt. Serve at once with either the Spicy Tartar Sauce or Walnut Sauce on page 28. Each sauce makes enough for about two dozen oysters.

Spicy Tartar Sauce

WE LOVE THE BASIC TARTAR SAUCE *served with fish and chips in restaurants all over New England, but this slightly spicy version, made with homemade mayonnaise, is worthy of grilled oysters.*

YIELD: 1¹/₂ CUPS

1 cup mayonnaise (see Herb Mayonnaise, page 49, but omit the herbs)
2 tablespoons finely chopped red onion
¹/₄ cup finely chopped dill pickles
1 teaspoon lemon juice
1 teaspoon Tabasco or Sriracha sauce
Kosher salt and freshly ground black pepper

Combine all the ingredients in a small bowl and mix gently. This sauce will keep in the refrigerator for up to two days.

Walnut Sauce

WALNUT SAUCE IS TRADITIONALLY *served with fried oysters in Turkey, but it's also great with oysters hot off the grill anywhere.*

YIELD: 1¹/₄ CUPS

2 garlic cloves
1 cup toasted walnuts, skins removed
1 tablespoon lemon juice or white wine vinegar
¹/₄ cup olive oil
Kosher salt and freshly ground black pepper

In a food processor, pulse the garlic until finely chopped. Add the walnuts and lemon juice and pulse again. Drizzle in the olive oil and season with salt and pepper to taste. (You can also use a mortar and pestle to mix the ingredients or simply mince them finely with a knife.) This sauce will keep in the refrigerator for up to two weeks.

BROILED OYSTERS *with* SCALLOPS, PANCETTA, *and* BAY LEAVES

THIS COMES FROM AN OLD YANKEE RECIPE WITH PLENTY OF BACON BUT HERE *the bay leaves and pancetta give it a stylish Mediterranean twist. Having scallops and oysters together is a part of a classic shore dinner and echoes the customs of Native Americans centuries ago, but it's also a twist on the traditions of a Maine shore dinner when seafood and meats are cooked together. Tiny bay scallops are great for this dish, but you can use larger sea scallops cut in half. Either way, use the largest oysters you can find.*

YIELD: 6 SERVINGS (12 SKEWERS)

12 bamboo skewers

24 bay scallops, "foot" muscle removed

24 oysters, shucked into a bowl

12 thin slices pancetta

12 bay leaves

2 tablespoons olive oil

Kosher salt and freshly ground black pepper

Preheat the broiler or grill. Assemble the skewers by alternating two scallops and two oysters on each, weaving one strip of pancetta between the seafood and placing the bay leaf in the middle of the sequence. Drizzle the skewers with the olive oil and sprinkle with the salt and pepper to taste. Broil or grill until cooked through, 1 to 2 minutes per side.

POACHED OYSTERS *with* CREAM *and* CHERVIL

THIS SIMPLE DISH, ACCENTED BY DELICATE CHERVIL, IS SO ELEGANT THAT IT'S *hard to believe how easy it is to make. It takes minutes to prepare and makes an impressive opener for a dinner party when you've got other things on your mind than worrying about the first course. The secret is not to overcook the oysters, just warm them slightly.*

YIELD: 6 SERVINGS

1 cup heavy cream
1 tablespoon finely chopped shallots
24 oysters, shucked into a bowl with their liquid
1 teaspoon lemon juice
2 teaspoons finely chopped chervil
Kosher salt and freshly ground black pepper
6 sprigs chervil, for garnish

Combine the cream and shallots in a nonreactive saucepan over medium heat and bring to a gentle boil. Cook the mixture until reduced by one-third, 5 to 8 minutes. Add the oysters, oyster liquid, lemon juice, and chervil. Lower the heat to a simmer and gently poach for 1 minute. Season with salt and pepper to taste. Divide the oysters and cream evenly onto warm plates or bowls. Garnish with chervil sprigs.

BROILED OYSTERS *with* BACON *and* HERBS

THIS DISH WORKS AS A NICE PASSED APPETIZER IF USING SMALL OYSTERS OR AS *a first course with larger, plumper oysters. Two of our favorite food groups—tarragon and bacon— are included here!*

YIELD: 4 TO 6 SERVINGS

24 oysters on the half shell
6 strips bacon, cooked and chopped
1 cup panko breadcrumbs
4 tablespoons unsalted butter, melted
$^1/_4$ cup grated Parmesan cheese
$^1/_2$ tablespoon chopped fresh tarragon
$^1/_2$ tablespoon chopped fresh thyme
Kosher salt and freshly ground black pepper

Preheat the broiler. Arrange the opened oysters in their shells on a cookie sheet. Combine the bacon, breadcrumbs, butter, cheese, tarragon, and thyme in a bowl. Add salt and pepper to taste. Spoon the breadcrumb mixture evenly over the oysters. Broil until golden brown and serve at once.

The oyster sorter separates the oysters by size.

OYSTER FRITTERS *with* REMOULADE

THIS OLD-FASHIONED FRITTER RECIPE DOES NOT REQUIRE A DEEP FRYER. INSTEAD, *a heavy pan is used to make a raised pancakelike fritter. Half the old Yankee recipes you'll read begin with a well-worn cast-iron pan and the other half will open with fritters. Here's one of our favorites from this tradition. Remoulade sauce is a rich and nostalgic pairing for this classic appetizer or main meal. The sauce is a natural accompaniment to fish in general, and we see it in many regional American cuisines from New Orleans to our own Aroostook County. Serve with our Coleslaw with Caraway Seeds (page 213).*

YIELD: 6 SERVINGS

FRITTERS

1 cup vegetable oil

2 cups all-purpose flour

2 teaspoons baking powder

1 teaspoon salt

$1/2$ teaspoon paprika

$1/4$ teaspoon finely ground black pepper

1 cup milk

2 large eggs, lightly beaten

$1 1/2$ cups shucked oysters, drained and roughly chopped

REMOULADE

1 cup mayonnaise (see Herb Mayonnaise, page 49, but omit the herbs)

1 tablespoon chopped red onion

1 tablespoon finely chopped gherkins (cucumbers)

$1/2$ tablespoon whole grain mustard

1 teaspoon Dijon mustard

$1/2$ teaspoon Spanish paprika

$1/4$ teaspoon Tabasco or Sriracha sauce

Kosher salt and freshly ground black pepper

FOR THE FRITTERS: Heat the vegetable oil in a heavy cast-iron or stainless steel skillet until it reaches 350°F on a frying thermometer. Meanwhile, combine the flour, baking powder, salt, paprika, and pepper in a bowl. Combine the milk, eggs, and oysters and add to the dry ingredients; gently mix until just combined. Drop the batter by tablespoons into the hot oil. Turn when the fritter is golden brown on one side and then cook on the other side. Drain on paper towels and serve with the remoulade sauce.

FOR THE REMOULADE: Combine all the ingredients in a bowl. The sauce can be stored, covered, for two days in the refrigerator.

OYSTERS *with* "OYSTER PLANT" SOUP

OYSTER PLANT IS AN OLD NAME FOR SALSIFY, A ROOT VEGETABLE THAT GROWS *well here. It's a bit like a parsnip or a rutabaga. Some say it has a light oysterlike flavor and that's how it got its name. To us it certainly doesn't look or taste like oysters, but it definitely tastes good alongside them. When washing and peeling the salsify, be sure to submerge it at once into the cream-and-milk mixture so it does not discolor.*

YIELD: 6 SERVINGS

24 oysters
1^1/$_2$ cups heavy cream
1^1/$_2$ cups whole milk
3 cups roughly chopped salsify or parsnips
1 tablespoon unsalted butter
^{1}/$_2$ cup finely chopped Spanish onion
^{1}/$_4$ teaspoon ground nutmeg
1 teaspoon lemon juice
Kosher salt and freshly ground black pepper
2 tablespoons chopped chives, for garnish

Shuck the oysters into a bowl with their liquid and set aside in the refrigerator. Mix the cream and milk in a bowl and add the salsify as soon as it is peeled and chopped. Melt the butter over medium heat in a nonreactive saucepan. Sauté the onion in the butter until it is translucent, about 3 minutes. Add the salsify mixture and cook until soft, about 5 minutes. Allow the mixture to cool slightly and then purée in a blender until smooth. Return the mixture to the pot and bring to a simmer. Add the nutmeg, lemon juice, and salt and pepper to taste. Add the oysters to the pot and gently simmer for 1 minute. Divide the soup into six warm bowls. Garnish with the chives and serve.

MAINE'S TASTY OYSTERS

AINE'S WATERS SUPPLY US WITH A WONDERFUL ARRAY OF TASTY oysters, each with its own flavor and texture. In creeks and estuaries from north to south in the state, oyster farms are growing and harvesting some of the best bivalves in the country. Some of the more fertile areas for oysters are Pemaquid, Glidden Point, and Hog Island around the Damariscotta River. In the surrounding finger estuaries, oysters are farmed, growing from "spat" to "seed" in oyster beds throughout the region. It takes over three years for a Maine oyster to mature, and the result is a marvelous flavor and texture. It's in this area that the Glidden Midden, thirty feet high and 150 feet long, shows us a history of Native American aquaculture over two thousand years old. Some of the shells found there are over a foot long.

In these brackish waters you'll find the oyster we call Belon, one that is really the European flat transplanted from the Belon River in France to Boothbay Harbor, Maine, in the 1950s. The oysters became wild and the flavor reflects that wildness. It took thirty years for the oysters to adapt to our harsh waters, but now that they're here, they're considered some of the best in the world. They're not for everyone, though. The flavor is strong, with a marked brininess and a metallic hint that stands up to any sauce.

Damariscotta oysters are a bit more mainstream and come from primarily farmed and harvested waters, although some can be found wild. This is another salty oyster, but with a marvelous, chewy texture. Glidden Point oysters have a deep cup, hard shells, and a great heft to them, as well as a light brine. They grow deep in the cold waters so the shell is dense and hard. Also found in the deep waters are the Pemaquids, firm and chewy with a light flavor but a deep brine. The larger the better for these. Closer to the New Hampshire border are the Spinney Creek oysters: plump, clean, sweet, and salty all at the same time.

CHOOSING AND HANDLING OYSTERS

NOT ALL OYSTERS LOOK OR TASTE ALIKE, BUT THEY ALL NEED TO be fresh and safe to eat. Pick up your favorite oyster. It should feel heavy and dense, like it's very full. It should also be completely shut, not at all popped open or cracked. You might notice a briny smell, but there should never be a strong odor.

By law, oysters must be sold live and you'll know it's live if it is shut tight. If the shell is loose, it's dead, so throw it away. Also throw away any oysters with broken shells.

It's best to eat the oysters within twenty-four hours. Keep the live oysters stored large shell side down in a mesh bag or an open container in the refrigerator, covering the oysters with a damp cloth. Be sure to keep them out of airtight containers or they'll die. When you open oysters, be sure to keep that delicious oyster juice, the "liquor." If shucked and kept in their own liquor, they can be kept in the refrigerator for a few hours. Make sure there's no cloudiness or sour odor. We're not sure why you'd keep them for so long, though, we can hardly wait to get home when we've picked up a brace of Maine oysters.

NEWFANGLED CLAM BOIL
with Sausage, Corn, and Beans

THIS IS OUR TAKE ON ONE OF THE OLDEST NEW ENGLAND DISHES, SUCCOTASH— *which dates back to the Native Americans who planted corn and beans together so the vines of the beans could run up the cornstalks. When harvested, the two were cooked together in a dish they called M'Sickquatash, which means "maize not crushed or ground." To this we have added another dash of history, spicy Portuguese sausage brought to New England by seafaring settlers in southern Massachusetts.*

YIELD: 6 SERVINGS

1 tablespoon olive oil

10 ounces linguiça or other spicy sausage, coarsely chopped

4 pounds littleneck clams, scrubbed well

2 cups fresh corn, cut from the cob

1 cup fresh or frozen lima beans

2 cups chicken or vegetable stock

4 tablespoons ($^1/_2$ stick) unsalted butter

Kosher salt and freshly ground black pepper

In a large sauté pan with a tightly fitting lid, heat the oil over medium heat. Add the chopped sausage and cook until done, 5 to 8 minutes. Add the clams, corn, beans, and stock. Cover and cook over high heat until the clams open, 4 to 5 minutes. Remove the clams with tongs to a platter or individual plates. Add the butter to the vegetables and swirl to combine. Season with salt and pepper to taste. Spoon the vegetable mixture evenly over the clams and serve at once.

STEAMED CLAMS *with* PARSLEY *and* GARLIC

THIS CLASSIC CLAM RECIPE IS SIMPLE AND DELICIOUS, WHICH EXPLAINS ITS *appeal. Clams have such an assertive taste that it would be hard to imagine too much garlic. Sautéing the garlic first adds extra flavor. Serve with crusty bread to sop up the broth.*

YIELD: 6 SERVINGS

1 tablespoon olive oil
2 tablespoons finely slivered garlic cloves
4 pounds littleneck clams, scrubbed well
1 cup dry white wine
1 cup bottled clam juice
Kosher salt and freshly ground black pepper
1 cup Italian parsley leaves, washed and dried

Heat the oil in a large sauté pan that has a tightly fitting lid. Sauté the garlic over medium heat until just slightly golden. Add the clams, wine, and clam juice. Cover and increase the heat to high. Cook until the clams open, 3 to 5 minutes. Season with salt and pepper to taste. With a slotted spoon, transfer the clams to a platter or into six individual bowls. Add the parsley to the broth and spoon the broth over the clams.

CLAMS *with* SHALLOTS, BACON, *and* TARRAGON

NEVERMIND LOBSTER; CLAMS ARE A PRIMARY ATTRACTION IN MAINE. IN THE *summer, Route 1 is lined with busy clam shacks from the New Hampshire border to Canada, and along the shore, clambakes are nightly events. Locals and visitors alike dig for clams from mud flats at low tide. (The amateurs are the ones without tall rubber boots, which protect you from itchy sand fleas!) There are many great clams to be had in Maine, especially tender, nut-brown mahogany clams.*

YIELD: 6 SERVINGS

10 strips bacon, chopped
1 cup thinly sliced shallots
4 pounds clams, scrubbed well
2 cups chicken or vegetable stock
1 tablespoon chopped fresh tarragon
Kosher salt and freshly ground black pepper

Using a large pan with a tightly fitting lid, cook the chopped bacon over medium heat until crispy. Remove the bacon from the pan with a slotted spoon and drain on paper towels. Pour off all but 1 tablespoon of the fat and return the pan to the stove. Cook the shallots in the bacon fat until golden brown. Put the clams, stock, and tarragon in the pan with the shallots. Cover and cook over high heat until the clams are opened, 3 to 5 minutes. Transfer the clams to a platter or six individual bowls. Pour the cooking liquid over the clams evenly.

CLAM CHOWDER *with* THYME

NOTHING SAYS NEW ENGLAND LIKE CLAM CHOWDER, OR "CHOWDAH" AS WE SAY
*here. Every family has its own recipe, and when we think of clam chowder, we think of sitting by the
shore in stormy weather with a bowl of rich, thick comfort food. In one bowl there are ingredients
from the farm, sea, and garden, including bacon, dairy, potatoes, and plenty of fresh herbs.*

YIELD: 6 SERVINGS

5 slices thick bacon (about $^1/_3$ pound), chopped

2 tablespoons extra virgin olive oil

$^1/_4$ cup sliced garlic cloves

1 cup chopped shallots

$1^1/_2$ cups chopped onions

2 cups clam juice

1 tablespoon chopped fresh thyme

1 cup milk

$^1/_4$ cup lemon juice, divided

2 cups peeled and diced potatoes

2 cups cream

2 cups chopped clams, juice reserved

2 teaspoons kosher salt

1 teaspoon freshly ground black pepper

Sauté the bacon in a sauté pan until just crisp. Remove the bacon with a slotted spoon and
set aside. In a medium saucepan heat the olive oil and then sauté the garlic, shallots, and
onions. Add the clam juice and thyme. Add the milk and cook for 10 minutes. Purée the
mixture in a food processor. Add 2 teaspoons of the lemon juice. Return the pureed mixture to the saucepan. Add the potatoes and cook until tender. Add the cream and the clams
and cook on low heat until the clams are done, about 10 minutes. Add the reserved juice
from the chopped clams, the salt, pepper, the remaining 2 tablespoons of lemon juice, and
the bacon and heat through. Divide among six cups or bowls and serve at once.

SCALLOPED CLAMS *with* MAINE POTATOES *and* YAMS

UNTIL THE 1950s MAINE WAS THE LARGEST PRODUCER OF POTATOES IN AMERICA, *and when you taste our potatoes you'll know why. To us, Maine potatoes have a clean, sweet taste that lends itself to all kinds of cooking, and in this dish they don't get lost. We've updated the recipe with yams, which originally come from South America and add a nutty quality and a good color contrast. This easy casserole is a hearty side dish that can easily be translated into a dinner with the addition of a side salad, such as Warm Dandelion Greens Salad (page 209).*

YIELD: 6 SERVINGS

CLAMS AND POTATOES

4 tablespoons unsalted butter

1 cup finely chopped Spanish onion

2 cups milk

1 medium Maine potato, peeled and cut into $^1/_2$-inch dice

1 medium yam, peeled and cut into $^1/_2$-inch dice

$^1/_8$ teaspoon cayenne

2 cups shucked clams

2 tablespoons chopped chives

$^1/_2$ cup grated sharp Cheddar cheese

BREADCRUMB MIXTURE

4 tablespoons unsalted butter

1 cup panko breadcrumbs

$^1/_2$ teaspoon crushed red chili flakes

FOR THE CLAMS AND POTATOES: Preheat the oven to 450°F. Melt the butter in a heavy saucepan. Sauté the onions in the butter until soft and translucent. Add the milk and heat to simmer. Add the potato and yam and cook them slowly until just soft, about 15 minutes. Add the cayenne and the clams and mix well.

FOR THE BREADCRUMB MIXTURE: Melt the butter in a sauté pan over medium heat. Add the breadcrumbs and the red chili flakes. Sauté until golden.

Spoon the potato and clam mixture into a 2-quart casserole. Sprinkle chives on top; then add the cheese and then the breadcrumb mixture. Bake for 15 minutes. Serve at once.

CLAMS *with* CHINESE BLACK BEANS *and* GINGER

WHEN CLARK LIVED IN BEIJING, HE AND HIS FRIENDS USED TO RIDE THEIR BIKES *to a famous old restaurant called the Roast Meat Restaurant. In the winter they had a pot-bellied stove steaming with Shao Xing wine. Shao Xing isn't very well known to Americans, but, like sake, it's made from rice. In China there are many different grades, but here usually the only one available is just good for cooking. Clams have a big briny flavor that goes well with this wine, as does the rich flavor from the Chinese black beans, and we enjoy melding our Asian food experiences with our wonderful Maine ingredients.*

YIELD: 6 SERVINGS

2 cups chicken stock

$^1/_2$ cup beer, like an amber ale

$^1/_4$ cup Shao Xing cooking wine or dry sherry

$1^1/_2$ tablespoons soy sauce

1 tablespoon sherry vinegar

48 littleneck clams

3 tablespoons finely chopped garlic cloves

3 tablespoons finely chopped ginger

2 teaspoons Chinese black beans

1 cup chopped scallions

8 tablespoons (1 stick) unsalted butter, softened

1 cup finely chopped tomato

Kosher salt and freshly ground black pepper

Mix the stock, beer, wine, soy sauce, and vinegar in a large saucepan with a tightly fitting lid. Add the clams and steam over medium-high heat, covered, in the liquid until open, about 5 minutes. Remove the clams from the liquid and place them on a large platter or in a large bowl. Add the garlic, ginger, and black beans to the pan. Bring to a boil over high heat and then add the scallions. Lower the heat to medium and whisk in the softened butter. Add the tomato and the salt and pepper to taste. Increase the heat to high and bring the mixture back to a boil. Place the clams back into the liquid and stir. Portion out clams into individual bowls, eight in each, and divide the liquid over each portion. Serve at once.

FRIED CLAMS *with* BREAD *and* BUTTER PICKLES

PICKLES ARE A BIG PART OF NEW ENGLAND AND MAINE TRADITION BECAUSE *cucumbers in the summer are so abundant they really need to get used up. Having brightly flavored cucumbers in the winter is a crisp reminder of summer's bounty. The sweet and sour of these pickles offset the rich fattiness of the fried clams. Serve with our Spicy Tartar Sauce (page 28) or Hot Sauce (page 51) and a bit of bread and butter pickles on the side.*

YIELD: 6 SERVINGS

FRIED CLAMS

3 cups canola oil, for frying

36 shucked clams

2 cups cornmeal

BREAD AND BUTTER PICKLES

2 cups Champagne vinegar

1 teaspoon fennel seed

$^1/_2$ cup sliced onions

2 garlic cloves, cut in half

$^1/_2$ teaspoon Coleman's mustard powder

$^1/_2$ teaspoon turmeric

1 cup sugar

2 tablespoons kosher salt

4 cups sliced cucumbers, in $^1/_4$-inch slices

FOR THE FRIED CLAMS: Heat the oil in a deep fryer or deep pan to 350°F. Toss the clams in the cornmeal and rub the cornmeal into the clams until a light crust forms. Immerse the clams into the oil, six at a time, and remove with a slotted spoon or basket strainer. Drain on a paper towel.

FOR THE BREAD AND BUTTER PICKLES: Combine the vinegar, fennel, onions, garlic, mustard, tumeric, sugar, and salt in a large nonreactive pot over the stove and bring to a boil over high heat. Place the cucumbers in a bowl. Pour the hot mixture over the cucumbers and allow to cool to room temperature. The pickles can be jarred or placed in a sealed container in the refrigerator for up to three days.

CLASSIC MAINE STEAMERS
with DRAWN BUTTER

IN LOBSTER POUNDS ALL OVER MAINE, STEAMERS ARE EVERYONE'S OPPORTUNITY *to roll up their sleeves and dig in. Eating with gusto is encouraged. Have these with crusty garlic bread or our Bread Sticks (page 262). The cornmeal removes any grit.*

YIELD: 6 SERVINGS

3 pounds clams
$^{1}/_{4}$ cup cornmeal
$^{1}/_{2}$ pound (2 sticks) unsalted butter, melted

To clean the clams, place them in 1 gallon of water with the cornmeal and soak overnight. Pick the clams out of the liquid. Rinse off the cornmeal and place the clams in a pot with 1 cup water. Cover and cook the clams on medium to high heat for 2 to 3 minutes past the point at which they open. Remove the clams from the water and reserve the cooking liquid to wash and clean each clam before dipping into the melted butter.

CRAB CAKES *with* HERB MAYONNAISE

CRAB CAKES ARE ONE OF THOSE THINGS THAT ARE EITHER LIGHT AND ETHEREAL *and you love them, or they turn into lead balls you absolutely hate. We've been serving this version— our secret recipe—in our restaurants for over twenty years, and it's always a hit. Use whatever herbs you like in the mayonnaise—our favorite is tarragon.*

YIELD: 6 (ONE-CAKE SERVINGS)

CRAB CAKES

12 ounces peekytoe crabmeat, picked and checked for shells

$1^1/_2$ tablespoons lemon juice

$1^1/_2$ cups sour cream

5 tablespoons all-purpose flour, divided

6 tablespoons unsalted butter

$1/_4$ cup finely chopped Spanish onion

$1^1/_2$ cups panko breadcrumbs

2 teaspoons kosher salt

3 tablespoons canola oil

HERB MAYONNAISE

5 large egg yolks

Juice from one lemon, about 3 tablespoons

$3/_4$ cup olive oil

$1/_4$ cup extra virgin olive oil

Kosher salt and freshly ground black pepper

$1/_4$ cup finely chopped fresh herbs, such as chives, cilantro, dill, chervil, tarragon

FOR THE CRAB CAKES: Mix the crabmeat, lemon juice, sour cream, and 3 tablespoons of the flour in a bowl. Melt the butter in a sauté pan over medium heat. Sauté the onions in the butter until soft. Add the breadcrumbs and salt and sauté until golden. Remove the onion and breadcrumb mixture from the sauté pan and cool on a cookie sheet. Stir into the crab mixture. Form into cakes. Dredge the cakes in the remaining 2 tablespoons of flour. Heat the canola oil in a large skillet over medium-high heat. Fry the crab cakes until golden brown, about $1^1/_2$ minutes on each side.

FOR THE HERB MAYONNAISE: Combine the egg yolks and lemon juice in the bowl of a food processor fitted with a metal blade. Process the mixture for 20 seconds. With the machine running, add both of the olive oils, drop by drop, and then slowly increase to a steady stream as the eggs and oil become emulsified. If the mixture gets very thick, thin it with a tea-spoon of ice water. The consistency should be a little thinner than store-bought mayonnaise. Season with salt and pepper to taste and then add the herbs, mixing the mayonnaise briefly once again. Store in a tightly sealed container in the refrigerator for up to a day.

CRAB SALAD *with* GARDEN GREENS

ON A HOT SUMMER DAY WHEN THE GARDEN IS FILLED WITH A PLETHORA OF *greens and you don't want to be laboring over a hot stove, this makes an elegant luncheon salad or summer dinner. Adjust the amounts to make more for a heartier dinner. The crabmeat must be super fresh, which you can tell by its lack of odor except for a light, briny aroma. In no way should it be strong smelling or slimy. If it is, don't bother. Keep the crab fresh in a bowl of ice while you assemble the ingredients. We like our garden greens for this salad just plain and simple, but feel free to toss them with a light vinaigrette or just a squeeze of lemon.*

YIELD: 6 SERVINGS

12 ounces crabmeat

2 teaspoons coarse-grain mustard

$^1/_3$ cup mayonnaise (see Herb Mayonnaise,
   page 000, but omit the herbs)

2 tablespoons sour cream

1 teaspoon sweet paprika

1 tablespoon finely chopped Spanish onion

1 teaspoon chopped garlic cloves

$^1/_2$ teaspoon kosher salt

$^1/_3$ cup chopped celery

6 cups greens

Combine the crabmeat, celery, mustard, mayonnaise, sour cream, paprika, onion, garlic, salt, and celery in a bowl and mix well. Divide the greens among six plates and place a mound of the crab mixture on the greens. Serve at once.

CRAB FRITTERS *with* HOT SAUCE

FRITTERS—OR SPOON CAKES, SIZZLERS, JOLLY BOYS, HOLY POKES, HUFF JUFFS, *whatever you call them—are Maine favorites, and Mainers use many varieties of seafood and vegetables to make savory versions of these fried treats. Our recipe is a more luxe version of the Maine classic, and the hot sauce is a good contrast to the creamy crab and dough. The egg whites make them oh so fluffy.*

YIELD: 12 FRITTERS (2 PER PERSON)

FRITTERS

1^1/$_2$ cups cornmeal

1^1/$_3$ cups all-purpose flour

1 teaspoon sugar

1 teaspoon kosher salt

1 teaspoon freshly ground black pepper

5 large eggs, separated

1 cup milk

4 tablespoons (^{1}/$_2$ stick) unsalted butter, melted

^{1}/$_3$ cup sour cream

^{1}/$_3$ cup finely chopped Spanish onion

12 ounces crabmeat, cleaned and picked

1 cup canola oil

HOT SAUCE

1 cup sugar

1 tablespoon chile flakes

1 tablespoon sweet paprika

1 cup sliced onion

4 garlic cloves, sliced

2 tablespoons salt

1 teaspoon cumin seed

1 cup red wine vinegar

^{1}/$_2$ cup Worcestershire sauce

FOR THE FRITTERS: Mix the cornmeal, flour, sugar, salt, and pepper in a large bowl. In a separate bowl whip the egg whites until just stiff. Lightly beat the egg yolks in a medium bowl. Stir in the milk, butter, and sour cream, and then pour into the dry ingredients. Add the onion and the crabmeat and stir to combine. Gently fold in the whipped egg whites. Heat the canola oil in a heavy cast-iron or stainless steel pot until it reaches 350°F on a frying thermometer. Drop the tablespoons of the batter into the hot oil. Turn when the fritter is golden brown on one side, about 2 minutes and then cook on the other side for about 2 more minutes. Drain on paper towels and serve with the hot sauce on the side.

   FOR THE HOT SAUCE: Combine all of the ingredients in a heavy saucepan over medium heat and cook until reduced by half and slightly syrupy. Let the syrup cool to room temperature and purée in a blender.

BOILED CRAB *with* DRAWN BUTTER

THERE'S A GREAT DEBATE ABOUT WHAT DRAWN BUTTER REALLY IS—IS IT JUST *melted butter or is it clarified butter—separated butter with the solids removed? We prefer to use clarified butter and call it drawn so that's where the debate ends for us.*

YIELD: 6 SERVINGS

1 gallon water
2 tablespoons salt
6 (1-pound) crabs, such as blue stone, sand, or peekytoe
$^1/_2$ pound (2 sticks) unsalted butter

Bring the water and the salt to a boil in a large pot. Add the crabs and boil them until bright pink, 10 to 15 minutes. Remove the crabs from the pot with long tongs or a slotted spoon.

For the drawn butter, melt the butter in a double boiler over low heat and cook for 10 minutes. Pour the butter through a fine sieve, discarding the white part.

Crack the crabs with a mallet and pull off the top shell. Twist off the claws and tap gently with a mallet to crack the claws. Remove the meat with picks. Break the body into sections and pull out the meat with your fingers or a pick. Serve the crab at once with the drawn butter.

SNUG HARBOR STYLE CRAB

IN THE 1980S WHEN MARK WORKED AT THE WHISTLING OYSTER, A FAMOUS OLD *tea house from the turn of the century in Perkins Cove, he was always looking for ways to update this old Yankee standby. This is our favorite of all his renditions, and the real secret is no secret at all— using the best, freshest ingredients. The original dish can easily turn into something less than appetizing, but our version is not only tasty but looks enticing too.*

YIELD: 6 SERVINGS
CRABMEAT

8 tablespoons (1 stick) unsalted butter

$1/2$ cup sliced scallions

2 cups sliced mushrooms

2 cups peeled and sliced celery

$1/2$ cup all-purpose flour

$1^1/2$ quarts (6 cups) cream

1 teaspoon Worcestershire sauce

1 teaspoon sherry vinegar

$1^1/2$ tablespoons diced pimento

$1^3/4$ teaspoons kosher salt

$1/8$ teaspoon freshly ground black pepper

3 cups crabmeat, cleaned and picked

BREADCRUMB TOPPING

8 tablespoons (1 stick) unsalted butter

$1/2$ teaspoon salt

1 cup panko breadcrumbs

FOR THE CRABMEAT: Preheat the oven to 350°F. Melt the stick of butter in a heavy saucepan over medium heat, and add the scallions, mushrooms, and celery. Add the flour and cook for 3 minutes, stirring constantly. Slowly add the cream, stirring constantly, and reduce the heat. Add the Worcestershire sauce, sherry vinegar, pimento, salt, and pepper. Simmer, stirring slowly for 20 minutes, until thickened. Let the mixture cool to room temperature.

FOR THE BREADCRUMB TOPPING: Melt the butter in a sauté pan over medium heat. Add the salt and stir well. Add the breadcrumbs and cook until lightly golden. Layer the ingredients in six (8-ounce) ramekins starting with the cream mixture, then about 2 ounces of crab, another layer of the cream mixture, 2 more ounces of crab, and 2 more ounces of cream mixture. Top with 2 ounces of the breadcrumb mixture. Bake until bubbling, about 20 minutes.

CRAB CHOWDER *with* CORN AND CELERY

CLAM CHOWDER'S RICHER AND SNOBBIER OLDER SISTER, THIS CRAB CHOWDER *is bright with fresh herbs mingled with the delicate crabmeat. The herbs lighten the dish, and we like to keep that theme going by serving this with our "Everything in the Garden" Salad (page 211) and Caraway Bread (page 263).*

YIELD: 6 SERVINGS

6 ears of corn

2 quarts (8 cups) heavy cream

8 tablespoons (1 stick) unsalted butter

$1^{1}/_{2}$ cups chopped Spanish onion

1 cup chopped celery

3 teaspoons kosher salt, divided

1 teaspoon chopped fresh thyme

1 tablespoon chopped fresh tarragon

2 tablespoons chopped fresh chervil

$^{1}/_{4}$ cup plus 2 tablespoons chopped chives, divided

3 tablespoon lemon juice

16 ounces crabmeat, cleaned and picked

$^{1}/_{4}$ cup chopped tomato, for garnish

Cut the kernels off the corn cobs (about 4 cups corn kernels) and set aside. Pour the cream into a heavy saucepan over medium heat. Place the cobs into the cream and simmer until reduced by one-fourth, about 30 minutes. Remove the cobs and add the corn kernels. Cook for 4 minutes.

Melt the butter in a small skillet over medium heat. Add the onions, celery, and 1 teaspoon of the salt and sauté until the onions are translucent, about 5 minutes. Add to the corn and cream. Cook for 1 minute. Add the thyme, tarragon, chervil, and 2 tablespoons of the chives and cook for 5 minutes. Add the lemon juice and the remaining 2 teaspoons of salt.

Place half the crab in the soup and divide the remaining crab among six bowls. Divide the chowder among the six bowls, pouring it over the crab with a ladle. Garnish with the remaining $^{1}/_{4}$ cup of chives and the chopped tomato.

CRAB PARFAIT

EVEN THE MOST STAUNCH "LOCAVORE" HAS TO THROW SOMETHING FROM OUTSIDE *his or her own state into a dish. So, we've layered some of our favorite Mexican ingredients, from our own homegrown cilantro to ripe avocado, into this festive "parfait." This is a knockout, show-stopping dish to serve at lunch, brunch, and special occasions.*

YIELD: 6 SERVINGS

$^3/_4$ cup extra virgin olive oil

$^1/_4$ cup lime juice

3 tablespoons chopped cilantro

1$^1/_2$ cups chopped tomato

10 ounces crab, cleaned and picked

1$^1/_2$ cups shredded lettuce

$^3/_4$ cup diced ripe avocado

1 cup chopped scallions

6 whole romaine lettuce leaves from the heart, for garnish

Make a dressing by whisking together the olive oil, lime juice, and cilantro in a small bowl. Divide the remaining ingredients among six Champagne flutes or other tall glasses. Layer some tomato, crab, lettuce, avocado, and scallion. Halfway through filling, pour half of the dressing over the ingredients equally among the glasses. Continue to layer the ingredients until the crab is on top. Top with the rest of the dressing and garnish with romaine lettuce leaves placed into the glass.

THE OYSTER FARMER

HE'S DESIGNED BARGES AND BOATS AS A MARINE ARCHITECT, but Dr. Chris Davis' heart belongs to what's under the water—fresh oysters. Traversing the chilly waters of the Damariscotta River, where one of the oldest oyster shell middens still towers on the bank, Chris brings hundreds of thousands of sweet, briny oysters to maturity each year through Pemaquid Oyster Company. The company sells oysters to over thirty restaurants in Maine, and many are in large cities throughout the U.S. and Canada. Chris, who got his PhD in marine biology, studying ways to breed oysters faster in the cold Maine waters, founded the company in 1995 with Colby College alumni Carter Newell and Jeff McKeen, as well as three other partners.

He raises the oysters from the size of grains of sand until they are big enough for us to slurp down with hot sauce and a cold glass of beer. The oysters are raised near the dock in Damariscotta village in long vessels that can circulate the water among the developing young until they are about a half-inch in size. Then they are moved to mesh bags, one thousand oysters in each, where they can mature during the summer. In late fall, when the oysters are about an inch long, they are moved to the bottom of the river where they attach and hibernate for a year on the company's licensed ten acres of "bottom." The following September, after a span of about two and a half years they are plump ready to eat.

About fifteen thousand of those oysters go to the Pemaquid Oyster Festival, which the partners founded in 2001. The proceeds went to firefighters working in New York after 9/11. In 2003, they founded the Ed Myers Marine Conservation Fund, benefiting science education in Maine schools. The festival is now the main fundraiser for the fund, named after Edward Myers, a Walpole resident who pioneered aquaculture in the Damariscotta River. The money is used to continue his vision of having a sustainable working waterfront as well as protecting the marine environment.

Chris is also the Executive Director of the Maine Aquaculture and Innovation Center, which promotes applied aquaculture research and assists in the formulation of policies that help to benefit the industry, helping Chris and his company grow those sweet juicy oysters for Mainers and those from away to enjoy.

Chapter 2 **THE SEA**

*I*n our travels we've met people who didn't know the state of Maine, but they sure knew Maine lobster. We dined at San Domenico, one of Italy's most celebrated restaurants, a few years ago, and the first course, to our amusement, was Maine lobster. Our lobster is served in the waterside restaurants in Hong Kong and on the plates in front of Arab sheiks dining in Dubai. It's one of the world's great luxury foods, but all we have to do is go down to the harbor to get it. Over the years one of the greatest pleasures in our lives has been getting to know the hard-working people who have made Maine culture world famous. The lobstermen and women are a part of the American heritage, part of its mythology, and a big part of what makes America great.

Getting to know Maine has come hand in hand with getting to know these people, like our lobsterman Ted Johnson. We've been out on his boat many times and nothing beats that experience. But for Ted and all the lobstermen and women, it's not an easy job. The weather is freezing cold, there are territorial wars, and they're out there all alone. It's a tough job, and we're privileged to be able to get to know them at home, to share a meal at their own tables.

In both of our Maine restaurants, it's the real guy just off the boat who comes by and brings in a load of flapping lobsters. Steam billows off their cold shells as they come from the chilly sea into our toasty kitchen. It's a joyful thing and makes us feel extremely connected. It makes us want to cook even more. MC Perkins Cove is literally a stone's throw from the lobster boats, and our lobstermen stop off for a "little pop" after a hard day before we start service. We're happy to be able to provide a place for them to relax.

Of course, there's much more in our seas than lobster. Gems like the Maine shrimp—here for a brief visit each year in winter—are some of the delights we get every day from just off the dock. Fish such as haddock and cod are being regulated in terms of how they are caught, and we support that local fisherman who goes out and casts a line rather than dragging a net across the sea floor. For all of our restaurants we work with our purveyors and with the state, along with groups like the Maine Lobster Council, The Monterey Bay Aquarium, and The Smithsonian Institution to ensure the future of Maine's fish and lobster.

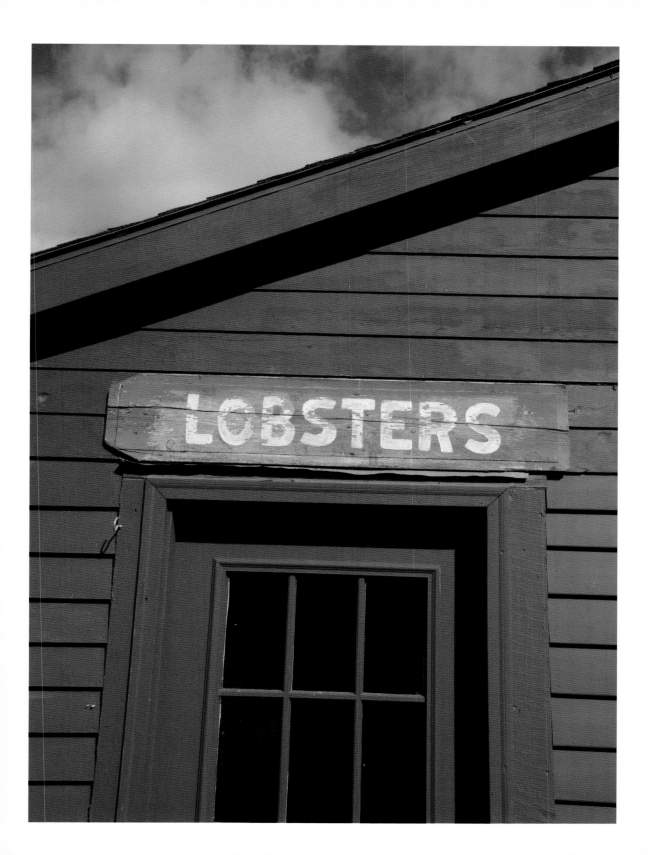

CLASSIC LOBSTER ROLLS

WHEN MAKING A TRUE MAINE LOBSTER ROLL, CERTAIN CRITERIA NEED TO BE
met. The bun must be a "top-loader," buttered and grilled, and there must be enough mayonnaise to coat the lobster liberally. In our opinion, most people just don't add enough mayo. Travel up and down the coast of New England and you'll encounter many versions. In fact one of our favorites is not served in Maine at all, but in New York City at Rebecca Charles' Pearl Oyster Bar. In our version we like to use a lemon mayo and sprinkle plenty of fresh herbs from the garden on top. Serve these with a pickle and French fries.

YIELD: 6 SERVINGS

$^1/_2$ gallon water

$^1/_4$ cup kosher salt

4 live lobsters (about $1^1/_4$ pounds each)

$1^1/_2$ cups mayonnaise (see Herb Mayonnaise, page 49, but omit the herbs)

3 tablespoons lemon juice

6 top-loading hot dog buns

3 tablespoons unsalted butter

$^1/_4$ cup finely chopped fresh tarragon

$^1/_4$ cup finely chopped fresh parsley

$^1/_4$ cup finely chopped fresh chervil

$^1/_4$ cup finely chopped fresh chives

To prepare the lobsters, fill a large heavy pot or standard clam steamer pot with the water and the kosher salt. Set over high heat and bring to a boil. Place the lobsters in the pot and cover tightly. Boil for 14 minutes. Remove the pot from the heat and carefully pour the lobsters and the water into a deep sink or colander. Cover with ice for about 10 minutes. Take the meat out of the shell (see How to Eat a Lobster, page 83).

Cut the lobster meat and place in a bowl. Toss with the mayonnaise and lemon juice. Slather the outside of the rolls with the butter and quickly grill on both sides either in a skillet or on an outdoor grill. Fill the grilled rolls with the lobster salad. Combine the herbs, mix well, and sprinkle over the salad. Serve immediately.

BOILED LOBSTER *with* DRAWN BUTTER

SOMETIMES THE SIMPLEST THINGS ARE THE BEST, SO WHAT MORE CAN WE SAY?
Serve this with our Coleslaw with Caraway Seeds (page 213) and another Maine classic, well, a classic everywhere, Deviled Eggs (page 188).

YIELD: 6 SERVINGS

$1/2$ gallon water
$1/4$ cup kosher salt
6 ($1^1/4$-pound) lobsters
$1/2$ pound (2 sticks) butter
6 lemon wedges

Fill a large heavy pot or standard clam steamer pot with the water and the kosher salt. Set over high heat and bring to a boil. Place the lobsters in the pot and cover tightly. Boil for 14 minutes. Remove the pot from the heat and carefully pour the lobsters and the water into a deep sink or colander.

FOR DRAWN OR CLARIFIED BUTTER: Cut the butter into cubes. Slowly heat the butter in a small saucepan until the butter is completely melted and the solids have foamed to the top, about 10 minutes. Remove from the heat. Skim the foam from the top of the clear golden liquid underneath or pour through a fine sieve until you reach the white solids. Discard the solids. Let cool. Use the clarified butter as a dip for the lobsters. Serve with lemon wedges.

LOBSTER BISQUE

ALTHOUGH BISQUE USUALLY IMPLIES A SMOOTH CREAMY SOUP WE LIKE TO LEAVE *some potatoes and onions in the soup to give it a bit more texture. You will find that this bisque certainly is creamy and smooth with some surprising contrasts.*

YIELD: 6 SERVINGS

3 ($1^1/_4$-pound) lobsters
$^1/_2$ pound (2 sticks) butter
$^1/_2$ cup finely chopped Spanish onion
$^1/_4$ cup all-purpose flour
1 quart (4 cups) whole milk
4 cups diced potatoes (about $1^1/_4$ pounds)
2 cups clam juice or lobster stock
1 quart (4 cups) heavy cream
$^1/_2$ cup mixed herbs (such as chives, tarragon, thyme)
$^1/_4$ cup fresh lemon juice (about 3 lemons)
Kosher salt

Cook and pick the lobsters and reserve the lobster meat and shells. In a large nonreactive saucepan melt the butter over medium heat. Add the onions and sauté until soft. Stir in the flour and cook slowly for 5 more minutes, stirring constantly. Heat the milk in a saucepan over medium heat until just hot and then add the hot milk slowly to the onion and butter mixture. Cook over medium to low heat for about 15 minutes, or until it begins to thicken. Add the potatoes and the clam juice and keep at a simmer until the potatoes are done.

In another nonreactive pan combine the lobster shells and the heavy cream. Bring to a simmer and reduce the heat. Simmer for 15 minutes. Strain the cream from the shells and discard the shells. Set aside.

Chop the lobster meat by slicing the tails and claws, leaving the knuckle meat whole. Chop the herbs. Add the lobster cream to the potato and milk mixture. Keep at a low simmer and add the lobster meat, the herbs, lemon juice, and salt to taste. Serve in six warm bowls.

LOBSTER STEW
with BELL PEPPERS *and* CORN

WHEN CORN WAS FIRST PLANTED AT ARROWS, CLARK AND EXECUTIVE CHEF, *Justin Walker, were out in the garden looking at the tops of the stalks one day and saw no corn cobs. By that time of the season there should have been plenty, and they were concerned they weren't going to get any corn. Growing up in Ohio—which is corn country—I came out and said, "Are you two out of your minds? The corn comes from the sides of the stalk!" I got a good laugh out of their gaff, and after they looked where they were supposed to, they saw that we did indeed have plenty of corn. You don't get corn in Maine until almost September—there's no "knee high by the Fourth of July" here—so the wait seems endless. When it does come in, it's just great. Things taste so much better when eaten in season and locally because you're craving them. This dish takes advantage of a few of our local gems and its colors show off the season. Cook your own lobster or make it easy on yourself and buy freshly cooked and picked meat.*

YIELD 6 SERVINGS

6 ears fresh corn

1/2 pound (2 sticks) unsalted butter

1 cup chopped Spanish onion

1/4 cup all-purpose flour

4 cups milk

1 small yellow bell pepper, seeded and diced (about 1 cup)

1 small red bell pepper, seeded and diced (about 1 cup)

2 cups half-and-half

1 teaspoon kosher salt

2 cups chopped lobster meat

2 tablespoons chopped fresh chives

Freshly ground black pepper

Shuck the corn, clean it of silk, and then remove the kernels (about 4 cups) with a sharp knife. Melt the butter in a saucepan over medium heat and sauté the onion in the butter until soft. Add the flour and cook for 5 minutes, stirring occasionally until it becomes a light tan color. Warm the milk in another saucepan and whisk into the flour mixture. Slowly bring the mixture to a boil. Turn down the heat and simmer for 5 minutes. Add the corn, 1/2 cup of the yellow bell pepper, and 1/2 cup of the red bell pepper. Stir in the half-and-half and simmer until the corn is soft. Add the salt and cook until thick, about 10 minutes. Add the lobster meat and the remaining red pepper. Serve in large bowls. Garnish with the remaining yellow pepper and the chopped chives. Season with black pepper to taste.

LOBSTER SHORTCAKE
with RUM VANILLA SAUCE

FOR MANY YEARS THIS HAS BEEN A SIGNATURE DISH THAT WE OFTEN TAKE ON THE *road to events and TV shows. It brings together many of the traditions of the seafaring Mainers of old, involving the Triangle Trade when New England ports would send rum produced here to Africa to trade for slaves. The slaves would be sold in the West Indies for sugar and molasses, which would complete the circle—the sugar and molasses came right back to New England to make—you guessed it— more rum. One of the by-products of this triangle was an infusion of some of the more exotic ingredients we now find here. In this recipe we also hearken back to Maine's bustling spice trade, which brought even more flavors from exotic lands to our plain Yankee cooking. This dish can be an elegant way to start a lavish dinner, as we like to do, or it can be a main dish with our Celery Root Salad (page 201).*

YIELD: 6 SERVINGS

SHORTCAKE

1^1/$_2$ cups all-purpose flour

1^1/$_2$ teaspoons baking powder

^{1}/$_2$ teaspoon baking soda

1 teaspoon salt

12 tablespoons (1^1/$_2$ sticks) very cold butter, cubed

^{3}/$_4$ to 1 cup buttermilk

^{1}/$_4$ cup heavy cream

LIME VANILLA RUM SAUCE

^{1}/$_2$ cup lime juice

^{1}/$_2$ cup rice wine vinegar

^{1}/$_4$ cup dark rum

1 serrano chile, seeded and finely chopped

^{1}/$_2$ vanilla bean, split lengthwise

^{1}/$_4$ cup finely chopped shallots

1 tablespoon finely sliced fresh ginger

^{1}/$_2$ pound (2 sticks) unsalted butter, softened

Kosher salt and freshly ground black pepper

CURRIED SHALLOTS

8 shallots, peeled and thinly sliced

1 teaspoon finely chopped fresh ginger

1 serrano chile, seeded and finely chopped

1 teaspoon turmeric

1 tablespoon Madras curry powder

1 teaspoon kosher salt

1 cup rice wine vinegar

LOBSTER

3 (1^1/$_4$-pound) lobsters, boiled and meat removed

^{1}/$_2$ pound (1 stick) butter

FOR THE SHORTCAKE: Preheat the oven to 325°F. Combine the dry ingredients in a bowl. Cut the butter into the dry ingredients. Add the buttermilk, a bit at a time, until a soft dough holds together. Roll the dough to a $\frac{1}{2}$-inch thickness and cut with a 3-inch round cutter. Make 12 cakes. Brush with cream and bake until lightly brown, about 15 minutes. Cool on a rack.

FOR THE LIME VANILLA RUM SAUCE: Combine the lime juice, vinegar, rum, chile, vanilla bean, shallots, and ginger in a saucepan. Cook on medium heat until reduced by two-thirds. Reduce the heat to low and whisk in the softened butter. Season with salt and pepper to taste. Strain through a fine sieve and discard solid ingredients. The sauce can be held in a warm place for up to 1 hour.

FOR THE CURRIED SHALLOTS: Place all the ingredients in a stainless steel pot and bring to a boil. Turn off the heat and cool. These can be made a day ahead and kept in the refrigerator.

FOR THE LOBSTER: Split each lobster tail in half. Melt the butter over medium heat. Add the lobster and heat gently until the lobster is warmed through, 3 to 4 minutes.

To assemble the dish: Spoon half of the sauce evenly onto six warm plates. Split each shortcake and place the bottom half on each plate. Top each shortcake with one-half of a tail, a claw, and knuckle meat. Top with the remaining sauce and then with the top of the shortcake. Divide the curried shallots among the plates.

THE SUSTAINABLE LOBSTER

WE ALL KNOW THAT MAINE IS FAMOUS FOR LOBSTERS, AND WE'D like to keep it that way. To keep our lobsters populating the frigid Atlantic Ocean, Maine regulates how lobsters are caught and kept. You won't see one of those twenty-five pounders in a restaurant in Maine; our lobstermen are required to throw them back.

Regulations vary in the Atlantic states, but in Maine any lobster under $3\frac{1}{4}$ inches, a "short," gets thrown back into the water as well as those over five inches. In addition, "scrubs," female lobsters with eggs attached under the tail, are clipped or notched in the flipper so that they are identified and thrown back as well.

Lobsters can only be legally caught in lobster traps, or "pots," to discourage trawling. There's an eight-hundred-pot limit to each inshore license to prevent over-fishing, and lobstermen pull in up to four hundred pots a day and only between sunrise and sunset.

Lobstermen must also have distinctly marked buoys so that they can tell whose pots are whose down below, and these patterns and markings are displayed on the lobster boat as well. Hauling up anyone else's pot is against the law, and there are territorial disputes between lobstermen that self-regulate this too.

It's hard work hauling up those large, heavy lobster pots in cold, often rough seas. They work every day of the year, but Maine is the largest supplier of lobsters in the country and it's an important part of our economy. All of that hard work pays off in sweet, tender lobster, so when you crack open a steamy lobster tail, give it a squeeze of lemon, dip it into hot butter, and raise a glass to our lobstermen who are out there bringing them all in and following the laws so our lobsters keep on coming.

LOBSTER *in a* "PAPER BAG" *with* GREEN CURRY

THIS DISH COMES FROM OUR TRAVELS IN SOUTHEAST ASIA. USING A REALLY FRESH *green curry and hints of lime and coconut with Maine's fresh shellfish was a no-brainer for us. Heating the ingredients in paper is a gentle way to cook, and you can make it ahead of time and then bake them at the last minute. For a dramatic effect at a dinner party, open the paper bags at the table, serving the sauce on the side. Your guests will gasp when the steam is released, bringing the aroma of lobster and spices to the room.*

YIELD: 6 SERVINGS

GREEN CURRY SAUCE

1 cup cilantro leaves, washed and picked

$^1/_2$ cup basil leaves, washed and picked

$^1/_4$ cup parsley, washed and picked

$^1/_2$ tablespoon peeled and finely chopped fresh ginger

3 shallots, peeled and finely chopped

1 (8-ounce) can unsweetened coconut milk

1 serrano pepper (about 2 teaspoons), stem removed, seeded, and finely chopped

$^1/_2$ cup canola oil

Juice of 3 large limes (about 6 tablespoons)

Kosher salt and freshly ground black pepper

LOBSTER

6 (18 x 13-inch) sheets parchment paper

1 large zucchini squash (about 6 ounces), julienned and seeds discarded

6 (1$^1/_4$-pound) lobsters, boiled and picked (page 65)

1 large yellow (summer) squash (about 6 ounces), julienned and seeds discarded

6 tablespoons unsalted butter, divided

1$^1/_2$ teaspoons kosher salt, divided

Freshly ground black pepper

FOR THE GREEN CURRY SAUCE: Place all the ingredients into a blender and blend until smooth. Set aside.

FOR THE LOBSTER: Prepare the paper "bags." Fold one parchment sheet in half, shorter end to shorter end. Using as much of the paper as possible, start at the upper folded edge and cut out a heart shape (as if making a valentine in grade school). Discard the remainder of the paper. Continue for the remaining five bags. Lay the left side of the heart over the right side. Starting at the top of the heart, fold down the edge section by section, crimping down the edge as you go. Continue folding and crimping until you reach the bottom and the bag is fully sealed. At the bottom, twist the pointy end of the heart and tuck under. Place a baking sheet in the oven to warm.

Divide the squash into six portions. Place each portion (about 4 tablespoons) inside the heart on the right side. Add the meat of each lobster on top of the squash. Top each with 1 tablespoon butter, $\frac{1}{4}$ teaspoon salt, and a pinch of pepper.

Place the bags on the cookie sheet in the oven. Bake for 8 minutes and remove from the oven. To serve, cut a hole in the center of the bag about 6 inches across, leaving part of the cut intact to create a flap. Roll back the flap and present the bag at the table. Serve the green curry sauce on the side, or drizzle some on the bag contents at the table or before serving.

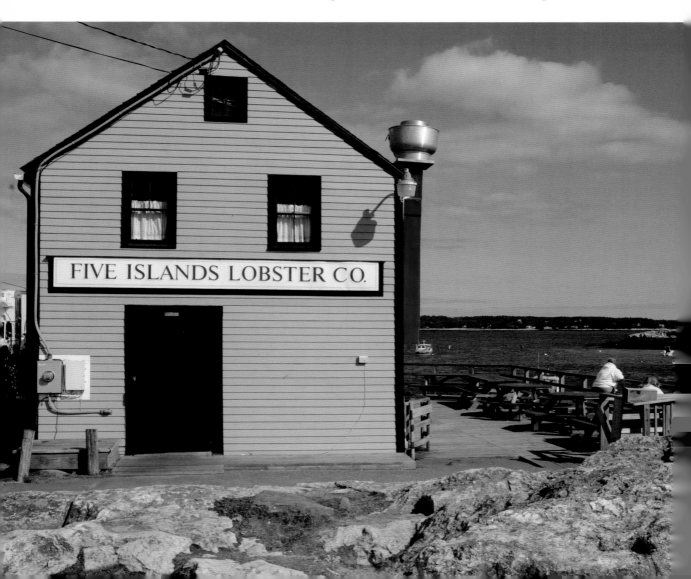

LOBSTER MAC 'N' CHEESE

COMFORT FOOD, MAINE STYLE—THAT'S THE IDEA BEHIND THIS SLIGHTLY UPSCALE
version of an American classic. The rich buttery flavor of lobster marries perfectly with creamy pasta. It's a good way to use "culls"—the cheaper lobsters often available in summer that are missing a claw or are otherwise less then perfect looking. This could be a first course, or a simple main meal for the family. Serve with our Warm Dandelion Greens (page 000), Coleslaw with Caraway Seeds (page 000), or some simple sliced cucumbers.

YIELD: 6 SERVINGS

$1^1/_2$ pounds uncooked elbow macaroni

2 cups heavy cream

$^1/_2$ cup grated Gruyere cheese

$^1/_2$ cup grated Monterey Jack cheese

$^1/_2$ cup grated Parmesan cheese

1 tablespoon chopped fresh chives

1 tablespoon chopped fresh parsley

2 lobsters, boiled (page 65), cooled, picked and coarsely chopped

Kosher salt

$^1/_2$ cup panko breadcrumbs

Preheat the oven to 350°F. Cook the macaroni according to the package directions in a large pot of boiling salted water. Drain, rinse, and set aside in a large bowl. Meanwhile, bring the cream to a boil in a large nonreactive saucepan. Add the cheeses, chives, parsley, lobster, and salt to taste to the cream. Stir to melt the cheese. Pour the mixture over the macaroni and stir to combine. Transfer to a 3-quart casserole dish, sprinkle with the breadcrumbs and bake until the casserole is bubbling, about 15 minutes. The dish can be made a day ahead and kept in the refrigerator, covered, until ready to use.

LOBSTER SALAD *with* MINER'S LETTUCE *and* CHIVE MAYONNAISE

MINER'S LETTUCE, ALSO CALLED WINTER PURSLANE, GROWS NATURALLY UNDER *trees. It has a velvety, intensely "green," almost grassy flavor that goes well with the sharp onion flavor from the chive and creaminess of the mayonnaise. If you can't find miner's lettuce, use mache or arugula for their distinctive character. This salad is wonderful to serve out on the patio with a chilly bottle of white wine.*

YIELD: 6 SERVINGS

CHAMPAGNE VINAIGRETTE
$^1/_4$ teaspoon kosher salt

$^1/_8$ teaspoon freshly ground black pepper

$^1/_4$ cup Champagne vinegar

1 cup olive oil

SALAD
$^1/_2$ cup chopped chives

12 tablespoons mayonnaise (see Herb
  Mayonnaise, page 49, but omit the herbs)

3 ($1^1/_4$-pound) lobsters, boiled and picked

6 cups miner's lettuce or other greens

3 slices each tomatoes, radishes, avocado,
  for garnish

FOR THE CHAMPAGNE VINAIGRETTE: Combine the salt and pepper in a bowl. Add the vinegar and whisk to blend the seasonings. Drizzle in the olive oil while whisking to bind the mix into an emulsion.

  FOR THE SALAD: Mix the chives with the mayonnaise and the lobster meat in a bowl. Toss the greens with the Champagne vinaigrette and divide onto each of six chilled plates. Top each plate with half a lobster tail, one claw, and one knuckle. Garnish with the tomato, radish, and avocado slices.

LOBSTER PLT

THE BLT IS ONE OF CLARK'S FAVORITE SANDWICHES AND ADDING LOBSTER MAKES *it a little more sophisticated. We call this a PLT because we use pancetta, a great salty contrast to creamy sweet lobster. Tarragon, our favorite herb, is so good with both lobster salad and tomatoes, so it's a double treat. We offer quantities for each ingredient here, but a PLT is a personal thing so add or take away whatever you like. Experiment with herbs and the many colors and varieties of tomatoes you'll find in the farmers' markets and make an event of it by laying out variations and letting family and friends assemble their own.*

YIELD: 6 SERVINGS

12 slices pancetta

12 ounces lobster meat

$1/2$ cup tarragon mayonnaise (see chive mayonnaise, page 78, and substitute tarragon for chive)

12 slices sourdough bread, toasted

12 arugula leaves

2 tomatoes, sliced

Preheat the oven to 350°F. Place the pancetta on a baking sheet and bake until crisp, about 10 minutes depending on thickness. Remove the pancetta and blot on paper towels. Toss the lobster meat with the tarragon mayonnaise until it's the consistency you like. Assemble the sandwiches with 6 slices toasted bread topped with lettuce, tomato, pancetta, and finally the lobster. Top with the other slices of bread.

BUTTER-POACHED LOBSTER
with JOHNNYCAKES

LOBSTER MEAT IS VERY DELICATE SO IT'S IMPORTANT NOT TO OVERCOOK IT AS *it will get rubbery and just plain fall apart, neither of which is very appetizing. Butter poaching, just warming the meat ever so gently in melted butter, coats the meat and the gentle heat prevents overcooking. It doesn't hurt that the lobster is infused with the buttery deliciousness we love. The trick is to cook the lobster in the shell just enough to get it out of the shell, but then finish cooking it in the butter. This dish is great for brunch, as a knockout appetizer, or an elegant fish course in a multi-course meal.*

YIELD: 6 SERVINGS

POACHED LOBSTER
$3^1/_4$ pounds lobster
$^1/_2$ pound (2 sticks) unsalted butter

JOHNNYCAKES
$1^1/_3$ cups milk

$1^1/_3$ cups water
$^3/_4$ cup plus 2 tablespoon cornmeal
1 teaspoon butter
$^1/_2$ teaspoon kosher salt
$^1/_4$ cup canola oil, divided

FOR THE LOBSTERS: Bring a large pot of water to the boil and plunge the lobsters into the water. Cook for 6 minutes. Pour the lobsters into a colander or deep sink and cover with ice. Remove the meat from the shell (page 83). Split the tails in half. Heat the butter in a saucepan over medium-low heat and add the lobster. Gently heat the lobster for 6 minutes.

FOR THE JOHNNYCAKES: Bring the milk and water to a boil in a saucepan. Gradually whisk in the cornmeal. Add the butter and the salt. Finish with warm water until the batter is the consistency of thick pancake batter. Remove from the heat, and let stand 10 minutes stirring occasionally. Heat 1 tablespoon of the canola oil in a skillet over high heat. When smoking hot pour in a small amount of batter, about 2 tablespoons. Cook until golden brown on each side and the edges are firm. Repeat in batches until you use all of the batter.

To assemble, place one cake on each of six plates, top with half of a lobster tail and then divide the rest of the lobster meat among the plates. Drizzle with the lobster butter from the poaching pan.

JOHNNYCAKES

OHNNYCAKES ARE AN OLD NEW ENGLAND DISH, AND THERE'S much debate as to whether they should be called "Journey Cakes." Mainers of old would take them on long trips because they just wouldn't spoil. Like any pancake, the first ones don't always come out right, but don't despair; it won't take many to get it just right. They're thin so use a lot of butter and be sure to use a perfect nonstick pan with no "wear or tear." While they used to be made with a cast-iron pan, this is one instance when modern technology is needed. They are not just for this more elegant dish, either. Have them at breakfast with jam, honey, or maple syrup and at lunch and dinner with stew or chowder.

LOBSTER COCKTAIL *with* HORSERADISH-TOMATO MAYONNAISE

THIS DISH IS VERY FESTIVE SO IF YOU'RE MAKING IT FOR FRIENDS THEY'LL BE *quite impressed. As we say in Maine, though, it's "wicked" easy to make. We suggest chives and parsley here, but please feel free to use anything coming up from your garden to liven up the flavors. The horseradish and tomato in the mayonnaise is a little play on classic cocktail sauce. Use eight-ounce Champagne flutes or glasses.*

YIELD: 6 SERVINGS

3 ($1^1/_4$-pound) lobsters, boiled and picked (page 65)

$1^1/_2$ cups Champagne vinegar

$4^1/_2$ tablespoons sugar

$1^1/_2$ tablespoons salt

$1^1/_2$ tablespoons ground horseradish

6 tablespoons mayonnaise (see Herb Mayonnaise,
    page 49, but omit the herbs)

$1^1/_2$ cups chopped tomatoes

6 lemon wedges

$^1/_8$ cup chopped fresh parsley

$^1/_8$ cup chopped chives

Chill the lobster meat. Mix the Champagne vinegar, sugar, and salt in a saucepan and bring to a boil. Add the horseradish and simmer for 5 minutes. Remove the mixture from the heat and chill. To layer the cocktail, start with 1 teaspoon mayonnaise in the bottom of each flute or glass. Add 1 teaspoon tomato, 1 teaspoon horseradish mixture, a bit of the lobster, mayonnaise, horseradish, part of the tail, mayonnaise, tomato, horseradish, lobster claw, mayonnaise, and horseradish. Top with 1 tablespoon of the Champagne vinaigrette. Add a lemon wedge and snips of parsley and chives on top. Serve chilled.

HOW TO EAT A LOBSTER

CRACKING A LOBSTER SEEMS DAUNTING TO SOME, BUT IT'S REALLY quite simple. We often look at the cartoonlike drawings on the paper place mats at typical lobster pounds in New England, but we think they're just designed to confuse you further. Just start with the tail. Hold the tail as if the lobster is swimming away from you. Twist to remove the tail. With two hands, push the tail together until the top of the tail cracks; then flip the tail over and place two thumbs in the ridge of the tail and push outward until the entire shell comes off.

Now, twist off the arms. Discard the body and reserve it for stock or keep as a garnish. Twist the claws off the arms. Place the arms on a cutting board and cut along the lines separating each knuckle with a heavy-duty chef's knife. Using your fingers or a chopstick, push the meat out of each knuckle. Use the heavy end of the knife to hit the claw gently until it's cracked all over like an egg. You may want to cover the claw with a towel before hitting it to keep the juice from flying. Remove the meat from the claw. Twist the small part of the claw with your hand until it comes away from the flesh and then gently twist the larger part and pull it out from the shell. Using your fingers, pull the cartilage from inside of the claw out as well.

As for the thin legs, just give it up, man! There are fanatics who like to suck the meat out of the legs and, if you feel so inclined, go ahead. We know they always show that on the place mats, but we think it's just too much trouble.

THE LOBSTERMAN

TED JOHNSON HAS ALWAYS LED A DOUBLE LIFE—AS A BUILDER AND as a lobsterman. Lobstering came first. He started fishing at age thirteen when a friend of his father's who had a lobster boat let him play around in the skiff. That's when he got his first two traps. Although his mother was scared he would drown, lobstering was now in his blood. When Ted finished high school he realized he also wanted to build and for decades he built houses and boats, lobstering for six months of the year. It was a lifestyle that fit into his personality—he's an independent man and he says he didn't like working for other people. Being out on the lobster boat fit into his view of life as did the building. At age sixteen he built his own house, clearing the land with an ax. He used a shovel to dig out the foundation.

Now Ted's retired from building and can spend more time lobstering, but he says he doesn't really know anyone who can make a living just lobstering. Many of his fellow lobstermen have "regular" jobs that pay the bills and benefits so they can get out on the water and pull in the traps. Ted says he sees more lobsters now than he did in years past because many of the lobster predators are gone due to dragging as a fishing technique. He says more people are trying to get into lobstering despite the limit on licenses, and he's got to keep buying his license each year or lose it.

There's also more competition than in the past. More independent people coming into the business and advances in technology are putting pressure on his way of life, a way of life that can often be very dangerous. Ted says he's been lucky through the decades. He's been "hung up" a few times, but he always got out of it. In some years, men die on the water, men who get caught in ropes and are pulled down because of the repetitive nature of hauling. Ted says pulling up the traps and letting them down over and over again can make you careless. He always carries a sharp knife and has a knife at the stern of the boat in case he goes overboard, but he's been lobstering a long time and still enjoys doing it.

CLASSIC SHORE DINNER

MOST PEOPLE DON'T HAVE TIME TO GO DOWN TO THE BEACH AND DIG A PIT— *if it's even allowed. This is our way of doing the lobster shore dinner using the family barbecue. Ask your fishmonger for seaweed or go gather your own.*

YIELD: 6 SERVINGS

FIRE PIT

Newspaper

1 (25-pound) bag charcoal

12 pieces dry firewood

1 (5-gallon) bucket of river rocks
  or pumice stones

10 pounds fresh seaweed

FOOD

12 small Maine or new potatoes, scrubbed

12 ears sweet corn, husk on, soaked
  overnight in salted water

6 chorizo sausage links

6 ($1^1/_4$ -pound) lobsters

36 littleneck clams

1 pound (4 sticks) unsalted butter,
  made into drawn butter (page 52)

FOR THE OUTDOOR FIRE PIT: Start a fire using newspaper and charcoal. Once the charcoal is flaming, add wood and allow it to burn down until you have a large amount of coals. Place the river rocks or pumice stones around the coals in a ring and place some in the coals themselves, being careful not to extinguish the fire. Add half of the seaweed on top.

    FOR THE FOOD: Place all of the food on top of the seaweed and then cover with the rest of the seaweed and steam until the ingredients are cooked, about 1 hour. Remove the seaweed and take out the food. Serve each guest 1 lobster, 6 clams, 1 sausage link, 2 ears corn, and 2 potatoes with the drawn butter.

PIT COOKING

VERY INDIGENOUS CULTURE SEEMS TO HAVE HAD A METHOD OF cooking which involved burying the bounty of the land and sea, and cooking with hot rocks, wood, and whatever else was around for fuel. In the Hawaiian Islands you'll find the Kalua pig. Traditionally, it's roasted in a pit with hot rocks and banana leaves and buried to cook for five hours. Here in Maine, we have the shore dinner or clam bake. To find the antecedents of the New England feast, one needs to look no further that the Native Americans who taught the settlers to cook in this manner. The early Native Americans created pits dug into clay soil. They lined them with rocks and then put on a layer of aromatic leaves, which further enhanced the flavor of meat and shellfish and kept in the steam. The Penobscot tribe here in Maine taught the settlers how to bake beans underground by digging a fire pit in which to bury a bean pot and cook them overnight. The Bean Hole dinner is still a tradition today, and New Englanders still have the clam bake and the shore dinner. In summer, tourists flock to clam bakes to get a taste of that tradition.

In creating a fire pit, a large hole is dug in the ground and stones are placed inside to line it and build up a wall and to provide a ledge on which to place a grill. The cooking stones are laid in the pit's center along with the wood that will get them piping hot. Once the stones are glowing, it's necessary to let the fire burn down and to create a bed of embers. Next, comes a layer of seaweed on the stones and finally the food. Steamers, mussels, lobsters, potatoes, corn, sausages, onions, and really anything you like, alternating layers of seaweed and food. Then the entire pit is covered with canvas that has been soaked in sea water, and the food is allowed to cook for hours, steaming in all the great flavor.

Pit cooking is slow and laborious, but also a festive way to prepare our local seafood, sausage, and potatoes. While some Mainers have a dedicated area behind the house for their shore dinners, most of us don't want to dig up our own lawns and the park rangers frown on digging up the beaches with a big pit and a fire, so the New England Clam Boil came into being. Just cook it all in a big pot on the stove or try our middle-of-the-road version right in your kettle grill on the patio.

SCALLOPS

WHEREVER YOU GO AROUND THE WORLD, YOU FIND SOMETHING on a skewer; the Greeks call it souvlaki, the Turks call it shish kebab, and as we've traveled, we've always found fun ways to interpret these meals on a stick. Maine diver scallops are delightful because they're pure and unadulterated. Look for scallops that are dry and never dripping wet to ensure that they are fresh. We like to use the large U-10 size for these dishes, meaning ten to a pound. Here we offer three scallop-on-a-skewer recipes. Mix them up at a dinner party or outdoor lunch barbecue for more variety and fun.

GRILLED SCALLOPS *with a* LEMONGRASS SKEWER

YEARS AGO WE DISCOVERED WE COULD GROW LEMONGRASS EVEN THOUGH OUR *garden is in a Zone 4 growing area, and we did grow it—long before we could find it in the local super-market. It was very successful and we had plenty, so we found that if we cut it before a hard freeze and trimmed it, we could freeze it and keep it all winter. The oil from the lemongrass infuses the scallops with a hint of exotic lemon and a whiff of Southeast Asia.*

YIELD: 6 SERVINGS

18 U-10 scallops
6 lemongrass stalks
24 large basil leaves
2 tablespoons corn oil
Kosher salt and freshly ground black pepper

Heat the grill as hot as it will go. Each lemongrass skewer will have 3 scallops and 6 basil leaves. Fill each skewer with a scallop, 2 leaves, scallop, 2 leaves, scallop, 2 leaves. Baste each skewer with corn oil and season with salt and pepper to taste. Grill for 2 minutes on each side until the scallops are lightly browned.

SCALLOPS *on a* BROCHETTE *with* BAY LEAVES *and* ONION

THESE TAKE THE LEMONGRASS SCALLOP FROM SOUTHEAST ASIA TO SOUTHERN *Italy; same concept, but from cultures that are worlds apart.*

YIELD: 6 SERVINGS

18 pearl onions, peeled
2 tablespoons olive oil
18 bay leaves
18 U-10 scallops
18 lemon peel slices
6 (10-inch) bamboo skewers
Kosher salt and freshly ground black pepper

Heat the oven to 350°F. Toss the onions in the olive oil and bake in a casserole for 30 minutes, until just soft. Remove the onions from the oven and cool. Heat the grill as hot as it will go. Skewer the ingredients in order: 1 bay leaf, 1 scallop, 1 onion, 1 lemon peel. Repeat twice for each skewer. Grill until the scallops are lightly browned, about 2 minutes.

SCALLOPS WRAPPED *in* PANCETTA

COCKTAIL PARTY CIRCA 1960 ANYONE? WE HAD TO TAKE THOSE CLASSIC BACON *wrapped scallops and bring them up to date. Don't forget the Motown.*

YIELD: 6 SERVINGS

18 slices of pancetta, $1/16$ inch thick
   (to wrap around the scallop)
18 U-10 scallops
6 (10-inch) bamboo skewers
2 tablespoon clarified butter or canola oil
Kosher salt and freshly ground black pepper

Wrap the pancetta around each scallop. Skewer three scallops on each skewer. Sear the scallops in the butter or oil, 1 minute on each side and then 30 seconds on the edges to crisp the pancetta. Season to taste with the salt and pepper.

SCALLOPS *with* GRILLED TOMATOES *and* AÏOLI

SEAFOOD, TOMATOES, AND GARLIC ARE ESSENTIAL FOR A GREAT BOUILLABAISSE, *the classic French seafood stew. For this recipe we decided to take those delicious ingredients and create a much simpler version. It's a nice, light dinner with a salad and crusty bread. The aïoli is simply our mayonnaise recipe with plenty of nutty, sharp garlic added. Aïoli is also great with grilled vegetables.*

YIELD: 6 SERVINGS

6 plum tomatoes

18 U-10 scallops

3 tablespoons extra virgin olive oil

2 teaspoons chives, chopped, for garnish

2 teaspoons chervil, chopped, for garnish

$^1/_2$ cup aioli

AÏOLI

$1^1/_2$ cups mayonnaise (see Herb Mayonnaise, page 49, but omit the herbs)

3 garlic cloves, peeled and finely chopped

Heat the grill to medium hot. Slice the tomatoes in half, coat with oil, and grill 2 minutes per side. Pull off the charred skin. Grill the scallops until golden brown, 2 minutes per side. Serve on a large platter or individual plates and top with chopped herbs. Combine the mayonnaise and garlic cloves and mix well. Serve at once with aïoli on the side.

SCALLOPS *with* WILD MUSHROOMS *and* HERBS

THIS DISH GIVES YOU A CHANCE TO LEAVE THE FRESH GARDEN GREENS BEHIND *and move on to mushroom season. Maine's forests are filled with golden chanterelles, which you can find in your local market. They're the ultimate autumn mushroom, one many chefs consider the king of mushrooms—buttery, rich, and lovely to smell and touch. When the fall gives you the king of mushrooms and the sea brings the best scallops of the year, they simply must be combined. Toss this dish with fettuccine or linguine for an entree, or serve the scallops solo for a robust autumn appetizer.*

YIELD: 6 SERVINGS

$^1/_4$ cup drawn butter (page 65)
18 U-10 scallops
$^1/_4$ cup white wine
8 tablespoons (1 sticks) unsalted butter, divided
4 cups cleaned and sliced chanterelle mushrooms
$1^1/_2$ cups chicken stock
3 teaspoons chopped tarragon
3 tablespoons chopped fresh chervil or parsley

Heat the clarified butter in a sauté pan until smoking hot. Sauté the scallops for 2 minutes per side and then remove from the pan. Add the white wine to the pan, scraping off the caramelized scallop bits and juices. Add 6 tablespoons of the butter. Sauté the mushrooms in the butter until just soft and the liquid is almost gone, 3 to 4 minutes. Add the chicken stock and cook until the mixture is reduced by half. Add the herbs. Toss the scallops in the sauce to warm. Finish with the remaining 2 tablespoons of butter. Divide the scallops onto six warm plates, top with sauce and mushrooms, and serve at once.

SAUTÉED SCALLOPS *with* ROASTED SHALLOT CRÈME FRAÎCHE

Roasting shallots—the sweeter, milder sister gems of the onion— makes them soft and even sweeter. Wrapping the shallots in foil makes it easy—you can't mess anything up or overcook them, but do cook them until they are absolutely soft. We offer our recipe for crème fraîche, which is terrific on grilled peaches. When mixed with herbs and spices, it can jazz up many dishes, but you can use sour cream or an even a mix of sour cream and heavy cream. Serve this dish with our Root Cellar Gratin (page 275) or Carrot and Parsnip Purée (page 277). A chilled brown ale or a locally brewed IPA would be great too.

YIELD: 6 SERVINGS

CRÈME FRAÎCHE
1 cup heavy cream
$1/8$ cup yogurt
$1/8$ cup buttermilk

SCALLOPS
6 ounces (about 8) shallots, peeled
1 teaspoon olive oil

$1/4$ teaspoon kosher salt
$1/4$ teaspoon freshly ground black pepper
1 teaspoon chopped fresh thyme
2 teaspoons lemon juice
1 cup crème fraîche or sour cream
3 tablespoons unsalted butter
18 U-10 scallops

FOR THE CRÈME FRAÎCHE: Whisk the ingredients together in a bowl and let sit for 30 minutes. Chill.

FOR THE SCALLOPS: Preheat the oven to 350°F. Toss the shallots with the olive oil, salt, and pepper. Place the shallots on a large sheet of foil, sprinkle with the thyme, and fold the foil over and seal to form a packet. Place in the oven and roast until soft, about 20 minutes. Remove the shallots from the foil, cool to room temperature, and then purée them in a food processor. Add the lemon juice to the shallots and mix into the crème fraîche. Melt the butter in a skillet. Add the scallops and sauté in the butter until golden brown, about 2 minutes each side. Divide the scallops onto six plates and serve with the shallot crème fraîche on the side.

BAKED SCALLOPS *with* POTATOES

CASSEROLES WITH BAKED FISH ARE SOMETHING MANY OF US GREW UP WITH. *They offer a quick, easy way to make something really good for family, company, or one of those frequent pot-luck gatherings. This one is a no-hassle winter dish, hearty and delicious. Serve it with our warm Brussels Sprout Salad (page 121), Warm Dandelion Greens Salad (page 209), or the Fried Green Tomatoes (page 204).*

YIELD: 6 SERVINGS

2 pounds fingerling potatoes

1 teaspoon chopped fresh thyme

3 tablespoons melted unsalted butter, divided

8 U-10 scallops

$^3/_4$ cup crème frâiche (opposite page)

Kosher salt and freshly ground black pepper

4 ounces Parmesan cheese, thinly shaved

3 tablespoons panko breadcrumbs

Preheat the oven to 375°F. Cook the potatoes in a pot of boiling water until just tender. Drain, let cool, and slice into coins. Toss with the thyme and 1 tablespoon butter. Slice the raw scallops into $^1/_4$-inch slices. In 6 (4-ounce) ramekins, assemble the ingredients in layers beginning with potatoes at the bottom, a dollop of crème frâiche, salt and pepper to taste, sliced scallops, potato, shaved Parmesan, another layer of scallops, a dollop of crème frâiche, and finish with potato slices. Sprinkle $^1/_2$ tablespoon panko breadcrumbs on each ramekin and drizzle with the remaining melted butter. Bake for 30 minutes and serve at once.

CHILLED SCALLOPS *with* CITRUS

WHEN THE FIRST WARM DAYS COME TO MAINE AND THE CITRUS KEEPS ROLLING IN *from far and wide, this early spring dish can't be beat. It's a fun dish to serve with fruity cocktails, just put it out on a platter at the bar or on the kitchen table (where everyone gathers anyway) and it will just blow everyone away. Light, healthy, and packed with flavor, people are really starting to understand this kind of "cooking" where the juices from citrus do all the work. Serve with iced Cold River Vodka, a favorite in Maine.*

YIELD: 6 SERVINGS

1 lime

1 lemon

2 oranges

Juice of 1 lemon (about 2 tablespoons)

Juice of 1 lime (about 2 tablespoons)

1/2 cup extra virgin olive oil

12 large scallops

1 tablespoon chopped chives

1 teaspoon chopped fresh cilantro

Peel the citrus fruits and divide into sections. Mix the juice of the lemon and lime in a bowl. Whisk in the olive oil. Add the lime, lemon, and orange sections and toss with the scallops for 3 minutes. Add the herbs. Slice the scallops to 1/4-inch thickness. Serve at once.

SCALLOPS *with* PAPPARDELLE, MARJORAM, *and* ROASTED GARLIC

IF FISH OR SHELLFISH CAN MAKE A TRUE NEW ENGLAND STICK-TO-YOUR-RIBS *dish, this is the one to do it. Marjoram is an intense, earthy herb more commonly paired with meats, but it's great in robust cooking of any kind. Pairing rich scallops with this herb just works. Pappardelle is great with this dish because the wide noodles give the wine sauce and marjoram something to stick to so the flavors weave throughout the dish. Go ahead and impress your friends with your knowledge of wine pairing and serve this with a Chianti or a pinot noir.*

YIELD: 6 SERVINGS

3 large heads garlic, broken into cloves, husks intact
2 tablespoons olive oil
1 teaspoon kosher salt plus more to taste
18 U-10 scallops
2 tablespoons extra virgin olive oil
$1^{1}/_{2}$ cups chicken stock
$1^{1}/_{2}$ cups white wine
1 teaspoon marjoram
2 teaspoons unsalted butter
6 cups pappardelle, cooked
Freshly ground black pepper

Preheat the oven to 375°F. Toss the garlic cloves with the olive oil and 1 teaspoon salt and heat in the oven for about 15 minutes. Remove the garlic, let cool, and peel. Sauté the scallops in the extra virgin olive oil, 2 minutes per side. Remove the scallops and discard the oil. In the same pan, bring the chicken stock and the wine to a boil and cook to reduce the liquid by half. Add the marjoram and whisk in the butter. Combine the scallops, the sauce, and the garlic in a large bowl and then toss with the pasta. Season with salt and pepper to taste. Serve on a platter or divide between six heated individual plates.

SCALLOPS *with* CORN PUDDING

MAINERS LOVE TO MAKE PUDDING OUT OF ANYTHING, AND THEY'LL CALL IT A *million things—slump, puffets, dowdy, even seventh heaven. They make it with plenty of wholesome farm products—vegetables, milk, eggs, and flour—and we love puddings just as much as everyone else.*

YIELD: 6 SERVINGS

CORN PUDDING

1 cup sour cream

2 large eggs

2 cups all-purpose flour

1 cup cornmeal

1 tablespoon baking powder

1 teaspoon kosher salt

2 cups corn kernels

1 cup milk

SCALLOPS

2 tablespoons unsalted butter, melted

18 U-10 scallops

Kosher salt and freshly ground black pepper

BUTTER SAUCE

$1/4$ cup white wine

$1/4$ cup freshly squeezed lemon juice

8 tablespoons (1 stick) unsalted butter

FOR THE CORN PUDDING: Preheat the oven to 400°F. Mix the sour cream and eggs in a bowl. Mix the flour, cornmeal, baking powder, and salt in a separate bowl. Add the sour cream and egg mixture to the dry ingredients. Add the corn and milk and mix well. Pour the batter into a 2-quart, 9-inch round buttered baking pan. Bake for 45 minutes.

FOR THE SCALLOPS: Melt the 2 tablespoons of butter in a medium skillet over medium heat. Sauté the scallops in the butter until they get a nice crust on either side, about 2 minutes each side. Season with salt and pepper to taste.

FOR THE BUTTER SAUCE: Mix the wine and the lemon juice in a skillet over medium heat and cook to reduce the liquid until syrupy. Remove from the heat and add the butter, one chunk at a time, whisking until combined. You might need to bring the pan back to the heat to get it all melted but if you do, keep it over a very low heat. Serve the scallops with a wedge of corn pudding and top the scallops with the butter sauce.

SHRIMP COCKTAIL

IF WE COULD SAY, "'NUFF SAID" ABOUT ANY RECIPE, IT WOULD BE THIS ONE. IT'S
everybody's favorite, including ours and great as an appetizer or a poolside snack. If Maine shrimp are in season, we especially like to use them in a shrimp cocktail because they arrive only in the winter, making the sweet little shrimp a delicacy. If you're ambitious, you can buy them unpeeled, but after you do it once, you might just pay a bit extra and ask your fishmonger to do it the next time—it's meticulous work.

YIELD: 6 SERVINGS

SHRIMP

1 carrot, peeled and sliced

1 celery stalk, sliced

$^1/_2$ Spanish onion, sliced

6 garlic cloves, peeled and sliced

2 sprigs fresh thyme

1 teaspoon chili flakes

2 bottles beer, not a dark beer

1 tablespoon olive oil

2 cups water

3 pounds Maine shrimp, peeled

COCKTAIL SAUCE

1 cup ketchup

1 tablespoon fresh lemon juice

2 tablespoons fresh-grated horseradish, or prepared will work

1 teaspoon finely ground black pepper

Tabasco sauce to taste (some like it HOT!)

FOR THE SHRIMP: Place the carrot, celery, onion, garlic, thyme, chili flakes, beer, olive oil, and water in a large pot and bring to a rolling boil. Add the shrimp and cook until the flesh is white, about 1 minute. Strain the shrimp from the liquid and cool the shrimp on a parchment-lined cookie sheet in the refrigerator. When cool, serve with the cocktail sauce.

FOR THE COCKTAIL SAUCE: Combine all of the ingredients in a bowl. The sauce can be kept up to one week, tightly sealed, in the refrigerator.

SHRIMP DUMPLINGS *with* SWEET CHILI SAUCE

IN CHINESE CUISINE ANYTHING CAN BE MADE INTO A DUMPLING, AND THEY'RE *always a great way to impress a crowd. Maine shrimp are so special and delicate they really work in Asian preparations. If you have people over who like to cook, have all the ingredients ready and have your guests help with the assembly. Save the cooking for yourself so they actually get to the table. The dumplings are hard to resist when they come out of the water. We like to serve the dumplings with a sweet chili sauce from Thailand. It's a spicier version of a sweet-and-sour sauce.*

YIELD: 6 SERVINGS

10 ounces raw Maine or other small shrimp, shelled

$1/2$ cup finely chopped cabbage

$1/4$ cup chopped fresh cilantro leaves

2 tablespoons sugar

2 teaspoons finely chopped fresh ginger

1 tablespoon sweet chile paste

2 teaspoons soy sauce

1 teaspoon sesame oil

36 wonton wrappers, fresh or frozen then thawed

2 large eggs, lightly beaten

$1/4$ cup cornstarch

6 quarts water

1 tablespoon vegetable oil

1 tablespoon kosher salt

Thai sweet chili sauce

In a bowl combine the shrimp, cabbage, cilantro, sugar, ginger, chile paste, soy sauce, and sesame oil. Mix well with a wooden spoon. Spoon $1/2$ teaspoon of the mixture into the center of a wonton wrapper. Keep the remaining wrappers covered with a clean kitchen towel or plastic wrap to prevent drying. Using a pastry brush, coat two adjacent edges of the wrapper with the beaten egg. Fold the wrapper over to form a triangle and seal the edges, pushing out any air. Join the two opposite points into a closed "bishop's hat," pointy and joined at the top to completely seal the joint with a dot of beaten egg. Transfer to a cookie sheet lined with parchment paper, sprinkle with cornstarch, and cover with a clean kitchen towel. Repeat the process until all the filling is used. The dumplings will keep in the refrigerator for up to 3 hours.

Bring the 6 quarts of water, the oil, and the salt to a boil in a large pot. Work in batches to avoid overcrowding the pot, if necessary. Place the dumplings in the pot and cook until soft and the filling is cooked through, about 2 minutes. Remove with a slotted spoon and transfer to a cookie sheet. Cover with foil to keep warm while cooking the remaining dumplings. Serve at once with the sweet chili sauce.

SEARED SHRIMP *with* GARLIC *and* TOMATOES

THERE ARE MANY WAYS TO SERVE THIS SIMPLE, ELEGANT DISH—AS A LIGHT *summer appetizer followed by a white bean soup or a big green salad, with fresh pasta with butter, or with our Corn Pudding (page 102). When tomatoes are at their best and you can get different varieties in many colors—such as the smoky Purple Cherokee, the sharp-tasting Green Zebra with it's green and yellow pattern, the deep-red round Brandywine with a slightly tart taste, or the White Queen with it's pale yellow color—then go all out and use them all in this dish.*

YIELD: 6 SERVINGS

2 tablespoons extra virgin olive oil, divided

1 cup slivered garlic

12 ounces large U-25 shrimp

3 cups quartered tomatoes, various types

$^1/_2$ cup white wine

Kosher salt and freshly ground black pepper

2 cups chopped loose herbs, such as garlic chives or fennel tips

Heat 1 tablespoon of the oil in a large sauté pan over high heat. Add the garlic and sauté, stirring vigorously until browned, 1 to 2 minutes. Add the shrimp, and cook until the shrimp are white. Stir in the tomatoes. Add the white wine. Drizzle the remaining tablespoon of olive oil over the shrimp. Remove from the heat and season with salt and pepper to taste. Divide the shrimp and tomatoes among six plates and sprinkle with chopped herbs. Serve at once.

CLASSIC SHRIMP SALAD
with RUSSIAN DRESSING

THIS IS A DISH YOU MIGHT FIND IN AN OLD TURN-OF-THE-CENTURY BOSTON *cookbook when Mainers started getting a little more gussied up and recipes like this began to crop up that were a little less colonial, and a little more worldly. Salads like these seem to have fallen out of favor in the past thirty years, but when you prepare it you'll realize why it was a favorite for so long and why classic dishes like this one are coming back, modern style. The Russian dressing is rich and luxurious, and the Maine shrimp dot the dish with bursts of sweetness.*

YIELD: 6 SERVINGS

RUSSIAN DRESSING

1 tablespoon whole-grain mustard

1 teaspoon Dijon mustard

1 tablespoon lemon juice

$1/4$ cup finely chopped Spanish onion

$1/4$ cup tomato paste

1 tablespoon sweet paprika

$1/2$ teaspoon cayenne

1 cup mayonnaise (see Herb Mayonnaise, page 49, but omit the herbs)

$1/2$ cup sour cream

1 teaspoon Sriracha

2 teaspoons ketchup

SHRIMP SALAD

24 ounces Maine or other small shrimp, cooked and peeled

6 large lettuce leaves

3 tomatoes, sliced

3 large hard-boiled eggs, each cut into 6 slices

6 sprigs chervil and 6 sprigs parsley, for garnish

FOR THE RUSSIAN DRESSING: Combine all of the ingredients in a bowl, mix well, and set aside.

FOR THE SHRIMP SALAD: Toss the shrimp with 10 tablespoons of the dressing. Place one lettuce leaf on each of six small plates and divide the dressed shrimp on each leaf. Surround each leaf with a half of a sliced tomato and three slices of hard-boiled egg. Add 1 tablespoon of Russian dressing to each plate. Cover the remaining Russian dressing and refrigerate. Garnish the salads with chervil and parsley. Serve at once.

GRILLED SHRIMP *with* LEMON, OLIVE OIL, *and* BLACK PEPPER

BLACK PEPPER IS THE SIMPLEST SPICE TO USE, AND ONE OF THE EASIEST OF ALL *to find and store. It's on every table, but it's often forgotten as a pronounced part of a dish. When we visited Cambodia, once the largest producer of black peppercorns, we found it to be an integral part of the cooking there. It gives shrimp an exotic flavor when used as a major part of the dish, and we think you'll be surprised at just how complex the flavor of black pepper really is. In colonial times pepper was hard to get in Maine and was highly prized, but now we can go to town and grind away. Serve these shrimp with our aïoli (page 96) and with boiled potatoes or jasmine rice.*

YIELD: 6 SERVINGS

48 U-15 shrimp with the shell on
6 tablespoons extra virgin olive oil
6 tablespoons lemon zest
$1^1/_2$ teaspoons freshly ground black pepper
6 teaspoons lemon juice
1 teaspoon kosher salt
12 bamboo skewers
Olive oil for drizzling
2 lemons, sliced, for garnish

Marinate the shrimp in a bowl in the olive oil, lemon zest, and black pepper for 1 hour. Heat the grill to as hot as it will go. Add the lemon juice and salt to the shrimp. Place four shrimp on each skewer. Grill for 2 minutes on each side. Drizzle with olive oil and garnish with lemon slices.

SHRIMP *with* SALT PORK, ONION, *and* POTATOES

WE LOVE TO READ OLD COOKERY BOOKS FROM MAINE AND NEW ENGLAND, AND *they all include fatback, the part of the pig used to make lard and salt pork as well as a part of the sausage making tradition. Mainers live in an adverse environment and in the old days, nothing was wasted. Now, Americans are afraid of fat, but used in small amounts, it's a great way to add flavor to any dish as well as honor our new artisan food sensibility. This dish is a kind of hash, a very New England dish as thrifty Yankees and frugal Mainers, then and now, use leftovers to create great next-day dishes. Serve this dish at brunch with a poached egg on top.*

YIELD: 6 SERVINGS

3 ounces fatback (or butter), diced
1 cup finely chopped Spanish onion
6 baby Yukon Gold potatoes
Kosher salt and freshly ground black pepper
1 tablespoon canola oil
2 teaspoons clarified or drawn butter (page 65)
2 tablespoons unsalted butter
12 ounces shrimp, peeled
2 teaspoons chopped chives, for garnish
2 teaspoons chopped tomato, for garnish

In a sauté pan over medium heat, cook the fatback for 5 minutes. Pour off the excess fat. Add the onion and sauté until translucent. In a pot of water, boil the potatoes until tender. Drain and then cut the potatoes into $1/4$-inch slices. Place the potatoes in the pan with the fatback and onions. Season with salt and pepper to taste. Cook until the potatoes are golden and then set aside. In a sauté pan heat the canola oil and clarified butter over high heat until smoking. Add the shrimp and cook for 1 minute. Lower the heat and add the butter. Add the potato and onion mixture to the shrimp. Divide between six heated plates and garnish with chives and tomato. Serve at once.

IN *the* SHELL
BOILED SHRIMP *with* SPICES

SPICES WERE A BIG THING WHEN THEY FIRST CAME TO THIS COUNTRY. WHEN *Maine ship captains returned from the Far East, they brought back more exotic influences. We, too, have the wanderlust, and one of our more exciting experiences was in Indonesia where we had shrimp with turmeric, which gave the shrimp a touch of orange flavor. Combining our travels with that spice heritage of old, we can come up with some great ways to meld the Far East and Maine, as in this spicy dish. It's a great casual party food and unexpectedly participatory; everyone gets their hands dirty, and it's a great way to break the ice.*

YIELD: 6 SERVINGS

$^1/_2$ gallon water

6 tablespoons sliced garlic

2 tablespoons kosher salt

3 tablespoons whole coriander

3 tablespoons chili flakes

3 tablespoons Madras curry

3 tablespoons cumin seed

1 cinnamon stick

1 tablespoon ground cloves

3 tablespoons mustard seed

24 U-15 shrimp, shell on

Bring the water to a boil in a large pot with the garlic and salt. Meanwhile, toast the coriander, chili flakes, curry, cumin, cinnamon, cloves, and mustard seed in a large sauté pan with no oil over medium heat until the aroma is apparent, about 5 minutes. Add the spices to the water. Drop in the shrimp and cook for $1^1/_2$ minutes. Strain the water through a sieve, leaving the shrimp and all the spices. Serve the shrimp and spices either hot or cold on a large platter.

SHRIMP ROLL *with* HERBS *and* CELERY

A FUN ALTERNATIVE TO THE LOBSTER ROLL, THIS TREAT USES OUR SWEET MAINE *shrimp in season, so it's a great way to bring summer to the cold-weather months. If they're not in season, use small rock shrimp instead or large shrimp cut into good-size pieces. Serve one roll per person or as party food cut into smaller pieces.*

YIELD: 6 SERVINGS

2 quarts water

3 tablespoons kosher salt

24 ounces Maine shrimp, peeled and cleaned

1 cup chopped celery

5 tablespoons mayonnaise (see Herb
  Mayonnaise, page 49, but omit the herbs)

5 teaspoons chopped chives

5 teaspoons chopped chervil

$1^1/_2$ teaspoons lemon juice

6 top-loading hot dog buns

2 tablespoons unsalted butter, melted

Boil the water and the salt in a large pot. Reduce the heat, add the shrimp, and cook for 1 minute. Drain and chill the shrimp. In a bowl, toss the shrimp with the celery, mayonnaise, chives, chervil, and lemon juice. Brush the outside of the buns with melted butter and grill or toast in a pan. Fill the buns with the shrimp salad and serve.

SHRIMP SALAD
with CELERY ROOT *and* LEMON

CELERY ROOT IS ONE OF THOSE THINGS THAT SEEMS TO BE POPPING UP IN TRENDY *restaurants everywhere, but looking at this large, earth-covered bulb can be daunting for the home cook. It's actually very easy to work with. Just wash it and cut off the outside layer, and then shred it with a mandolin or food processor. To cook it but still leave a light crunch, blanch it quickly in boiling water to bring out the flavor and soften it. Its delicate flavor is a perfect accompaniment for seafood. Serve this salad with chilled Champagne or a citrusy Belgian beer.*

YIELD: 6 SERVINGS

2 quarts water

3 tablespoons kosher salt

$2^1/_4$ pounds Maine shrimp, shelled and cleaned

4 cups julienned celery root

24 cherry tomatoes, sliced $^1/_4$ inch thick

1 Granny Smith apple, julienned

6 tablespoons mayonnaise (see Herb
 Mayonnaise, page 49, but omit the herbs)

$^1/_4$ cup sugar

$^1/_4$ cup Champagne vinegar

14 basil leaves, shredded

Juice of 1 lemon (about 2 tablespoons)

24 Bibb lettuce leaves

Boil the water and the salt in a pot. Add the shrimp and cook for 1 minute. Drain the shrimp and chill on a cookie sheet in the refrigerator. Blanch the celery root in a pot of boiling salted water for 4 minutes. Drain the celery root and chill in an ice bath. As soon as the celery root is cold, remove it from the ice bath and place in a bowl. Toss with the shrimp, tomatoes, apple, mayonnaise, sugar, vinegar, basil, and lemon juice. Arrange four lettuce leaves on each plate and top with the shrimp salad.

SHRIMP *with* SHELLING BEANS *and* HAM

THE BEANS IN THIS DISH SEEM VERY SOUTHERN, BUT IN ANY REGION WHEN YOU *garden, one of the fun things to do is to watch the beans grow. They're so pretty as they wind their stalks around arbors and trellises and their beautiful blossoms tell you there is something wonderful coming. In Maine, this happens at the end of the season, and one of our favorites is the cranberry bean because of the deep red color. You can't get much more Maine than mixing beans and ham, and this is an updated way to present this pair. The beans are fresh and the ham lightly cooked, creating a light ragout. We suggest using white, gigante, or fava beans because they're sturdy and plump.*

YIELD: 6 SERVINGS

1 quart water

1 tablespoon kosher salt

6 cups fresh shelling beans (white, gigante, favas)

3 tablespoons olive oil

36 U-15 shrimp

$1^1/_2$ cups ham, cut into $^1/_4$-inch cubes

6 tablespoons chopped fresh parsley

6 tablespoons chopped chives

6 tablespoons chopped fresh thyme

$1^1/_2$ cups chicken stock

3 tablespoons lemon juice

4 tablespoons unsalted butter

Combine the water and salt in a pot over high heat. Add the beans, bring to a boil, and cook salt for 30 minutes. Drain the beans and set aside. Heat the olive oil in a sauté pan until almost smoking hot and then toss the shrimp in the pan for 30 seconds. In another large, heavy pot, place the ham, herbs, chicken stock, and lemon juice. Add the beans to the pot and heat. Add the shrimp and the butter and cook through until the butter is melted. Serve in six bowls on a large platter.

SUSTAINING THE SEA

IN MAINE, WE ARE VERY PROUD OF OUR STATE'S LONG COMMITMENT to husbanding the ocean's resources. As early as 1872 Maine passed its first law protecting lobsters. In 1874 a minimum size limit was established. In 1917 harvesters began "notching" the tails of egg-bearing females to protect them from harvest. And in 1961, in a landmark law, dragging the sea floor for lobsters was banned to eliminate both unwanted by-catch and damage to the sea floor.

Maine has not just been interested in protecting the sea for lobsters. Harvests of Maine shrimp, one of the great delicacies of the sea, are strictly regulated. In the Damariscotta region of Maine, a tremendous resurgence in oyster farming has emerged in the last two decades. The innovative oystermen and women of this region have employed environmentally sound methods of raising these coveted byvalves. Just thirty years ago, Maine had few oysters left, but now we have a thriving, healthy oyster supply in our state.

Overfishing and pollution are causing many of our fish species to become depleted. Marine habitats are damaged through dredging and trawling the sea floor. Destroying the sea floor eliminates the place where marine life lives and breeds. Bycatch is also an environmental concern. When ocean trawlers pull up many species of fish at once, the fish are sorted and rejected and many varieties are thrown back often dead or in distress. This is a tragic waste of the world's marine life. Now, efforts are being made to use solutions like trapdoors in nets or sound to keep unwanted species away.

There are ways we can all help to ensure our fish species thrive. At our restaurants we work closely with the best purveyors and local fishermen who share our vision of a sustainable marine environment. We see ourselves as "ambassadors of sustainability." We are involved with a number of groups that help protect our sea life, including the Monterey Bay Aquarium and the Maine Lobster Council, but you can help just by being aware of what fish you buy and how they are caught or raised. We never serve bluefin tuna, Chilean sea bass, orange roughy, or other endangered species, in any of our restaurants.

When shopping for seafood, take along the Seafood Watch Guide found at SeafoodWatch.com. Shop only from reputable markets that make an effort to support the sustainability of our seas. We encourage you to buy fish that are pole caught rather than netted and find seafood harvested in a carefully controlled manner, such as Maine shrimp. Some farm-raised fish is better than others: consult your fishmonger. Wild fish harvested in a sustainable manner is best. If you want to make a recipe from this book but can't find sustainable fish, choose another recipe until sustainable fish is available. It's that important.

Every time we cook from the sea, we make an impact; so if we all work to cook what is sustainable, then we can really make a change.

HADDOCK SANDWICH *with* TARTAR SAUCE

THIS IS CLASSIC MAINE SHORE FOOD BUT MAKING IT WITH THE RIGHT INGREDIENTS *and freshly caught haddock will elevate it from average to sublime. In Maine, we have endless debates about who makes the best fried fish and tartar sauce and no one seems to agree. We think the debate ends here. A frosty mug of great ale with this sandwich wouldn't hurt to help make you agree.*

YIELD: 6 SERVINGS

TARTAR SAUCE

$1/2$ cup finely chopped red onion

$1/2$ cup chopped gherkins

2 cups mayonnaise (see Herb Mayonnaise, page 49, but omit the herbs)

Juice of 1 lemon (about 2 tablespoons)

1 teaspoon freshly ground black pepper

FISH

1 cup panko breadcrumbs

Kosher salt and freshly ground black pepper

1 tablespoon unsalted butter

6 (6-ounce) haddock fillets

6 white rolls or 12 slices sourdough bread, buttered

Lettuce and tomato slices, optional

FOR THE TARTAR SAUCE: Combine all the ingredients in a bowl, mix well, and set aside.

FOR THE FISH: Preheat the oven to 400°F. Combine the breadcrumbs with salt and pepper to taste. Lightly coat the haddock with the seasoned breadcrumbs. Heat the butter in a large ovenproof sauté pan until bubbling. Sear the haddock in the butter, about 2 minutes on each side. Place the pan with the haddock in the oven until the haddock is browned, about 4 minutes. Toast the buttered rolls or bread on a griddle. Place one piece of the fish on one side of a slice of sourdough or roll. Top with tartar sauce and the remaining bread slice. Add lettuce and tomato if desired.

BAKED LEMON-THYME FLOUNDER

MANY PEOPLE THINK OF FLOWERS AS BEING JUST ORNAMENTAL, BUT THE *flowering herb—lemon thyme—in this recipe brings together the flavor attributes of lemon with one of our favorite herbs. Adding a squeeze of lemon brings in even more layers of flavor. Lemon thyme might be a bit hard to find, but it's worth seeking out and it's certainly easy to grow in a window box or small garden. If you can't find it, don't despair; just use regular thyme and an extra squeeze of lemon.*

YIELD: 6 SERVINGS

2 cups finely ground panko breadcrumbs
2 teaspoons kosher salt
$^1/_4$ teaspoon freshly ground black pepper
6 (6-ounce) flounder fillets
4 tablespoons melted unsalted butter or olive oil, divided
2 tablespoons chopped fresh lemon thyme

Preheat the oven to 400°F. Combine the breadcrumbs with the salt and pepper. Dip the fish in 3 tablespoons of the melted butter or olive oil then into the seasoned breadcrumbs. Lightly oil a cookie sheet with the remaining butter or olive oil and place the fish on the sheet. Sprinkle the chopped thyme over all. Bake until brown, 10 to 12 minutes, and serve.

SALMON WIGGLE, OUR WAY

THIS IS ONE OF THOSE OLD DISHES MAINERS LOVE TO HATE BECAUSE IT'S ONE *that can go horribly wrong if you overcook it. Don't cook that salmon and peas to mush like Mom used to—it might ruin it for your future generations. The traditional old menu for the Fourth of July is fresh salmon, new peas, boiled potatoes, and hard-cooked eggs with one cup of medium thick white sauce. We've jazzed that old dish up a bit with herbs and some non-traditional red pepper.*

YIELD: 6 SERVINGS

8 tablespoons (1 stick) unsalted butter

$^1/_2$ cup all-purpose flour

2 cups sliced mushrooms

$^1/_2$ red onion, finely chopped (about $^1/_2$ cup)

2 cups chicken or vegetable stock

2 cups heavy cream

2 cups fresh peas

$^1/_3$ cup diced red bell pepper

$^1/_8$ teaspoon cayenne pepper

$^1/_4$ teaspoon ground nutmeg

$^1/_2$ cup chopped fresh chives

1 pound salmon, cut into $^1/_2$-inch chunks

1 teaspoon lemon juice

Melt the butter in a large sauté pan over medium heat and slowly add the flour, whisking until it thickens, about 5 minutes. Add the mushrooms and onions and turn the heat to low. Continue to cook, stirring occasionally. In a pot, heat the chicken stock and the cream. Add the cream mixture to the onion mixture, whisking in slowly. Cook on low heat until thick, about 5 minutes. Add the peas and the bell pepper. Stir to mix. Add the cayenne, nutmeg, and chopped chives. Add the salmon and cook for 5 minutes. Finish with the lemon juice. Serve at once.

HALIBUT *and* BRUSSELS SPROUT SALAD

CLARK'S FATHER HATED BRUSSELS SPROUTS. HE GREW UP IN THE DEPRESSION, *and back then he had to eat many a Brussels sprout. He'd often say it was his least favorite vegetable. When we said we were going to serve him Brussels sprouts one night, he was discouraged, but this dish completely changed his mind. He loved it. The Brussels sprouts come out fresh, crisp, and buttery and when you brown the halibut well, it's nice and flaky inside, a perfect complement for the buttery salad.*

YIELD: 6 SERVINGS

BRUSSELS SPROUTS SALAD
48 medium Brussels sprouts
4 tablespoons unsalted butter
1 teaspoon kosher salt
$^1/_4$ teaspoon freshly ground black pepper

HALIBUT
$^1/_2$ cup all-purpose flour
1 teaspoon kosher salt
$^1/_4$ teaspoon freshly ground black pepper
6 (6-ounce) thin halibut fillets
4 tablespoons ($^1/_2$ stick) unsalted butter

FOR THE BRUSSELS SPROUTS SALAD: Separate the Brussels sprouts into leaves by removing the tough outer leaves and coring the sprouts. Coring is easier if you cut the sprouts in half then cut out the hard center. Remove the tender inner leaves and reserve. Melt the butter in a large sauté pan over medium heat and add the Brussels sprouts. Cook slowly, stirring frequently until just tender and bright green, about 3 minutes. Season with the salt and pepper and serve with the halibut.

   FOR THE HALIBUT: Combine the flour, salt, and pepper and mix well. Dredge the halibut in the seasoned flour. Heat the butter in a very large nonstick sauté pan over medium heat. Sauté the fish, a few pieces at a time, until it is browned, about 3 minutes per side. Keep the fish warm while you finish cooking the remaining fillets. Divide the fish on six plates and garnish with the warm salad.

GRILLED SALMON
with GREEN BEANS *and* CORN

IT'S SUMMER, SUMMER, SUMMER WHEN THE CORN AND BEANS ARE COMING OUT *of the garden and those fresh-from-the-garden vegetables are great with seafood. All you need to do is fire up the grill and create a ragout, which can also be done on the grill.*

YIELD: 6 SERVINGS

4 tablespoons unsalted butter
6 ears of corn, cleaned of silk and kernels cut off (about 4 cups)
1 cup chicken stock
1 cup peeled, seeded, chopped tomato
2 tablespoons chopped thyme
1 pound green beans
Kosher salt and freshly ground black pepper
6 (6-ounce) pieces salmon fillet
$^{1}/_{4}$ cup olive oil

Heat the grill as hot as it will go. Melt the butter in a large sauté pan over medium heat and sauté the corn for 1 minute. Add the chicken stock, tomato, and thyme. Boil 1 quart salted water and add the green beans. Blanch the green beans in boiling water for 3 minutes. Drain the beans and add to the corn. Season with salt and pepper to taste. Brush the salmon with the olive oil and season with salt and pepper to taste. Grill the salmon until cooked, about 5 minutes on each side. Divide the bean and corn mixture onto six plates. Top with grilled salmon and serve.

CIDER-POACHED SALMON *with* APPLES

AUTUMN IN NEW ENGLAND IS GORGEOUS, AND THE HIGHWAYS ARE CLOGGED
with RVs and retirees coming north to catch the spectacular colors before they fade. At Arrows in the fall, we're blessed by numerous old apple trees that give us apples for cooking and cider. Our chef Justin Walker has a hundred-year-old cider press, and it's a fun group enterprise to gather apples for the cider for many dishes, including this one. Salmon and apples go well together whether the salmon is poached or smoked.

YIELD: 6 SERVINGS

1 gallon apple cider

2 teaspoons rosemary

2 tablespoons thyme

$^1/_4$ cup plus $^1/_4$ teaspoon brown sugar

2 tablespoons fennel seed

1 tablespoon kosher salt

1 tablespoon freshly ground black pepper

6 (6-ounce) salmon fillets

$^1/_2$ pound (2 sticks) unsalted butter

1 quart (about 6) cooking apples, such as Macintosh, cored and sliced

Heat the cider in a nonreactive, wide-bottomed saucepan and reduce the liquid by half. Add the rosemary, thyme, brown sugar, fennel, salt, and pepper to the cider. Bring to boil. Reduce the heat to a simmer. Gently place the salmon in the liquid. The liquid should be steaming, but not moving. Cook the salmon for 6 minutes. Heat the butter in a sauté pan. Add the apples and sauté until golden, about 2 minutes. Remove the salmon from the cider liquid with a slotted spatula. Place the salmon on six heated plates and garnish with sautéed apples.

FINNAN HADDIE, RUTH'S WAY

CLARK'S FATHER WAS A SCOT AND HIS MOTHER NORWEGIAN, SO HIS FAMILY *alternated between many different kinds of Northern European breakfasts. People were always surprised by the unique breakfast dishes that appeared on their table like the light donut-like pancake called* ebelskivers, blintzes, *and of course,* finnan haddie, *named for a fishing village of Finnan in Scotland. There, the fish was originally smoked over peat, and it's still often served poached in milk for breakfast. You can find smoked haddock at a good fish market and some upscale supermarkets. The cream cuts some of the potency of the smokiness, dryness, and saltiness of the fish. Haddock is readily available here. Settlers ate smoked fish, which was hung on the barn door in just about every household. Cooking dried meats and fish in milk softened them and brought them back to life. Serve this like you would creamed chipped beef on toast—if you still do that—but on a toasted English muffin and with some thick bacon or sausages.*

YIELD: 6 SERVINGS

3 cups half-and-half

12 ounces smoked haddock cut into large chunks

6 tablespoons unsalted butter

1^1/$_2$ cups finely chopped Spanish onions

1^1/$_2$ cups panko breadcrumbs

1 teaspoon kosher salt

Dash of freshly ground black pepper

Juice of 1 lemon (about 2 tablespoons)

1^1/$_2$ cups finely diced potato

Chopped chives, for garnish

Preheat the oven to 350°F. Put the half-and-half in a saucepan over medium heat, add the fish, and cook until the liquid is reduced by half and the fish is soft. Remove the fish and reserve the finnan haddie cream. Melt the butter in a small skillet over medium heat and add the onions. Sauté until translucent. Add the breadcrumbs, salt, and pepper. Cool to room temperature. In a 2-quart baking dish, place the haddock, finnan haddie cream, lemon juice, and the potato. Bake for 20 minutes. Garnish with the chives. Serve with a toasted English muffin.

BACON-WRAPPED COD *with* HOMINY CAKE

HOMINY IS CORN PRESERVED WITH LYE, MADE FROM AN OLD COOKING TECHNIQUE *used to preserve and bring dried corn back to life. The Cherokees made hominy grits by soaking corn in a weak lye solution and beating it with a corn beater called a* kanona. *Hulled corn is a favorite old New England dish made from yellow corn, while hominy is made from white corn. Elderly New Englanders may still tell stories of peddlers who used to sell hulled corn and horseradish. Today hominy can be purchased in two forms—hulled and ready to cook, or in tins ready to just heat and serve. Either is an excellent change from potatoes. You can find it in the supermarket in tins, almost always in the Mexican food section. We've included it in this updated fish stew.*

YIELD: 6 SERVINGS

HOMINY

$2^1/_2$ cups hominy

2 large egg yolks, lightly beaten

2 tablespoons all-purpose flour

1 teaspoon sugar

$^1/_4$ teaspoon kosher salt

$^1/_8$ teaspoon freshly ground black pepper

$^1/_4$ teaspoon sweet paprika

1 teaspoon baking powder

2 egg whites

$^1/_2$ cup canola oil, divided

COD

6 (6-ounce) cod fillets

6 strips thick-cut smoked bacon

2 tablespoon canola oil

2 tablespoons unsalted butter

FOR THE HOMINY: Combine the hominy, egg yolks, flour, sugar, salt, pepper, paprika, and baking powder in a bowl and mix. In another bowl, beat the egg whites to stiff peaks. Gently fold the egg whites into the hominy mixture. Heat $^1/_4$ cup of the canola oil in a nonstick sauté pan. Spoon one-sixth of the hominy into the pan, flipping the cake when golden brown and firm to the touch on one side, about 1 minute per side. Cook the remaining hominy cakes, adding more canola oil when needed. Place the cakes on a cookie sheet while making the entire batch.

    FOR THE COD: Wrap each piece of cod in a slice of bacon. Heat the canola oil in a large nonstick sauté pan over medium heat. Add the butter and when melted and foaming, add the cod. Sauté until the bacon is lightly crisp and the cod is cooked through, about 5 minutes on each side. Place one hominy cake on each plate and top with the bacon-wrapped cod. Serve.

COD CAKES *with* TARTAR SAUCE

NEW ENGLAND'S ECONOMY WAS BUILT ON COD—IT WAS ONE OF THE COMMODITIES *we exported along with rum in the Triangle Trade. People used to say you could walk on the backs of the cod they were so plentiful. Unfortunately, the stock of cod is severely diminished today, but efforts are being made to save it.*

YIELD: 6 SERVINGS

20 ounces cod, coarsely chopped
$^1/_2$ cup fresh lemon juice
6 tablespoons unsalted butter, divided
$1^1/_2$ cup finely chopped Spanish onion
Kosher salt and freshly ground black pepper
$1^1/_2$ cup panko breadcrumbs
1 cup all-purpose flour
1 cup sour cream
3 tablespoons chopped chives

Toss the fish in the lemon juice in a bowl. Melt 1 tablespoon of the butter in a sauté pan over medium heat. Sauté the onion in the butter until translucent. Season with salt and pepper to taste. Stir in the breadcrumbs and then set the mixture aside to cool.

Combine the breadcrumb mixture and the fish. Stir in the flour, $^1/_4$ cup at a time, to bind, but be careful to use just as much as you need to hold the cakes together. Add the sour cream and the chopped chives. Form into six "cakes." Heat the remaining butter in a large nonstick sauté pan and sauté the cakes on each side until golden brown, about 3 minutes on each side. Serve with tartar sauce (see page 118).

PAN-FRIED TROUT

THE STOUT FLAVORS OF CHINESE SHAO XING WINE INSPIRED THIS DRAMATIC *dish, and it has become a signature dish in our restaurants where we often combine influences from our trips to Asia with classic Maine dishes and ingredients. One can catch trout in New England and our own Maine brook trout is delicious. In China, a whole fish is a sign of prosperity so we came up with this rendition using Maine's freshwater fish and always serve it whole, sometimes to the dismay of our guests.*

YIELD: 6 SERVINGS

$1/4$ cup plus 3 tablespoons
    canola oil, divided

1 tablespoon minced fresh ginger

1 tablespoon sliced garlic

$1/2$ cup chicken stock

$1/2$ teaspoon Shao Xing wine
    or sherry vinegar

$1/2$ tablespoon soy sauce

$1/8$ cup sesame oil

1 cup all-purpose flour

2 tablespoons sesame seeds

2 teaspoons kosher salt

6 (8- to 10-ounce) whole boneless trout

3 tablespoons unsalted butter

1 tablespoon Chinese fermented black beans

$1/4$ cup chopped scallions

2 tablespoons chopped tomato

Julienned scallions, for garnish

Cilantro sprigs, for garnish

Preheat the oven to 450°F. Heat 3 tablespoons of the canola oil in a large nonreactive saucepan over medium heat. Sauté the garlic and ginger. Add the chicken stock, wine, soy sauce, and sesame oil. Cook until the liquid is reduced by half and set aside.

Combine the flour, sesame seeds, and salt in a bowl, and dredge the trout in the breading mixture. Heat the remaining $1/4$ cup canola oil in a large, nonstick sauté pan over medium-high heat. Fry the trout both sides until golden brown, about 3 minutes on each side. Place the trout on a cookie sheet, and bake in the oven for 4 to 5 minutes. While baking, bring the chicken stock mixture to a simmer and whisk in the butter, black beans, chopped scallions, and tomato. Cook until heated through, about 2 minutes. Divide the sauce onto six plates and gently place a trout on each plate. Garnish with scallions and cilantro.

PLANK-ROASTED TROUT *with* ROSEMARY

PLANK ROASTING IS A NATIVE AMERICAN METHOD OF COOKING. IT LENDS ITSELF *to modern cooking because it's quick and easy and the wood imparts a subtle flavor. It's a fun presentation as well. The board should be plain cedar, untreated by any chemicals. Just go to your hardware store and tell them what you're using it for. Be sure to "marinate" the boards ahead of time with a small amount of oil. And save them—the boards can be reused even if they're a little charred. Serve with jasmine rice or parslied new potatoes and lemon wedges.*

YIELD: 6 SERVINGS

6 (10-ounce) whole cleaned trout, heads off
6 cedar planks
$^1/_2$ cup olive oil
Kosher salt and freshly ground black pepper
12 rosemary sprigs

Preheat the oven to 350°F. Split the trout and place skin side down on the plank. Sprinkle the trout with olive oil and salt and pepper to taste. Place rosemary sprigs on top of each trout.

Roast on the plank until cooked through and opaque, about 10 minutes. Place one plank with trout on each of six plates.

SAUTÉED STRIPED BASS *with* BACON *and* ONIONS

OK, WE'VE SAID IT BEFORE BUT PORK, FAT, AND ONIONS ARE ALL OVER TRADITIONAL *Maine cooking, so we just couldn't resist offering it again this time with striped bass. Slowly cooking the onions and bacon together adds a bold full-bodied flavor to a delicate white fish, and again, it's a kind of winter or cold-weather food for when you want a heartier dish.*

YIELD: 6 SERVINGS

18 strips of thick bacon (about 9 ounces), chopped
1 cup finely chopped Spanish onion
$^1/_2$ cup all-purpose flour
Kosher salt and freshly ground black pepper
6 (6-ounce) fluke fillets
2 tablespoons canola oil, divided
$^1/_4$ cup finely chopped chives
2 tablespoons lemon juice

Cook the bacon in a large nonstick sauté pan until just crisp, about 4 minutes. Add the onions and lower the heat. Stir and sauté until the onions are translucent, about 5 minutes. Remove the onions and bacon from the pan, and reserve 2 tablespoons of the bacon fat and discard the rest. Season the flour with a dash of salt and pepper. Dredge the fluke in the seasoned flour. Heat 1 tablespoon of the oil in the pan with 1 tablespoon of the bacon fat and sauté 3 of the fluke fillets until browned on both sides. Add the remaining tablespoon of oil and the remaining bacon fat and sauté the remaining fillets. Place one fillet on each of six plates. Top with the bacon and onions and then the chopped chives and a sprinkle of lemon juice.

Chapter Three **THE FOREST**

*O*ur house sits right where the southern and the northern forest come together, between Mt. Agamenticus, one of the largest undeveloped forests in coastal New England, and the sea. It's one of the most diverse ecological areas as well with an impressive variety of rare plant and animal species like wild onions, winterberry, and sassafras as well as myriad wild mushrooms and ferns. We walk in it, run in it and we're privileged to have it right outside our back door. We have some of the best water we've ever tasted too, sweet and crystal clear from five watersheds that run off from the Mountain.

It's easy to think that this forest was untouched when the settlers arrived, but that's not the case. The Penacook tribe cultivated here and had a managed ecosystem. When the settlers came, Portsmouth, New Hampshire, and Southern Maine became wealthy because of the timber industry and cleared the land in a more industrial way for farming and orchards. Now, when we look out the back door of Arrows, we see forests that one hundred years ago we would not have seen. We see wild apple trees there from old orchards, overgrown meadows from past cultivation, and rock walls that separated pastureland.

This forest is really only about a century old, but it's rich with wildlife and with food. Even if the land isn't cleared for farms, Mainers will scour the forest floor for wild mushrooms, fiddleheads, thickets of wild blueberries and raspberries, cranberry bogs, acorns, and honey. And while Vermont and New Hampshire get all the credit, Maine has wonderful maple syrup as well.

Mainers really get giddy in the early spring when the grass turns green and we can hear the peepers in the long night. That's when the royal trio of the season begins to arrive—ferns with the curly, crunchy tops we call fiddleheads; sharp, wild onions known as ramps; and the exotic to some, but not at all to us, coveted morel mushrooms. Long into the fall, we go out with the staff to forage for golden peppery chanterelles, huge hen-of-the-woods growing from oak bark—yes, they do taste like chicken—and the robust black trumpets great for sautéing or even tempura. There are huge rocky fields of wild blueberries. We're bombarded with TV, tweets, and texts but what we really need to do is slow down and take a look at what's right outside. That hillside we're driving past at sixty-five miles per hour is filled with blueberries and look, that black and gray patch is filled with the most delicious mushrooms.

Then there is the game from the forest. We've become such an urban society that many

Americans avoid rabbit and venison or pheasant and quail. They think it's strong tasting and tough, but now local farms are raising these game animals and birds and they're delicious. It's really not what one thinks it is. It's flavorful and not loaded with fat and chemicals. It's easy to cook too. Cooking venison can be as simple as grilling a steak, or chicken. Every year we do game dinners, and frequently our diners are a little apprehensive, but when they sit at the table they start to see it as an opportunity to learn something they didn't know. We're learning all the time that all around us is this food that just tastes really good.

FIDDLEHEAD FERNS *with* BROWN BUTTER

BECAUSE OUR WINTERS ARE SO LONG, WE GET VERY EXCITED AT THE FIRST SIGNS *of spring. Out come the cell phones to take photos of those first signs only to have our friends on the West Coast ask us why we just sent them a picture of a bleak winter. One of the most enjoyable things to find when spring first arrives are the ferns in the forest, which seem to burst within minutes after we hear the first peepers and see the first purple crocus coming up through the dense earth. On the tops of the ferns are the fiddleheads, and we've found plenty of ways to cook them, although it's easy to cook them badly. It's important to cook them long enough, but they're hideous when undercooked too. Fern mush is no one's favorite. When cooked just right, and with brown butter that imparts a nuttiness to the super green fern, we wager you'll never find a better way.*

YIELD: 6 SIDE DISH SERVINGS

2 quarts water
$^1/_2$ teaspoon kosher salt
4 cups fiddleheads
4 tablespoons unsalted butter
$^1/_4$ teaspoon lemon juice
Kosher salt and freshly ground black pepper

Bring the water and salt to a boil in a large pot. Add the fiddleheads and blanch for 1 minute. Drain and plunge them immediately into an ice bath. Remove the fiddleheads as soon as they are cool. Melt the butter in a saucepan on medium-high heat and cook until just brown. Turn the heat to low and then add the lemon juice and the fiddleheads. Season with salt and pepper to taste and cook until the fiddleheads are fork tender. Serve at once.

FIDDLING WITH FIDDLEHEADS

THE COILED LEAVES OF THE FERN JUST BEGINNING TO BURST through the earth are called "fiddleheads" because they look something like the carved decorative piece on the top of a violin or cello. All ferns have them but the ostrich fern reigns supreme as the tastiest. We get them in Maine in the early spring and for just a few months you'll find them in salads, custards, omelets, quiche, and with grilled steak in just about every home in the state. We've even seen them made into ice cream.

The ostrich fern fiddleheads are about an inch in diameter with a deep groove on the inside of the stem and a light scale-like covering on the unfurled fern. Get them before they open and start to grow because at that point they're inedible. They should be very green and wrapped up tight. Some liken the flavor to asparagus, and they do have a "grassy," earthy flavor.

We find them near the banks of rivers and streams in our area and pick them when they are about an inch or two out of the ground. It's important to wash them well several times until the water runs clean. They can be steamed, boiled, sautéed, and pickled, but we have yet to make them into ice cream.

GRILLED RAMPS

LIKE THE FIDDLEHEADS AND MOREL MUSHROOMS, RAMPS ARE ANOTHER SIGN OF
*spring. At our restaurants we are excited to offer all three together as soon as they mature. While
they look like the average scallion, wild ramps have an intense onion flavor with a touch of sweetness.
These grilled ramps are great draped over meat or fish, or served as a first course in a salad.*

YIELD: 6 SIDE DISH SERVINGS

24 ramps
$^1/_2$ cup olive oil
1 teaspoon kosher salt
$^1/_4$ teaspoon freshly ground black pepper

Rinse the ramps and peel off the outer layer. Trim off the ends. Toss the ramps in the olive
oil and season with the salt and pepper. Grill lengthwise until slightly translucent, about 2
minutes each side. Serve at once.

MUSHROOM PIE

IT TOOK A LOT MORE OF OUR TIME THAN WE EXPECTED TO FIGURE OUT HOW TO *get this just right, but after many years, we nailed the texture and the moisture. You can use the common domestic mushroom if you're on a budget and it will still taste luxurious. Or if you like, use more exotic mushrooms—there are plenty in the supermarket or at the farmers' markets. A slice of mushroom pie and a salad with a green vegetable makes a great dinner. It's hearty enough for fall or winter and makes a good side dish for a holiday meal.*

YIELD: 6 SLICES

PIECRUST

2 cups all-purpose flour

8 tablespoons (1 stick) cold butter,
  cut into small cubes

1 teaspoon kosher salt

1 cup ice water

FILLING

4 tablespoons unsalted butter

1 cup finely chopped Spanish onions

1 pound domestic mushrooms, sliced

2 tablespoons all-purpose flour

2 cups heavy cream

1 teaspoon chopped fresh thyme

1 teaspoon chopped chives

1 teaspoon chopped fresh parsley

$1/2$ cup sour cream

$1/2$ cup grated Reggiano cheese

Kosher salt and freshly ground black pepper

1 cup grated Gruyère cheese

4 large eggs, beaten

FOR THE PIECRUST: Place the flour in a food processor and add the butter cubes, a few at a time, pulsing to mix. The piecrust can also be mixed by hand. Add the salt and pulse again. With the processor running, add the ice water, a little at a time, until the mixture begins to form a dough but is not too wet. It should just hold together. Place on a cutting board and knead six times until all the cubes of butter are incorporated. Make a ball, wrap in plastic, and chill for 1 hour. Preheat the oven to 375°F. Roll out the dough and press it into a 9-inch tart shell. Line the tart shell with parchment paper and fill with dried beans or a pie weight. Bake for 15 minutes.

    FOR THE FILLING: Increase the oven temperature to 400°F. In a skillet melt the butter over medium heat and then sauté the onions until translucent. Add the mushrooms and cook until all liquid is gone. Add the flour and cream. Cook until thick, 5 to 10 minutes.

Add the herbs, sour cream, and Reggiano cheese. Season with salt and pepper to taste. Let the mixture cool and then add the Gruyère cheese and the beaten eggs. Place the mixture in the pre-baked shell and bake until the crust is lightly brown and the filling is firm, about 20 minutes. Cool for 15 to 20 minutes. Slice and serve.

MUSHROOM SOUP *with* SOUR CREAM

THIS IS A DECADENT AND LUXURIOUS HOLIDAY DISH, THE PERFECT WAY TO START A *festive occasion. We often serve it as a first course for a Christmas meal, calories be damned! You can just walk it off the next day. Serve this with an old-fashioned wine pairing, such as a dry sherry, which is traditionally served with cream of mushroom soup. Lustau Solera from East India, unique but inexpensive, would be perfect.*

YIELD: 6 SERVINGS

6 tablespoons unsalted butter
1 cup finely chopped Spanish onions
2 pounds domestic mushrooms, sliced
1 quart chicken stock
2 cups heavy cream
1 cup sour cream plus some for garnish
Chives, for garnish

Melt the butter in a large soup pot over medium heat. Sauté the onions in the butter until soft. Add the mushrooms and cook until soft and dark brown. Add the chicken stock and cook for 10 minutes. Lower the heat, add the cream, and cook for 10 more minutes. Let cool to room temperature. Blend in a food processor or blender in batches until smooth. Incorporate a little of the sour cream in the mushroom purée, return it all to the soup pot and then add the rest of the sour cream to the soup. Warm the soup in a pot over medium heat. When hot, divide into bowls and top with a dollop of sour cream and chopped chives.

FORAGING

THERE'S NOTHING MORE ENJOYABLE THAN GOING THROUGH THE forest and finding something you can take home for dinner. We have many varieties of mushrooms in Maine, two thousand in fact, but only a few show up on the table in our restaurants. Don't go out and find your own unless you have proper training or go out with an expert, although foragers guard their favorite spots like Egyptian tombs. *Edible and Medicinal Mushrooms of New England and Eastern Canada* by Maine's own David L. Spahr or *Foraging New England: Finding, Identifying, and Preparing Edible Wild Foods and Medicinal Plants from Maine to Connecticut* by Tom Seymour are two books we suggest that will help get you started, but here are some of the mushrooms we like to find and taste. Some say you should never wash mushrooms with water, just sweep off the dirt with a small, soft brush, but it's okay to use a little water as long as you dry them immediately and well so the water isn't absorbed into the spongy mushroom. There's no need to peel them, in fact, peeling will remove much of their flavor.

PORCINI. Also called Cepe, Steinpilz, or King Bolete, you'll find these robust mushrooms in Italian and French cuisine as well as here in our own native New England fare. We get them in the early fall and love to use them in tarts, pasta dishes, and eggs.

OYSTER. With its hint of anise and thick flesh, autumn's oyster mushrooms are perfect with beef, pork, and lamb, but we also love them just sautéed in a rich first-pressed olive oil and drizzled with aged balsamic vinegar as a first course. They're particularly good in a stir-fry with Asian ingredients, a little ginger, a touch of soy, and some tender beef—an easy, delicious meal.

CHANTERELLE. There's gold in the forest during the late summer in Maine, and we look for these prized mushrooms long into the fall. They're meaty, fragrant with touches of peach and pepper, and are wonderful in all kinds of cooking. They're terrific in egg and potato dishes and can even be pickled.

BLACK TRUMPET. Just a gorgeous mushroom, purple-black, soft yet chewy, black trumpet has a subtle sweetness with a buttery finish. Sound a bit like a fine wine? We treat them that way, savoring the delicate trumpet all summer and fall. Use in soups, stews, and stir-fries, with fish, eggs, and poultry, or just sauté in fresh creamy butter.

HEN-OF-THE-WOODS (OR MAITAKE). Around Labor Day, this versatile mushroom looks like a scaly mess, some weighing as much as ten pounds, but they're absolutely delicious. Luckily, they dry well, so if your friends don't call "dibs" on some of your harvest, dry them or freeze them raw for winter cooking. Subtly flavored with a bit of a citrus, you can even grind them up into a powder after drying and use the powder as a seasoning.

CHICKEN-OF-THE-WOODS. Like Hen-of-the-Woods, these mushrooms grow around tree trunks and have a similar petal-like construction, but their flavor is very different. It does have a bit of chicken flavor and is great in pasta and risotto or simply sautéed in butter with garlic and herbs.

MOREL. All of Maine's edible mushrooms are delicious, so it's with some reluctance that we say, "We've saved the best for last," but we really have. The flavor of morels is so intense and unique, we count the days until they come up in the spring. Try these lightly breaded and fried just like tempura or, as always, simply sautéed in butter. They'll make a great flavoring for sauces for chicken, shrimp, and flank steak. Never eat these raw. Cooking takes away toxins. You'll also need to be more careful when cleaning; the deep grooves in these mushrooms hold plenty of hidden soil.

ROASTED QUAIL
with CHESTNUT STUFFING

WE ALWAYS ASSOCIATE WARM FAMILY HOLIDAYS WITH CHESTNUTS. THERE'S *something to the whole "chestnuts roasting on an open fire" thing, and they are delicious right out of the oven or hearth. We almost lost chestnuts in America due to a blight in the early 1900s, but since the 1930s, efforts have been made to bring them back. We're glad they're back so we can make this elegant dish, a terrific showcase for these sweet and nutty treats. No one's going to stuff a quail for a casual family night, but they will when company is coming or for a night of romance. This dish is lovely paired with our Mushroom Pie (page 139) or Mushroom Soup with Sour Cream (page 140). Serve it with a good quality Pinot Noir or an elegant red Burgundy. Serve two quail as a hearty main course or one for an appetizer or lighter supper.*

YIELD: 6 APPETIZER SERVINGS OR DOUBLE FOR 6 ENTRÉES

$1^1/_2$ cups chestnuts

$^1/_2$ pound (2 sticks) unsalted butter, divided

1 cup finely chopped Spanish onion

$^1/_2$ cup chopped celery

1 tablespoon chopped fresh thyme

4 cups diced and dried sourdough bread

$^1/_4$ cup chicken stock

6 (3-ounce) quail

Kosher salt and freshly ground black pepper

Score an X into the chestnuts and boil in a pot of water for 5 minutes. Peel them while hot, but not hot enough to burn your hands. After they are peeled, finely chop the chestnuts. Melt 12 tablespoons ($1^1/_2$ sticks) of the butter in a skillet over medium heat and sauté the onion, celery, thyme, and chestnuts until the onions are translucent. Put the diced bread in a large bowl and pour the chestnut mixture over the bread. Boil the chicken stock in a pot and pour it over the bread mixture. Wait for the stuffing to cool and then stuff each quail, dividing the stuffing equally.

While the stuffing is cooling, preheat the oven to 400°F. Place the quail in the oven on a cookie sheet greased with 1 teaspoon of the butter. Melt the remaining butter in a small skillet and pour on top of the quails. Season with salt and pepper to taste and then roast until the internal temperature of the stuffing is 130°F. Serve at once.

CORN FRITTERS *with* MAPLE SYRUP

FRITTERS ARE VERY BIG IN OLD-YANKEE COOKING AND WHILE FRIED FOOD WASN'T *a huge tradition in New England, there were some dishes you'd see over and over including donuts and boat steerers, but we just call them corn fritters. It might be worth your while to invest in a small deep fryer if you think you might make these or our crab or clam fritters on a regular basis. If not, just use a deep heavy pot and invest in a deep-fat thermometer. By adding corn and thyme to this pâte à choux pastry, you have a great "corn fritter."*

YIELD: 6 SERVINGS

1 cup water
$1/8$ teaspoon kosher salt
$1/8$ cup unsalted butter
1 cup all-purpose flour
5 eggs
2 cups shucked corn, blanched
2 teaspoons chopped fresh thyme
3 cups canola oil

Combine the water, salt, and butter in a heavy 2-quart saucepan and bring to a boil. Add the flour all at once and stir until very smooth with a wooden spoon, 1 to 2 minutes. Remove from the heat. Allow to cool for 3 minutes in the saucepan. Add the eggs, one at a time, beating with the wooden spoon thoroughly after each addition. The paste should be smooth and shiny. Allow to cool for about 10 minutes. Add the corn and thyme and stir in gently. Cook the dough by dropping tablespoons into a deep fryer. Cook until they float and are golden, about 3 minutes. You can practice with one to check the time by cooking and then breaking open to check for doneness. They should not be too runny or liquid inside.

GRILLED RABBIT
with JUNIPER *and* BAY LEAVES

RABBIT IS QUICKLY RESURGING IN POPULARITY IN AMERICAN COOKING. IT WAS *wildly popular until World War II. After that, Americans clamored to get their food out of a box, and we forgot that food didn't come out of TV tins or a cellophane package in the supermarket. Now, with the return to artisan-raised livestock and game, where the old ways have become new again, we can even get rabbit in the supermarket. There are some important things to keep in mind when cooking rabbit, and number one is that you have to brine rabbit to make it tender and not dry. It only takes about an hour and a half to brine and requires virtually no effort. It is also essential to marinate rabbit to keep it from drying out when grilling. Juniper and bay are a traditional combination when cooking wild game, and they impart intense, unexpected flavors. Ask your butcher to break down the whole rabbit for you.*

YIELD: 6 SERVINGS

9 quarts cold water

9 tablespoons kosher salt

24 peppercorns

3 rabbits, cut into hind legs and saddle, with rib cage removed

1 cup extra virgin olive oil

Kosher salt and freshly ground black pepper

24 bay leaves, crushed

$^3/_4$ cup juniper berries

Make a brine solution by combining the cold water with the salt and peppercorns. Place the rabbit pieces in the brine and let sit for $1^1/_2$ hours.

Remove the rabbit from the brine, and place the rabbit pieces in a bowl with the olive oil and sprinkle with salt and pepper to taste. Marinate for 30 minutes.

Meanwhile, heat a grill to medium high. Place the crushed bay leaves and the juniper berries in the rabbit. Grill until the meat is brown on one side, about 10 minutes, and then flip and brown the other side. Divide the rabbit among six plates and serve.

GRILLED VENISON
with HUCKLEBERRY SAUCE

HUNTING IS STILL A TRADITIONAL PART OF LIFE IN MAINE AND FOR MANY FAMILIES, *a necessity. There are now farmers who are raising venison, so it's available year-round. If your family isn't used to it, we're here to tell you, there's nothing weird about the flavor and texture of venison. In fact, many who've tried it for the first time say it's the "best tenderloin of beef" they've ever had. Nowadays, people are turning to leaner meats like bison and venison, and a saddle, the loin of the venison, is tender, lean, and delicious. The huckleberry sauce here adds brilliant color. We've had a bumper crop of huckleberries in our garden for a number of years. At first we used it in desserts, but then experimented, using it with savory dishes. It's very traditional in Yankee cooking to use fruits with meat, and it adds brilliant color and a lightly sweet flavor. Obviously this isn't a dish you'll make every day so crack open that great red Meritage wine, fine quality Cabernet, or red Bordeaux you've been saving for that special occasion. Serve it with our Root Cellar Gratin (page 275).*

YIELD: 6 SERVINGS

1 quart beef stock
2 cups fresh or frozen huckleberries
$^1/_2$ cup red wine vinegar
$^1/_2$ cup sugar
1 teaspoon kosher salt
$^1/_4$ teaspoon freshly ground black pepper
3 venison loins (about 2$^1/_2$ pounds total)
$^1/_4$ cup olive oil
Kosher salt and freshly ground black pepper

Simmer the beef stock in a heavy saucepan until the liquid is reduced to $^1/_2$ cup. Place the huckleberries, vinegar, sugar, salt, and pepper in a stainless steel pot and cook on medium heat until thick and syrupy. Add the reduced beef stock and simmer until combined.

Heat the grill as hot as it will go. Toss the venison in the olive oil and sprinkle with salt and pepper to taste. Grill the venison for 3 minutes per side for medium rare (about 5 minutes per side for medium). Take the venison off the heat and let it rest for 4 minutes. Slice the venison, place the sauce on a hot platter, and arrange the meat on top. Serve at once.

A MAINER'S THANKSGIVING

THANKSGIVING IN NEW ENGLAND MEANS GOING TO THE PLACE where it all started, and we like to include those classic ingredients in our holiday meal as well as dishes from our own family heritage. On our table we'll have our famous prosciutto paired with the old-time Johnnycakes and cranberries from nearby bogs with molasses as well as dishes from the sea, such as the delicate peekytoe crab, an ingredient that gives a nod to our seafarers.

Many Mainers take advantage of our natural food resources at Thanksgiving including oyster stuffing, mashed potatoes made from huge Maine potatoes, and cornbread using corn dried after the summer's harvest. In Maine at Thanksgiving time, bagging one of our native birds makes any Mainer a hero, at least at the dinner table. Their meat is richer than their domestic counterparts and they've been ranging on the delicious fruits of the forests for additional great flavor.

We're never surprised to see lobster on the Thanksgiving table either. While there might not have been any potatoes or even turkey at the first "thanksgiving," more like ducks and geese as well as venison, records do show that there were lobster and clams at the first harvest feast in 1621 at Plymouth. Every year the cry goes up, "Is lobster the new turkey?" It could very well be, but we wouldn't want to miss our turkey and stuffing.

Mark's Traditional Turkey Dinner

AT ARROWS, WE BRINE OUR TURKEYS IN AN ANTIQUE CLAW-FOOT bathtub because we need to cook so many for our annual Thanksgiving dinner. We think brining is crucial to making a moist turkey. When we were on the *Today Show* a few years ago they asked if we needed anything for our segment. We asked for an antique claw-foot bathtub, and they got us one! Al Roker had a blast throwing the turkeys into the tub. After dinner is served to our restaurant guests, and they've gone home happy, we sit down with the entire staff and have our own turkey dinner. It's our tradition to tell our most embarrassing story of the year, and there are some doozies. In Maine at Thanksgiving time, you'll see wild turkeys all over the place, trucking over the overpass on I-95 or right in the backyard.

Menu

PROSCIUTTO WITH POMEGRANATES

JOHNNYCAKES WITH PEEKYTOE CRAB

HERB-BRINED TURKEY WITH PEAR GRAVY

CRANBERRY COMPOTE WITH GINGER AND MOLASSES

BOSTON BROWN BREAD STUFFING WITH SAUSAGE AND TARRAGON

YUKON GOLD POTATO AND WILD MUSHROOM GRATIN

WARM BRUSSELS SPROUTS SALAD (PAGE 121)

CARAMEL-PUMPKIN PIE WITH MINCEMEAT ICE CREAM

Prosciutto with Pomegranates

YIELD: 8 SERVINGS

24 prosciutto slices
2 pomegranates, separated into pips
Extra virgin olive oil
Freshly ground black pepper

Divide the prosciutto slices among eight plates. Arrange the pomegranate pips decoratively around the plate. Drizzle with olive oil and sprinkle with freshly ground pepper to taste.

NOTE: To remove the pips, first peel the pomegranate by cutting off the top and then scooping out the core. Try not to disturb the seeds. Score the outer rind in quarters with a sharp knife. Pull apart the sections. Peel off the white skin around the seeds and invert the skin. The seeds will pop out. To make it easier, place the cut pieces in a bowl of cold water to separate the seeds. The white part will float.

Johnnycakes with Peekytoe Crab

YIELD: 8 SERVINGS

9 ounces fresh Peekytoe crabmeat
  or other fresh crabmeat
$3/4$ cup mayonnaise (see Herb Mayonnaise,
  page 49, but omit the herbs)
$1/2$ cup finely chopped fresh chives
$1^1/2$ teaspoons lemon juice
Kosher salt and freshly ground black pepper
Johnnycakes (page 80)

Mix the crabmeat, mayonnaise, chives, and lemon juice in a medium bowl to blend. Season the mixture with salt and pepper to taste. Make the Johnnycakes according to the recipe. Divide them among eight plates and top with the crab mixture.

Herb–Brined Turkey with Pear Gravy

YIELD: 8 SERVINGS

TURKEY

5 gallons water

1 (1-pound) box coarse kosher salt

$^1/_2$ cup whole black peppercorns

$^1/_2$ cup fresh thyme sprigs

$^1/_2$ cup fresh marjoram sprigs

$^1/_2$ cup fresh sage sprigs

12 bay leaves

1 (13-pound) turkey

4 tablespoons butter, at room temperature

Kosher salt and freshly ground black pepper

PEAR GRAVY

4 tablespoons unsalted butter

$^1/_2$ cup all-purpose flour

2 cups low-salt chicken broth

1 cup pear juice

2 tablespoons dark rum

Kosher salt and freshly ground black pepper

3 tablespoons chopped fresh marjoram

FOR THE TURKEY: Select a container large enough to hold the turkey. Add the water and the salt and stir until the salt dissolves. Stir in the peppercorns, thyme, marjoram, sage, and bay leaves. Add the turkey to the brine. Place a large plate on top of the turkey to submerge it. Place in a cold place and soak for 8 to 10 hours.

Remove the turkey from the brine. Rinse and pat dry. Preheat the oven to 450°F. Place the turkey on a rack in a large roasting pan. Rub the butter over the turkey. Season with salt and pepper to taste. Place the turkey in the oven and reduce the heat to 325°F. Roast until a thermometer inserted into the thickest part of the thigh reads 175°F, about 2$^1/_2$ hours. Transfer the turkey to a platter and tent with foil. Let stand at room temperature for 30 minutes before carving.

FOR THE PEAR GRAVY: Spoon off the fat from the drippings in the roasting pan, reserving $^1/_4$ cup of fat. Measure $^2/_3$ cup of pan juices and set aside. Melt the butter and the reserved fat in a large saucepan over medium heat. Mix in the flour. Stir and cook until light brown, about 2 minutes. Gradually add the chicken broth, pear juice, and the pan juices. Simmer until thickened, stirring frequently, about 10 minutes. Stir in the rum. Season with salt and pepper to taste. Sprinkle the turkey with marjoram and serve with the gravy.

Cranberry Compote with Ginger and Molasses

YIELD: 8 SERVINGS

4 cups fresh cranberries
$1^1/_2$ cups water
1 cup sugar
1 tablespoon finely grated fresh ginger
1 tablespoon finely chopped shallot
$^1/_4$ cup light molasses
Kosher salt

Combine the cranberries, the water, sugar, ginger, and shallot in a large heavy nonreactive saucepan. Stir over medium heat until the sugar dissolves. Cover the pan and cook until the berries burst, about 10 minutes. Stir in the molasses. Season with salt to taste. Cool to room temperature. Cover and chill until cold, about 5 hours. This dish can be made one week ahead if kept in the refrigerator.

Boston Brown Bread Stuffing with Sausage and Tarragon

YIELD: 8 SERVINGS

1 (16-ounce) can Boston brown bread, cut into $^1/_2$ -inch cubes.
$^1/_2$ pound soft Italian bread, crusts trimmed, cut into $^1/_2$ -inch cubes.
4 ounces Italian sausage, crumbled
4 tablespoons unsalted butter
$^3/_4$ cup chopped Spanish onion
$^1/_4$ cup chopped fresh chives
3 tablespoons chopped fresh tarragon
$^1/_2$ teaspoon kosher salt
$^1/_4$ teaspoon freshly ground black pepper
$1^1/_2$ cups low-sodium chicken broth

Preheat the oven to 250°F. Divide all the bread cubes between two rimmed cookie sheets. Bake until the bread is dry, about $1^1/_2$ hours. Transfer the bread to a large bowl. Sauté the sausage in a large sauté pan until cooked through and browned, about 12 minutes. Using a slotted spoon, transfer the sausage to paper towels. Discard all but 1 tablespoon of the drippings in the sauté pan. Add the butter to the sauté pan and melt over medium heat. Add the onion and sauté until soft, about 7 minutes. Add the sautéed onion, the chives, tarragon, salt, pepper, and sausage to the bowl with the bread. Toss to combine. This can be prepared one day ahead if covered and refrigerated.

Butter a 9 x 9-inch baking dish. Add the chicken broth to the bread mixture and toss to moisten. Transfer the stuffing to the buttered dish. Cover the stuffing with foil and bake for 40 minutes. Uncover and bake until lightly browned on top, about 20 more minutes.

Yukon Gold Potato and Wild Mushroom Gratin

YIELD: 8 SERVINGS

7 tablespoons unsalted butter, divided

12 ounces assorted fresh wild mushrooms, sliced

3 pounds Yukon Gold potatoes

$1^1/_2$ teaspoons kosher salt, divided

$3/_4$ teaspoon ground black pepper, divided

2 cups heavy cream

Preheat the oven to 375°F. Melt 6 tablespoons of the butter in a large sauté pan over medium-high heat. Add the mushrooms and sauté until brown and soft, about 6 minutes. Generously butter an 11 x 7-inch baking dish with the remaining butter. Peel and cut the potatoes into $1/_8$-inch-thick slices. Arrange two layers of potatoes in the buttered dish. Spoon one-third of the mushrooms over the potatoes. Sprinkle with $1/_2$ teaspoon salt and $1/_4$ teaspoon pepper. Repeat two more times with the same proportions of potatoes, mushrooms, salt, and pepper. Pour the cream over the potatoes. Cover the dish with foil and bake for 45 minutes. Uncover and continue baking until golden brown and set, about 20 minutes longer. Let stand 10 minutes before serving.

Caramel-Pumpkin Pie with Mincemeat Ice Cream

YIELD: 8 SERVINGS

CRUST

$1^1/_3$ cups all-purpose flour

1 tablespoon sugar

$1/_2$ teaspoon kosher salt

3 tablespoons chilled unsalted butter, cut into $1/_2$-inch cubes

3 tablespoons chilled lard, cut into $1/_2$-inch cubes

2 tablespoons (or more) ice water

FILLING

$2/_3$ cup sugar

2 tablespoons water

2 tablespoons unsalted butter

$^3/_4$ cup half-and-half

$^2/_3$ cup whipping cream

2 large eggs

1 large egg yolk

1 cup canned pumpkin puree

2 teaspoons ground cinnamon

$^3/_4$ teaspoon ground ginger

$^1/_4$ teaspoon ground cloves

$^1/_4$ teaspoon kosher salt

FOR THE CRUST, mix the flour, sugar, and salt in a food processor. Add the butter and the lard, using the pulse, and process until a coarse meal forms. Add 2 tablespoons of ice water and process until moist clumps form, adding more ice water by teaspoonful if the mixture is dry. Form the dough into a ball. Wrap the dough in plastic wrap and refrigerate for 1 hour.

Roll out the dough onto a floured surface until it's a 12-inch round. Transfer to a 9-inch diameter pie dish. Fold the overhang under the rim and crimp the edges decoratively. Chill for 1 hour.

Preheat the oven to 375°F. Bake the crust until the edges begin to brown, pressing the crust with the back of a fork if bubbles form, about 15 minutes. Cool slightly. Reduce the oven temperature to 350°F.

Meanwhile, make the filling. Dissolve the sugar in the water in a saucepan over medium heat. Increase the heat and boil

without stirring until the sugar turns dark amber, occasionally swirling the pan and brushing the sides with a pastry brush, about 7 minutes. Remove the pan from the heat. Whisk in the butter, 1 tablespoon at a time. Stir in the half-and-half and the cream, stirring until the caramelized bits dissolve.

Whisk the 2 whole eggs and 1 yolk in a bowl to blend. Whisk in the pumpkin, cinnamon, ginger, cloves, and salt. Gradually whisk the caramel mixture into the pumpkin mixture. Transfer the filling to the crust. Bake until puffed and set in the center, about 50 minutes. Cool the pie on a rack.

Mincemeat Ice Cream

YIELD: ABOUT 5$^1/_2$ CUPS

VANILLA ICE CREAM

2 cups heavy whipping cream

2 cups whole milk

1 vanilla bean, split lengthwise

10 large egg yolks

1$^1/_2$ cups sugar

MINCEMEAT

2 Golden Delicious apples (about 1$^1/_2$ pounds), peeled, cored, and cut into $^3/_4$-inch cubes

1$^1/_2$ cups raisins

1 cup pecans, toasted and chopped

1 cup sugar

$^3/_4$ **cup apple cider**

$^1/_4$ **cup Calvados (apple brandy)**

4 tablespoons unsalted butter

$2^1/_2$ **tablespoons fresh lemon juice**

1 cinnamon stick

1 teaspoon kosher salt

$^1/_2$ **teaspoon ground nutmeg**

$^1/_2$ **teaspoon ground cloves**

$^1/_2$ **teaspoon finely grated lemon peel**

FOR THE ICE CREAM: Mix the whipping cream and the milk in a large heavy saucepan. Scrape in the seeds from the vanilla bean and add the bean itself. Bring to a simmer and then remove from the heat. Whisk the yolks and the sugar in a bowl to blend. Gradually whisk the hot cream mixture into the yolk mixture.

Return the mixture to the saucepan. Stir over medium heat until the mixture thickens and leaves a path on the back of a spoon when your finger is drawn across, about 5 minutes. Strain this custard into a bowl and chill, covered, about 4 hours.

FOR THE MINCEMEAT: Bring all of the ingredients to a boil in a heavy saucepan. Reduce the heat to medium and cook until almost all of the liquid is absorbed, stirring frequently, about 15 minutes. Discard the cinnamon stick. Transfer the mixture to a bowl and refrigerate until cold, about 2 hours.

Process the custard in an ice cream maker. Transfer the ice cream to a bowl. Fold in 3 cups of the cold mincemeat. Cover and freeze until firm, about 4 hours.

TURKEY POT PIE

WHEN EVERYONE IS SICK OF LEFTOVERS, THIS IS SOMETHING DIFFERENT TO DO
*with turkey. Meat pies are very traditional European fare and our French Canadian neighbors love
to cook them too.*

YIELD: 6 SERVINGS

FILLING

8 tablespoons (1 stick) unsalted butter

1 cup chopped celery

1 cup chopped red onion

1 cup chopped carrots

2 cups quartered button mushrooms

1 tablespoon chopped fresh thyme

$^1/_2$ cup all-purpose flour

3 cups chicken or turkey stock

3 cups peeled, cubed potatoes, cooked

1 pound leftover roasted turkey, cut
  into 1-inch cubes

1 teaspoon kosher salt

$^1/_4$ teaspoon freshly ground black pepper

PASTRY

$2^1/_2$ cups all-purpose flour

1 teaspoon kosher salt

$^1/_2$ cup unsalted butter

$^1/_3$ cup ice water

FOR THE FILLING: Heat the butter in a sauté pan and sauté the celery, onion, carrots, mushrooms, and thyme for 2 minutes on medium heat. Add the flour and cook for an additional 3 to 4 minutes. Add the stock and slowly bring to a boil. Add the potatoes and turkey and remove from the heat. Pour the mixture into a shallow dish and allow to cool.

FOR THE PASTRY: Preheat the oven to 325°F. Place the flour and salt in a bowl and mix thoroughly. Cut the butter into $^1/_4$-inch cubes and add to the dry ingredients. Using your hands, cut the butter into the flour until the mixture forms pea-size pieces. Add the water and gently form into a dough, without over-mixing.

Once the filling is completely cool, roll out the dough into two pieces and place one piece in the bottom of a 10-inch pie pan. Place the turkey filling in the pan and cover with another layer of dough. Crimp the edges together to seal. Cut vents in the top layer of the dough to allow steam to escape. Bake until the filling is gently bubbling and until the crust is golden brown, about 25 minutes. Remove from the oven and let cool for 20 minutes before serving. Serve with all of your leftover vegetables or a salad.

TURKEY BREAKFAST SAUSAGE

TURKEY IS A HEALTHY ALTERNATIVE TO PORK AS WELL AS A SAVORY SUBSTITUTE *for those who don't eat pork. People tend to try to make turkey taste like pork in sausages but it's not like it at all so even if you love the usual pork sausage, try this in your sausage biscuits and gravy or with your eggs for a very different flavor. You don't even need to use casings, just make patties.*

MAKES 1 POUND SAUSAGE

1 tablespoon cornstarch

2 tablespoons cold water

$\frac{1}{4}$ cup finely chopped onion

1 teaspoon chopped garlic cloves

1 tablespoon chopped fresh sage

1 teaspoon ground nutmeg

$\frac{1}{2}$ teaspoon chili flakes

$\frac{1}{3}$ cup finely chopped fatback

1 pound ground turkey

2 tablespoons kosher salt

$\frac{1}{8}$ teaspoon freshly ground black pepper

$\frac{1}{8}$ cup maple syrup

Mix the cornstarch with the cold water. In a bowl mix together all of the other ingredients. Pour the cornstarch mixture into the turkey mixture and combine. Form into patties and sauté over medium-high heat or cook on a hot grill. Serve at once.

ROASTED DUCK *with* GARLIC *and* THYME

DUCK IS ONE OF THOSE DISHES THAT CAN TURN INTO A HORRIBLE FIASCO WITH *friends and family complaining it's greasy and tough, but this cooking method is just about fool-proof. The water keeps it tender and moist, and the heat removes the fat. Like all things, starting with the right ingredients is very helpful so be sure to choose a good-quality duck, such as a Long Island variety, and while duck freezes well, fresh is always best. Serve this duck with wild rice, our Peach Chutney (page 290), and roasted vegetables.*

YIELD: 6 SERVINGS

2 (5-pound) fresh ducks
6 garlic cloves, cut into $^1/_8$ -inch pieces
24 sprigs of thyme
3 teaspoons chopped fresh thyme
$^3/_4$ teaspoon kosher salt
$^3/_4$ teaspoon freshly ground black pepper

Preheat the oven 500°F. Stuff each duck with half the garlic and sprigs of thyme, divided evenly. Sprinkle the top of the duck with chopped thyme, salt, and pepper. Place $^1/_2$ inch of water in a roasting pan. Place the ducks in the roasting pan, breast side up, and place in the oven. Turn the temperature down to 400°F. Flip the duck after 30 minutes and again after another 30 minutes. The bird should appear golden brown and the leg should move easily. If it is not yet done, roast the ducks for another 15 minutes. Remove the ducks from the roasting pan and place on a cutting board. Allow the birds to rest for 10 minutes. Carve the ducks and give each person some of the breast meat, leg, and thigh.

ROASTED DUCK *with* LINGONBERRY SAUCE

MAINERS LOVE THEIR MEAT WITH FRUIT AND WE HAVE MUCH TO CHOOSE FROM.
Lingonberries are from even further north than Maine, far up in Canada, and they're often called high-bush blueberries. While they used to be stored in sawdust and peat in the old days, now you can get them in cans in the supermarket. They're much like cranberries and their bold tartness will cut the fat of the duck. Experiment with different berries from tart to sweet, such as raspberries and blackberries. Serve with our Corn Pudding (page 102), Root Cellar Gratin (page 275), or Grilled Ramps (page 138).

YIELD: 6 SERVINGS

2 cups red wine

1 cup port wine

2 cinnamon sticks

2 star anise

$^1/_4$ teaspoon ground cloves

$^1/_4$ teaspoon cardamom

Juice and zest of 2 oranges

Juice and zest of 2 lemons

16 ounces lingonberry jam

2 (5-pound) fresh ducks

Preheat the oven to 500°F. In a nonreactive saucepan over medium heat, cook the red wine, port, cinnamon, star anise, cloves, cardamom, orange juice and zest, and lemon juice and zest until the mixture is reduced by one-half. Remove the cinnamon sticks and add the jam. Stir and heat the sauce. Drizzle the sauce on the duck to baste and reserve some of the sauce for basting during cooking. Place $^1/_2$ inch water in a roasting pan. Place the ducks in the roasting pan and place in the oven. Reduce the temperature to 400°F. Flip the duck after 30 minutes. Baste periodically. Flip again after another 30 minutes. The bird should appear golden brown and the leg should move easily. If it is not yet done, roast the duck for another 15 minutes. Remove the ducks from the roasting pan and place on a cutting board. Allow the birds to rest for 10 minutes. Carve the duck and give each person some of the breast, leg, and thigh meat. Serve the remainder of the sauce on the side.

Chapter Four **THE FARM**

*T*he farm-to-table concept is not a new thing in Maine where Yankees have relied on what they grew and raised for centuries. Now, the idea of cooking and eating meats and vegetables supplied by local farms has once again become a major part of the Maine culinary landscape. As chefs we've always been quietly on the forefront of the farm-to-table movement, even before it was a "movement," out of necessity. We had to start our own farm in 1992 because when we arrived here almost two dozen years ago, not many farmers were thinking of selling to a local restaurant, and one of our goals was to find small producers in our area to build on. There weren't many back then but over the years we've developed relationships with producers who provide us with pigs and poultry, beef and lamb. We wanted to make prosciutto and we found a farmer down the road who had pigs. They turned out to be the best pigs we could ever hope to find and our prosciutto, aging in our rafters year after year, is a much anticipated treat. Another neighbor was cultivating honey, another was raising rabbits, and we created recipes around what was available. We found eggs nearby too, along with fresh creamy butter, and slowly we collected a group of local farmers and producers to supply the restaurant. We both have fond childhood memories of taking trips to farms, so going to these farms and creating dishes with their bounty was important.

It wasn't easy but, then again, we arrived at a bad time for farming. In the 1970s farms were disappearing to make way for strip malls and condos. Commerical farming never left the state, but it suffered during the Depression and then with the rise of industrial farming and suburban sprawl, our farmers had difficulty competing. Aroostook County used to raise more potatoes than anywhere else in the country, but now that honor goes to Idaho. The numbers tell it all. In the 1940s there were six thousand potato farms, but now there are less than five hundred. Despite the difficulties, farming never died. Small farms survived, and all over the state you can still drive around and see a house with a small barn, a yard with pecking chickens, and a plot of land with a vegetable garden. No matter how small, good food is growing. There's always been a presence, and now farming in Maine is going through a Renaissance with hundreds of small producers and farmers' markets weekly in winter and daily in summer all across the state.

Now, we have young farmers starting their own farms with livestock, poultry, and vegetables, and folks who have been around for decades are finding a revived interest from home cooks in buying and eating locally. Our neighbors Tom and Betsy Hasty at Breezy Hill Farm, who have been farming there since 1979, are good examples. This has been their way of life, and they are part of a history that has come full circle. They now supply pigs, beef, eggs, and butter regularly to area restaurants. We're lucky to have them just down the road because although our summers are short, we don't put the barbeque away until we have to make snow tracks to get to it. Many things are seasonal in Maine, including the sale of charcoal briquettes, but with all this great pork and beef around, we stockpile ours. On a cold winter night we'll still be out grilling a steak. We feel proud that these relationships have allowed farms to flourish and that they can now supply many other restaurants and help the local ethic grow.

PORK SAUSAGE *with* HOMINY

SAUSAGE IS FUN AND EASY TO MAKE AND YOU REALLY DON'T HAVE TO GO TO THE *fuss of putting it into casings. Just use patties or cook the meat loose and make a savory hash. The fun is in the ingredients. It's just ground pork, herbs, and spices so you can experiment with hot chili flakes, your favorite herbs, and even something more exotic like clove or cumin. If you want to grind your own pork, go right ahead, but to make this even easier, buy ground pork and go to town. Serve with our Warm Red Cabbage Salad (page 202) or Broccoli Casserole (page 208) to make a stick-to-your-ribs kind of dinner that's a bit different for casual family night. Make it ahead of time and it might even be considered fast food!*

YIELD: 6 SERVINGS

HOMINY

1 cup peeled garlic

2 cups milk

4 (15.5-ounce) cans hominy

$^1/_2$ cup chicken stock

1 cup chopped scallions

4 tablespoons unsalted butter

Kosher salt and freshly ground black pepper

SAUSAGE

$^1/_4$ teaspoon pepper flakes

$^1/_4$ teaspoon allspice

$^3/_4$ teaspoon kosher salt

$^1/_4$ teaspoon freshly ground black pepper

$^1/_4$ teaspoon rosemary

$^1/_4$ cup panko breadcrumbs

$^1/_3$ cup cream

2 teaspoons cornstarch

1 large egg

$^1/_3$ cup milk

1 pound lean pork

$^1/_4$ cup plus 2 tablespoons canola oil

FOR THE HOMINY: Poach the garlic and milk in a nonreactive saucepan over medium heat. Cook until the garlic is soft but not falling apart. Drain the hominy through a colander. In a large sauté pan, combine the chicken stock with the scallions and hominy and bring to a boil. Add the poached garlic and stir in the butter. Season with salt and pepper to taste.

FOR THE SAUSAGE: Combine all of the ingredients except for the $^1/_4$ cup canola oil in a food processor and blend. Form the mixture into six patties. Heat the $^1/_4$ cup canola oil in a large nonstick sauté pan and sauté the sausage patties until golden brown, about 2 minutes on each side. Divide the hominy mixture between six hot plates and place a sausage patty on each. Serve at once.

APPLES STUFFED *with* SAUSAGE

AT ARROWS, ANCIENT APPLE TREES SURROUND OUR GARDENS, AND WHEN PEOPLE *ask us what type apple they are, we just say, "old type." You can use any type that's native to your state or experiment with different varieties to change it up a bit. Stuffed apples make a fun breakfast, or a side dish to a rustic family-style dinner. It's perfect for one of those many pot lucks you're invited to and it's great for Thanksgiving when you're asked to bring your own specialty.*

YIELD: 6 SERVINGS

$^1/_4$ teaspoon pepper flakes

$^1/_4$ teaspoon allspice

$^3/_4$ teaspoon salt

$^1/_4$ teaspoon freshly ground black pepper

$^1/_4$ teaspoon rosemary

$^1/_4$ cup panko breadcrumbs

1 large egg

$^1/_3$ cup cream

2 teaspoons cornstarch

$^1/_3$ cup milk

$^1/_2$ pound lean ground pork

$^1/_4$ cup canola oil

6 large apples, cored and peeled

2 tablespoons unsalted butter, melted

Preheat the oven to 400°F. Combine the pepper flakes, allspice, salt, pepper, rosemary, breadcrumbs, egg, and cream in a food processor. Purée until smooth. Combine this mixture with the cornstarch, milk, and pork in a bowl. Heat the canola oil and sauté the sausage mixture until browned. Stuff the mixture into the apples. Place the apples in an ovenproof baking dish. Drizzle the apples with butter. Bake until tender when poked with a skewer, 20 to 30 minutes. The apples will start to crack open a bit.

SLOW-BRAISED PORK ROAST *with* ROASTED ROOT VEGETABLES

ROAST PORK SEEMS SIMPLE BUT IT CAN BE HARD TO MAKE JUST LIKE YOUR
Grandma used to. She used the cheap cuts and cooked it for a long, long time. This cooking technique is virtually foolproof. Searing and cooking slowly in the stock and the vegetables ensures that it's tender, moist, and full of flavor. It might take awhile but it's easy. Come home and cook while watching the evening news. With the roasted vegetables, it's also a one-dish dinner and one of our favorites for casual company and family.

YIELD: 6 SERVINGS

2 tablespoons all-purpose flour

Kosher salt and freshly ground black pepper

1 (3-pound) pork loin

¼ cup canola oil

2 tablespoons Dijon mustard

2 tablespoons whole-grain mustard

1 cup white wine

2 cups chicken stock

1 tablespoon kosher salt

10 peppercorns

6 sprigs rosemary

2 medium turnips, peeled and
cut into 1-inch wedges

3 medium yellow beets, peeled and
cut into 1-inch wedges

18 large pearl onions, peeled

6 small parsnips, peeled and cut
into 1-inch pieces

3 tablespoons unsalted butter

Preheat the oven to 400°F. Combine the flour and salt and pepper to taste and coat the pork loin with it. Heat the oil in an ovenproof casserole or Dutch oven over medium-high heat. Brown the loin on all sides. Using a spatula, coat the loin with the mustards. Add the white wine and chicken stock, salt, peppercorns, and rosemary. Add all of the vegetables. Cover the casserole and place in the oven. After 40 minutes, remove the parsnips, turnips, and onions and set aside, keeping warm. Turn the loin over and continue cooking for 30 minutes. Remove the beets and keep warm. Turn the loin over again. Cook until the internal temperature is 140 to 145°F for medium. Remove the loin from the pan. Pour the liquid in the pan through a sieve and return the liquid to the casserole. Place the vegetables on a serving plate. Slice the pork. Whisk the butter in the liquid and pour over the loin. Serve at once.

HAM *with* RAISIN SAUCE

THIS DISH GOES BACK TO THE OLD DAYS WHEN AT THE END OF THE GROWING *season a farm family no longer had the means to feed the pigs. That meant it was time to use the pigs and use all of them. Most parts of the pig were smoked and cured, and one of the most popular cuts was the ham, the meaty thigh and rump portion of the animal. Just about every carnivore you talk to loves pork, and ham is at the top of the ladder. Here we pair it with raisins from grapes that are native to Maine for centuries. Leif Ericson found Concord grapes when he came to America and they grow abundantly around our restaurant and house. The two traditions of drying and smoking come together again in this recipe to show us how clever our forebearers were and that these delicious traditions from our hearty, free-thinking, adaptable, and yes, thrifty ancestors remain with us. Just to bring in a little more history, we've added some of that New England rum to the mix. Hams are already "cooked" by curing, so just get your favorite brand, heat, and serve with this rich, earthy sauce.*

YIELD: 6 SERVINGS

1 (5-pound) ham

1 cup golden raisins

$^{1}/_{2}$ cup dried currants

$^{1}/_{2}$ cup dark rum

4 tablespoons unsalted butter

$^{1}/_{2}$ cup finely chopped shallots

$^{1}/_{2}$ cup finely chopped fresh ginger

$^{1}/_{4}$ cup all-purpose flour

3 cups apple cider

1 cup chicken broth

1 tablespoon whole-grain mustard

1 tablespoon Dijon mustard

1 tablespoon finely chopped thyme

1 teaspoon cider vinegar

Kosher salt and freshly ground black pepper

Preheat the oven to 375°F. Place the ham in a roasting pan and roast for 1 hour. Soak the raisins and currants in the rum until they are plump, about 20 minutes. Melt the butter in a saucepan. Add the shallots and the ginger, and sauté slowly until soft, about 10 minutes. Add the flour and cook for 5 minutes, stirring slowly. Add the apple cider and the chicken broth and cook until the liquid is reduced by one-half. Add the mustards, thyme, cider vinegar, and the raisin and rum mixture. Season with the salt and pepper to taste. Bring to a boil and serve with slices of ham.

HAM *with* FRIED APPLES

TANGY, CRISPY, FRIED APPLES ARE A GREAT FOIL FOR SALTY, SMOKY HAM, AND NO *matter where you live, there are many local apple varieties to choose from. Maine pomologists are still rediscovering heritage apple varieties that thrived hundreds of years ago. Not only do we have the more familiar Macintosh and Cortland apples, but also the rare purple Black Oxfords, Briggs Auburn with it's green skin and hints of banana flavor, and the juicy Fletcher Sweet coming back to life after centuries.*

YIELD: 6 SERVINGS

6 (6-ounce) ham steaks
1 cup all-purpose flour
1 teaspoon kosher salt
1 pinch freshly ground black pepper
3 large apples, cored and sliced to $\frac{1}{2}$ inch thick
12 tablespoons ($1\frac{1}{2}$ sticks) butter, divided
1 cup apple juice or cider
1 cup chicken stock
$\frac{1}{4}$ cup Cognac or brandy

Grill or sauté the ham slices until lightly brown, about 5 minutes on each side. Keep warm. Combine the flour, salt, and pepper in a bowl. Toss the apple slices in the flour and coat. Melt 8 tablespoons of the butter in a large sauté pan. Fry the apples in the butter over medium-high heat until light brown, about 2 minutes per side. Remove the apples from the pan. Add the apple juice, the stock, and the Cognac. Cook until the liquid is reduced by one-half. Add the remaining 4 tablespoons of the butter and whisk it into the sauce. Place the ham slices on individual plates or one large platter. Pour the sauce over the ham. Serve with the apples.

A HAM IN THE RAFTERS

WE STARTED CURING OUR OWN PROSCIUTTO BECAUSE IT WAS very expensive to buy, but we continued to make it just because we loved doing it. When we lived in San Francisco, there were bakeries that made much better bread than we could, places to get confections that were better than anything we could dream up, so when we first opened Arrows we thought, "Why would you make these things?" But then we discovered we couldn't find anything. There was no good bread, no great desserts, and even the fish was poorly handled. We had to make it all ourselves and find the right source for fish and meats.

We also wanted to be true to our environment. Here we were in this old farmhouse and as we became involved in the renovation of this colonial structure where we both lived and opened Arrows, we were intrigued by how the farmers before us lived and their old ways. People gave us books on their ways, so we started thinking about making food using their techniques. Again, it was all out of necessity. We wanted to serve the best, and we couldn't find it. We wanted to re-establish the way the original Maine farmers who built our house had lived, so we started making our own prosciutto. We had to close the restaurant in the winter because there was no business then so we hung the prosciutto in the dining room. To us our homemade variety is buttery, creamy, and less salty than store-bought prosciutto, and it tastes like the very essence of the ham. We've made it every year since 1989 in batches of two to four dozen and over the years we've refined our techniques. One of our proudest moments was when a little Italian lady from Emilia-Romana said our prosciutto reminded her of home.

CLASSIC YANKEE POT ROAST

THIS SUPER-EASY ONE-DISH DINNER MADE WITH AN INEXPENSIVE CUT OF *meat thrives on neglect. No fuss meals like this one go back hundreds, even thousands, of years. When we stand by the fireplace at Arrows, it's not hard to imagine the ancestor of our farm standing around an iron pot and tending the well-kept fire, taking in the aromas of cooking that filled the room. They waited for the pot roast to "catch on," sticking to the pot just enough to brown, giving the gravy a richness and a savory flavor that coats the lips. You don't need an iron pot to recapture the flavor. If you like using a slow cooker, try that or simply use the oven or stove top. While the cooking time is long, just start it in the morning and it's done when you get home.*

YIELD: 6 SERVINGS

1 cup all-purpose flour
$^1/_2$ teaspoon kosher salt
$^1/_2$ teaspoon freshly ground black pepper
1 (5-pound) chuck roast
8 ounces beef or pork fat
1 pound carrots, peeled and sliced
1 pound celery, sliced
2 pounds Spanish onions, sliced
8 cups (64 ounces) chicken or beef stock
1 (16-ounce) can tomatoes in juice
1 pint dark ale

Combine the flour, salt, and pepper on aluminum foil. Roll the roast in the seasoned flour. Melt the fat in a large casserole and brown the roast with the vegetables. Add the stock, tomatoes, and ale. If cooking on the stove top, cook for 2 hours on medium heat. If cooking in the oven, preheat the oven to 300°F and cook until a fork goes into the roast very easily, about $3^1/_2$ hours. Remove the roast from the casserole and slice. Place the sliced roast on a platter and garnish with the vegetables and braising liquid.

CLASSIC BOILED DINNER

IT GOES WITHOUT SAYING THE ADAGE "WASTE NOT WANT NOT" IS VERY APP- *ropriate when applied to Yankees. This dish is often used the next day to make red flannel hash. Boiled dinners were traditionally served twice a week in Maine from early fall until late spring on Mondays and Wednesdays. In our version of a one-plate meal the vegetables are added at different times so that each item is perfectly cooked at the end.*

YIELD: 8 SERVINGS

1 (4- to 5-pound) corned beef brisket

8 bay leaves

1 teaspoon whole black peppercorns

1 teaspoon mustard seeds

1 teaspoon fennel seeds

18 small potatoes

24 small boiling onions, peeled

4 small carrots, peeled and sliced

4 small parsnips, peeled and sliced

2 small turnips, peeled and sliced

$1/4$ cup olive oil

Kosher salt

Freshly ground black pepper

1 large head green cabbage, outer leaves removed and cut in 8 to 12 wedges (do not remove the core or the cabbage will fall apart while cooking).

Rinse the brisket under cold running water. Place the brisket in a large pot with the bay leaves, peppercorns, mustards seeds, and fennel seeds. Add cold water to cover the meat by 2 inches. Bring to a boil over medium-high heat and then reduce the heat to low. Simmer for about 30 minutes per pound of meat, 2 to $2^{1}/_{2}$ hours.

After the brisket has cooked for $1^{1}/_{2}$ hours, preheat the oven to 325°F. Toss the potatoes, onions, carrots, parsnips, and turnips in a large roasting pan with the olive oil. Season with salt and pepper to taste. Bake, uncovered, for about 45 minutes, turning the vegetables with a large spoon every 15 minutes, until lightly browned and tender when pierced with the tip of a knife.

Once the brisket is tender, after about 2 hours, add the cabbage to the pot and cook until tender, about 15 minutes. Remove the pot from the heat and transfer the cabbage to a large warm serving platter. Transfer the brisket to a cutting board and slice thinly across the grain, arranging the slices in the center of the platter. Arrange the roasted vegetables around the brisket and cabbage. Serve at once with mustard.

GRILLED FLANK STEAK *with* MOM'S SAUCE

CLARK'S MOM USED TO SERVE THIS SAUCE WITH GRILLED SALMON, AND IT'S A *favorite standby condiment in all three of our restaurants. It is terrific with salmon, but we think it's particularly tasty with flank steak, a flavorful cut of meat. By marinating the steak in the sauce you're adding even more flavor to this delicious cut of meat.*

YIELD: 6 SERVINGS

1 cup red wine vinegar
1 cup balsamic vinegar
$^{1}/_{4}$ cup Worcestershire sauce
$^{1}/_{4}$ cup soy sauce
$^{1}/_{2}$ cup firmly packed brown sugar
2 tablespoons whole-grain mustard
2 tablespoons blanched and chopped fresh rosemary
1 cup olive oil
1 cup extra virgin olive oil
Kosher salt and freshly ground black pepper
3 pounds flank steak

In a large bowl combine the red wine vinegar, balsamic vinegar, Worcestershire sauce, soy sauce, brown sugar, mustard, rosemary, both olive oils, and salt and pepper to taste. Whisk together until thoroughly blended. Reserve half the sauce for later use. Add the steak to the remaining sauce in the bowl and marinate for at least 1 hour or overnight. Heat the grill as hot as it will go and cook the steak for about 2 minutes on each side for medium rare (4 minutes per side for medium). Remove the steak from the grill and place on a cutting board. Allow the steak to rest for 2 minutes and then slice into half-inch slices. Serve at once with the reserved sauce.

BRAISED VEAL SHANKS *with* "FLOOR SAUCE"

"FLOOR SAUCE" IS ESSENTIALLY A SAUCE MADE WITH PURÉED BRAISED *vegetables, but we'll let you in on a little secret about how it got its name. When we made this sauce at Arrows, we couldn't think of a name for it until an eager young cook spilled it on the floor one day and as restaurant humor goes, he got a razzing and the sauce got a new name. You'll find recipes similar to this going back to Medieval cooking when sweet spices were popular, so if you really want to know what Charlemagne's food tasted like, we recommend adding some nutmeg, clove, and cinnamon to this recipe. What we do not recommend is pouring the sauce on the floor.*

YIELD: 6 SERVINGS

6 (1-pound) veal shanks

$1/4$ cup all-purpose flour

Kosher salt and freshly ground
   black pepper, for seasoning the flour

$1/4$ cup olive oil

1 bunch fresh thyme

4 stalks celery, peeled and chopped
   into 1-inch lengths

5 medium carrots, peeled and chopped
   into 1-inch lengths

1 large Spanish onion, about
   $1^1/2$ cups chopped coarsely

6 garlic cloves, peeled

$1/2$ teaspoon ground cloves (optional)

$1/2$ teaspoon ground cinnamon (optional)

$1/2$ teaspoon ground nutmeg (optional)

3 cups red wine

4 cups chicken stock

8 black peppercorns

1 tablespoon kosher salt

Preheat the oven to 350°F. Sprinkle the shanks with the flour and salt and pepper to taste. Heat the oil in a heavy ovenproof pot, such as a Dutch oven. Sauté the shanks on both sides. Add the thyme, celery, carrots, onions, garlic, the spices if desired, the wine, chicken stock, peppercorns, and salt. Cover the pot with a lid or foil. Cook in the oven for 3 to 4 hours.

   Remove the veal shanks from the pan. They should be soft and tender. Remove the thyme sprigs. Let the remaining ingredients in the pot cool for 15 minutes then carefully pour them into a blender. Blend until smooth. Divide the shanks onto six plates and ladle the purée over the shanks. Serve at once.

TENDERLOIN OF BEEF
with CHESTNUT SAUCE

THIS DISH IS JUST RIGHT FOR A SPECIAL OCCASION DINNER UTILIZING BOTH *the tenderest cut of beef and the sweet and nutty chestnuts we see around Christmas time. The flavor of the chestnuts is great with the mild luxurious beef, and they shine in this opulent, silky sauce. Serve this with our Chive Mashed Potatoes (page 280), Root Cellar Gratin (page 275), or Celery Root Salad (page 201).*

YIELD: 6 SERVINGS

2 cups sliced chestnuts

12 tablespoons (1^1/$_2$ sticks) unsalted butter, divided

1 cup Champagne vinegar

^{1}/$_4$ cup Cognac or brandy

4^1/$_2$ cups chicken stock, divided

1 teaspoon finely chopped fresh thyme

^{1}/$_8$ teaspoon freshly ground black pepper

6 (8-ounce) tenderloin steaks

^{1}/$_4$ cup olive oil

Kosher salt and freshly ground black pepper

In a sauté pan over medium heat, cook the chestnuts in 4 tablespoons of the butter until lightly caramelized, about 1 minute. Add the vinegar, Cognac, thyme, and pepper, whisking them into the pan. Add 4 cups of the chicken stock and simmer until the liquid is reduced to about 2 cups. Let the mixture cool to room temperature, place in a blender and purée until smooth. Strain the purée through a sieve. Heat the purée in a saucepan and add the remaining 8 tablespoons butter, whisking in piece by piece. Boil the remaining ^{1}/$_2$ cup of the stock in a small saucepan, and adjust the texture of the sauce if needed by adding the hot stock to make the sauce smooth.

Heat the grill as hot as it will go. Toss the steaks in the olive oil and sprinkle with salt and pepper to taste. Grill the steaks 4 minutes per side for medium rare. Serve with the sauce.

THE TAO OF BRAISING
(and other great ways to cook meat)

IN SUMMER, YOU WANT TO BE OUTSIDE GRILLING, BUT WE HAVE long winters here, so we have many months for two great cold weather ways to cook meat—braising and roasting.

Braising is also known as pot cooking, a method that combines both moist and dry heat. Food is usually seared first to caramelize the surface and then the meat is placed in a pot or pan in the oven with liquid and covered to ensure tenderness and intense flavor. Lamb shanks, veal shanks, and chuck roasts are great for slow, one-pot cooking, and it's one of the easiest techniques around. Just sear; then put the meat in a pot with herbs, wine, and some vegetables and turn the heat to low. A few hours later, dinner is ready and you've had time in between to catch up with the kids or take a long hot bath.

We do have some tips for great braising results. Marinating is always a good idea. It infuses the meat with flavor, and the acids in a marinade tenderize the meat. Searing is important too. You'll get a nice caramelized crust on the outside and the juices are sealed inside.

There are many ways to braise. Some like to use a countertop slow cooker, which you can just turn on and leave with minimal supervision. A heavy Dutch oven is good for stove-top braising and for oven cooking as well.

Your cooking liquid is a factor too. Water is fine but add flavor with stock, wine, or even a rich, dark juice. Using flavorful liquids while braising gives you a tasty gravy or sauce at the end when you take the pot out of the oven, remove the meat and vegetables and strain the rest. What's left is that intense flavor from long, slow cooking and meat that is as tender as can be from this ancient cooking method.

Roasting, a cooking method using dry heat, is another great way to prepare meats in the winter or on a rainy day because it warms up the kitchen. Cooking in the oven with high temperatures browns and caramelizes the surface of meats and fowl, adding great flavor. Most recipes will tell you to have the heat on high for the first part of cooking and then reduce the heat to ensure a moist meal. There are few things as delicious as a simple roasted chicken. We'll roast one in the afternoon and have enough for dinner and then lunch the next day in salads and in a sandwich with a little mayo and fresh herbs. They're the easiest thing in the world to roast, throw one in the oven with lemon and garlic, do the laundry, watch the news, and there's your dinner. Just place a little water in the bottom of the pan to give it some moisture and you're done.

Roasts like lamb and pork benefit from marinating ahead of time. A little olive oil, wine, and herbs give the meat flavor and break down the tendons for more tender meat. Using a heavy pan helps, too, because it allows the meat to cook evenly. Very fatty meats like prime rib should be placed on a roasting rack, but in general, it's fine to have the meat right in the pan. At the end, let the meat rest after removing it from the oven. It will cook for a few minutes more and keep in the juices if you wait about seven minutes before carving.

Using a small amount of fat or oil in a sauté pan is another great way to cook pork, chicken breasts, and much more. We like to sauté meats briefly all around on the top of the stove and then finish up in the oven. The quick heat cooking gets a good crust on the meat and the oven cooking ensures a moist and fully cooked inside. It's as easy as it gets.

Because of the long winters, we enjoy grilling so much more when the snow melts and warm weather finally arrives. At Arrows, one of the first things guests see after they've toured the garden is our big wood-burning grill. We add woods from our apple orchard and oak from the forest to give meats and fish extra flavors, and we're sure to marinate as well not only to impart more flavor but to keep food from sticking.

While some like the convenience of a gas grill, we prefer the smoke and flavor from a wood grill. With both, heat is important so be sure to have a thermometer to keep track of the temperature.

The direct cooking method is a bit like broiling where the foods are right over the source of the heat. If you're grilling something that doesn't need much time, such as vegetables, steaks, and small chicken pieces, just turn them once halfway through cooking and you're done.

If cooking food that takes much longer like a roast, ribs, or a whole pork loin, use indirect cooking so the entire roast is cooked evenly. If using a charcoal grill, just arrange the coals on one side of the grill or on either side, leaving the middle bare. The food goes over the bare space. Place a drip pan under the meat to catch fats and juices. For a gas grill, heat all of the burners and then turn off the middle burner under the food. For a two-burner grill, just light one side.

There are so many foods you can cook on a grill—fish, clams, lobster, vegetables, corn on the cob. If we could bake a cake on a grill we'd try it!

ROASTED CHICKEN *with* MARK'S CORNBREAD SAUSAGE STUFFING

THIS IS ONE OF MARK'S FAVORITE STUFFINGS. HE LOVES TO MAKE STUFFING *and is very particular about it, making his own cornbread or sourdough bread, making sure it's not too sweet and drying it just right so it doesn't get mushy. The right Italian sausage is also a must—a little hot sausage with a bit of sweet sausage to balance it out. Most things in busy restaurants are collaborations between the pastry department, savory department, and the chefs, but Mark lets no one help him with stuffing. He only makes it a few times a year and wants it all to himself. Believe us, you'll find the results are well worth the effort, and we've found ourselves on many a night forgoing the silverware and hovering over this dinner, picking at the meat and stuffing until it was all gone. You can substitute sweet and hot turkey sausage in the stuffing recipe if you prefer. Serve this with our Twice-baked Potatoes (page 281) and warm Brussels Sprout Salad (page 121). The roasted chicken is also great with the Brown Bread Sausage and Tarragon stuffing in our Thanksgiving dinner (page 152).*

YIELD: 6 SERVINGS

STUFFING
$^1/_4$ cup unsalted butter

$^1/_2$ cup finely chopped Spanish onions

$^1/_2$ cup peeled and finely chopped celery

8 ounces sweet Italian sausage, crumbled

8 ounces hot Italian sausage, crumbled

1 teaspoon chopped fresh tarragon

1 teaspoon chopped fresh thyme

1 teaspoon chopped fresh parsley

1 teaspoon chopped chives

1 cup chicken stock

2 cups cubed and dried cornbread, $^1/_2$-inch cubes

2 cups cubed and dried sourdough bread, $^1/_2$-inch cubes

ROASTED CHICKEN
1 (5- to 6-pound) chicken

1 tablespoon olive oil

1 teaspoon kosher salt

$^1/_2$ teaspoon freshly ground black pepper

FOR THE STUFFING: Preheat the oven to 350°F. In a large high-sided sauté pan over medium heat, melt the butter. Add the onion and celery and cook, stirring occasionally, until the onion is translucent, about 5 minutes. Add the sausages and cook until thoroughly cooked, about 10 minutes. Add the herbs and cook for 1 more minute. Add the stock and bring to a boil. Place the bread in a large bowl and pour the sausage mixture over the bread. Mix well. Place all of the ingredients in a buttered casserole and cover with foil. Bake for 30 minutes. Remove the foil and continue to bake for another 20 to 30 minutes, or until the top is brown and crispy.

FOR THE CHICKEN: Preheat the oven to 400°F. Place the chicken in a roasting pan and rub it with olive oil. Sprinkle it with the salt and pepper. Roast for 10 minutes and then reduce the temperature to 350°F. Roast until the leg moves easily when wiggled and the juices run clear when the thigh is pierced with a knife, about 1 hour. The internal temperature should be 170°F. Turn the chicken one-quarter turn every 20 minutes. Place the chicken on a cutting board and allow to rest for 2 minutes. Carve and serve with the stuffing.

GRILLED CHICKEN *with* JUSTIN'S COFFEE BARBECUE SAUCE

COFFEE IS A CLASSIC INGREDIENT IN ICE CREAM AND FLAN, BUT LIKE CINNAMON, *there's no reason its use in cooking must be limited to sweets. Justin Walker, our Executive Chef at Arrows, has found unusual ways to use coffee in savory cooking. This recipe may look complex, but you can make a big batch of this barbeque sauce and use it again and again. It's great with chicken but it's also fabulous with pork and beef ribs. Serve with the Warm Dandelion Greens Salad (page 209) or the Broccoli Casserole (page 208) and pair with a big bold Syrah or Cabernet.*

YIELD: 6 SERVINGS

1 tablespoon kosher salt

1 teaspoon cocoa powder

1 teaspoon Spanish paprika

1 teaspoon ground coffee

1 teaspoon ground nutmeg

1 teaspoon ground cloves

1/2 teaspoon ground cayenne pepper

1 tablespoon corn oil

1 Spanish onion, finely chopped

3 garlic cloves, finely chopped

1/2 cup red wine

1/2 cup brewed coffee

1/2 cup red wine vinegar

1/2 cup firmly packed brown sugar

2 tablespoons tomato paste

1 (16-ounce) can crushed tomatoes

6 chicken breasts, bone in

1/2 cup olive oil

Kosher salt and freshly ground black pepper

Mix the 1 tablespoon salt, the cocoa powder, paprika, ground coffee, nutmeg, cloves, and cayenne together in a small bowl. Heat the corn oil in a medium saucepan. Add the onions and the garlic and sauté until translucent. Add the red wine, brewed coffee, vinegar, brown sugar, and the dry ingredient mixture. Cook over medium heat until the liquid is reduced by one-half, 15 to 20 minutes. Mix in the tomato paste and the crushed tomatoes and cook for another 30 minutes over low heat.

Meanwhile, rub the chicken with the olive oil and the salt and pepper to taste. Grill the chicken until done on a barbecue, brushing the chicken occasionally with the sauce. Be sure to put plenty of sauce on the side for dipping. Serve at once.

DRUNKEN CHICKEN *with* LEMON GRASS *and* GINGER

WHEN WE ARE VACATIONING IN OUR HOME IN CALIFORNIA, WE LIKE TO BE OUT-
doors enjoying the sights and scenery. This is a way we've found to spend the day playing and still enjoy a delicious home-cooked dinner. In the morning before we go out, we put the birds in the marinade and when we return in the afternoon, we set them to steaming. While they're steaming we can make jasmine rice and one of our favorite greens, such as Bok Choy with Shiitake Mushrooms (page 203). When we're ready for dinner, all we have to do is fry the birds and "voila!" we have the ultimate fast "slow food" dinner.

YIELD: 6 SERVINGS

3 bay leaves

6 garlic cloves

1 tablespoon coriander seeds

1 tablespoon fennel seeds

1 tablespoon cumin seeds

2 tablespoons chopped fresh ginger

2 stalks lemongrass, chopped

3 sprigs thyme

$^1/_2$ teaspoon chili flakes

$^1/_2$ teaspoon black peppercorns

1 cup sliced Spanish onion

1 (750-milliliter) bottle white wine

$^1/_2$ cup sugar

$^1/_2$ cup kosher salt

6 ($^1/_2$-pound) poussin or Cornish game hens

2 cups canola oil

Combine all of the ingredients, except the hens and oil, in a large bowl and stir well until the salt and sugar is dissolved. Add the birds and let them marinate for 6 hours or overnight in the refrigerator.

Fill a large pot with 1-inch water and place the birds in the pot. Cover with a tight lid and let them steam for 20 minutes over high heat. Let the birds cool. When ready to eat, heat the canola oil in a large heavy saucepan over medium-high heat until a thermometer reads 350°F and then fry the birds, turning occasionally until crispy, about 5 minutes.

BRAISED LAMB SHANKS *with* CORN CAKES

CORN IS A NEW WORLD CROP, BUT IT'S HARD TO GROW HERE IN MAINE. WE *just keep waiting with baited breath until it's finally ready to pick. If you have a lot of corn and can't use it all, these corn cakes are a good way to spread the corn around. Freeze the corn in the summer and then in the winter make these cakes and serve it with another great winter dish, lamb braised all day. Lamb shanks are relatively inexpensive, and they just require a little trimming, which your butcher can do. Brown them up and put them in the oven and you have time for the corn cakes and to catch up on a few chapters of that novel you've been reading before dinner.*

YIELD: 6 SERVINGS

LAMB

1 cup all-purpose flour

Kosher salt and freshly ground
    black pepper

6 lamb shanks

3 tablespoons canola oil

2 cups chopped carrots

4 cups chopped celery

5 cups chopped Spanish onions

2 cups canned plum tomatoes

1 tablespoon chopped fresh rosemary

4 quarts chicken stock

2 cups red wine

CORN CAKES

6 tablespoons unsalted butter, divided

2 cups corn

2 cups all-purpose flour

1 teaspoon sugar

2 teaspoons salt

$^1/_4$ teaspoon freshly ground
    black pepper

4 large eggs

$^1/_2$ cup sour cream

$^1/_4$ cup milk

1 cup chopped onion

FOR THE LAMB: Preheat the oven to 350°F. Mix the flour and salt and pepper to taste in a bowl. In a heavy sauté pan heat the canola oil over medium-high heat. Dredge the shanks in the flour mixture and sauté in the canola oil until golden brown. Put the cooked shanks into a large roasting pan when done. Add the carrots, celery, onions, tomatoes, and rosemary to the roasting pan. Add the chicken stock and the red wine. Cover the pan with foil and braise the shanks in the oven for 3 hours. Turn the shanks once during cooking.

    FOR THE CORN CAKES: Prepare during the last 20 minutes of cooking the lamb. Heat

4 tablespoons of the butter in a sauté pan over medium heat and add the corn. Sauté the corn until tender, about 2 minutes. In a large bowl, combine the flour, sugar, salt and pepper. In a separate bowl, whisk together the eggs with the sour cream and milk. Add the corn and onions to the wet ingredients. Fold all of the wet ingredients into the dry ingredients and mix well. Heat the remaining 2 tablespoons of butter in a nonstick sauté pan over medium heat. Working in batches, place $\frac{1}{4}$ cup batter into the pan. Cook on both sides until golden brown, about 1 minute per side. Place the finished cakes on a cookie sheet and keep them warm. Divide the shanks and corn cakes among six plates and serve at once.

DEVILED EGGS

WE ALL GREW UP WITH DEVILED EGGS. OURS ARE JUST A BIT MORE DEVILISH *than others because we add some heat from Madras curry. We like to add chives, but any fresh herb will liven these up.*

YIELD: 6 SERVINGS

6 large eggs

$^1/_4$ cup mayonnaise (see Herb
    Mayonnaise, page 49, but
    omit the herbs)

$^1/_8$ cup sour cream

2 teaspoons Dijon mustard

$^1/_2$ teaspoon Madras curry powder

Kosher salt and freshly ground black pepper

1 tablespoon chopped chives, for garnish

Paprika, for garnish

Place the unshelled eggs in a saucepan and cover with cold water. Bring the water to a boil over medium heat and then lower to a simmer and cook for 10 minutes. Plunge the eggs immediately into ice water to stop the cooking. Remove the eggs from the ice water. Peel the eggs and slice in half lengthwise. Remove the yolks, place in a bowl, and smash with a fork. Add the mayonnaise, sour cream, mustard, curry powder, salt and pepper to taste. Spoon or pipe the mixture into the hollow of the half egg white. Garnish with chopped chives and paprika.

DOUBLE LAMB CHOPS *with* MINT RELISH

MINT WITH LAMB IS A CLASSIC COMBINATION ESPECIALLY IN MIDDLE EASTERN *cuisine. Of course, some of us have less than fond memories of the mint and lamb "combo" when Grandma served that wobbly sweet mint jelly. We make garden-fresh mint relish, which makes what people tend to think of as a winter meat into a summery one, because you can grill it outside. Serve with our Warm Dandelion Greens Salad (page 209), Celery Root Salad (page 201) or the Fried Green Tomatoes (page 204).*

YIELD: 6 SERVINGS

2 lemons	2 shallots
1 cup sugar	3 garlic cloves
2$^1/_2$ cups water, divided	1 serrano chile pepper, seeded and stemmed
2 tablespoons kosher salt	1 cup canola oil
2 cups Italian parsley leaves	Kosher salt and freshly ground black pepper
2 cups mint leaves	6 (5-ounce) double lamb chops

Slice the lemons into $^1/_8$-inch rounds and place them in a nonreactive saucepan. Add the sugar, 1$^1/_2$ cups of the water and the 2 tablespoons salt. Bring the mixture to a boil and then lower the heat and simmer for 15 minutes. Remove the pan from the heat and allow the mixture to cool to room temperature. Place the parsley, mint, shallots, garlic, chile pepper, canola oil, and the remaining cup of water in a blender. Add the cooled lemon mixture and blend into a smooth sauce. Add salt and pepper to taste. This can be kept in the refrigerator up to one day in a sealed, nonreactive container.

Heat the outdoor grill. Season the lamb chops with salt and pepper. Place the lamb chops on the grill and cook for 5 minutes per side for medium rare or 6 minutes per side for medium. Remove from the heat and serve at once with the mint relish.

SAUTÉED LAMB CHOPS
with Breadcrumbs and Apple Currant Chutney

THIS IS A TERRIFIC DISH FOR FALL, WHEN APPLES ARE CHEAP AND DELICIOUS. *We always have so many apples from our orchard that we just don't know what to do with them and wind up making everything from cider to apple pies. This recipe is one of the many we've come up with to use the plethora of the autumn bounty. We found that the sweet and vinegary flavor of the chutney works well with the pungent sautéed lamb chops. Almost any Indian chutney has currants or raisins in it, but instead of raisins, we prefer the intense flavor of the smaller dried currant.*

YIELD: 6 SERVINGS

CHUTNEY

3 tablespoons canola oil

1 red onion, peeled and chopped (about 1 cup)

$^1/_4$ cup currants

1 tablespoon Madras curry powder

2 tablespoons peeled and finely chopped fresh ginger

$^1/_2$ cup firmly packed brown sugar

$^1/_2$ cup cider vinegar

1 teaspoon Sriracha

4 cups peeled, cored, finely chopped apples

LAMB CHOPS

$^1/_2$ cup olive oil

6 lamb rack portions, 4 rib chops each

2 cups panko breadcrumbs

1 tablespoon finely chopped thyme

Kosher salt and freshly ground black pepper

FOR THE CHUTNEY: Heat the oil in a nonreactive saucepan over medium heat. Add the onion, currants, curry powder, and ginger and sauté until the onions are translucent, about 3 minutes. Add the brown sugar, cider vinegar, Sriracha paste, and apples. Cook, covered, for 5 minutes, stirring occasionally.

FOR THE LAMB CHOPS: Preheat the oven to 400°F. Heat the oil in an ovenproof sauté pan over medium heat. Dredge the chops in the breadcrumbs and sprinkle with thyme and salt and pepper to taste. Add the chops to the pan and sauté for $1^1/_2$ minutes per side for medium rare or 2 minutes per side for medium. Place the sauté pan with the lamb into the oven for 5 minutes, turning once. Remove the chops from the pan and serve at once with the chutney.

LOIN *of* LAMB *with* MADRAS CURRY *and* BROWN SUGAR PEARS

WE'VE TALKED ABOUT HOW NEW ENGLANDERS TRAVELED THE WORLD AND CAME *home with spices, and Indian spices seem to be a natural pairing with local lamb both in Asia and here in Maine. In Indian cookbooks and restaurants you'll find all sorts of lamb dishes, including vindaloo, which is usually served painfully hot. We find that the addition of the brown sugar and pears mellow out the curry and add a nice contrast.*

YIELD: 6 SERVINGS

2 tablespoons olive oil

1 tablespoon Madras curry

$^1/_4$ teaspoon kosher salt

Freshly ground black pepper

6 (5-ounce) portions lamb loin

2 tablespoons unsalted butter

$^1/_4$ cup firmly packed brown sugar

4 ripe pears, such as Anjou or Bosque, peeled, cored, and sliced

Preheat the oven to 400°F. In a large ovenproof sauté pan, heat the oil over medium heat. Combine the curry, the salt, and pepper to taste. Dust the pieces of lamb with the curry mixture. Sauté the lamb on each side for 1 minute and then place in the oven in the pan. Roast for 5 minutes. While the lamb is roasting, heat the butter and brown sugar in a sauté pan. Add the pears and sauté over medium heat until the pears are caramelized. Place the lamb loins on six heated plates and garnish with the pears.

THE FARMERS

THEY NAMED THEIR FARM BREEZY HILL BECAUSE NO MATTER HOW hot it got outside, there was always a nice breeze blowing. Sounds romantic, but when young newlyweds Tom and Betsey Hasty bought their seventy-five-acre farm in South Berwick, Maine, over thirty years ago it was admittedly in pretty rough shape. There was no barn back then and no bathroom in the main house so the first order of business was to put in that bathroom, quickly followed by the much needed barn. Tom sawed the wood to build that barn, and the couple started raising cows with a dream to one day have a dairy farm. Tom had graduated from the University of Maine with an agriculture degree but worked for twenty-seven years at a manufacturing company while working the farm. Betsey worked in a bank and later as a social worker while their children Ben and Abbie, now in their twenties, were growing up, but while working full time off the farm, the couple raised veal calves for the Massachusetts food stores Bread & Circus, and Betsey even sold butter and yogurt. They also sold beef by word of mouth and raised dairy replacement heifers for farmers who wanted to sell milk but didn't have the room to raise heifer calves. The Hastys became quasi-foster farmers, caring for the calves until milking age and then bringing them back to the parent farm.

While Ben and Abbie grew, Betsey canned the fruits and vegetables from the garden, they raised a pig or two and some chickens, and with a freezer, a garden, their canning "put away," and a beef cow, as well as enough wood to heat the house, they could sustain themselves and their family on what they grew and raised at Breezy Hill, but they still needed to work "outside" the farm. Then life changed dramatically. Five years ago Tom and Betsey started raising pigs for local restaurants, tapping into the rapidly growing demand for artisan food and farm-raised livestock in restaurants, and that's when the farm really began to take off as a working venture. What was always a way of life would now become finally, a way to make a living.

Pigs were the real interest for the restaurants, and it is a more desirable choice for small farmers over raising cows, which can take up to three years to be ready for market. Most restaurants don't want six hundred pounds of meat. Pigs take only about six months to mature and restaurants can make a variety of products for the restaurant table from a two-hundred-pound pig, including prosciutto, sausage, head cheese, and salami. Tom likes the Landrace/Yorkshire cross pigs for their good consistency, growth rate, and fat-to-meat ratio, but he also raises many other breeds, including Duroc, Berkshire, Hampshire, and Canadian Cross. The pigs are treated well. Their pens are cleaned daily, and they are fed a grain diet of balanced nutrients and minerals, with a supplement of cheese curd, yogurt, and vegetable scraps.

The Hastys sell pigs to more than a dozen restaurants in the area. They say that compared to the huge dairy farms of some of their friends from college, Breezy Hill has always seemed like small potatoes, but now the farm has become more than a full-time job, raising as many as thirty-five pigs a year for area restaurants and individuals. In local restaurants, it's now a sign of quality and pride to be able to print "pork from Breezy Hill Farm" on the menu, and Tom and Betsey Hasty have been able to realize a life-long dream of living off the land.

SPICY LAMB SAUSAGE

ONE OF THE FIRST THINGS WE LEARNED TO MAKE FOR THE OPENING OF JEREMIAH
Tower's renowned restaurant Stars was this delicious sausage. There we served it with oysters on the half shell, but you can serve it with just about anything you like. It makes a great unique dinner paired with our hominy (page 164) and the Warm Red Cabbage Salad (page 202).

YIELD: 6 SERVINGS

$1^1/_2$ tablespoons olive oil
1 cup finely chopped Spanish onions
1 pound ground lamb
1 pound ground pork
1 tablespoon Spanish paprika
1 tablespoon cumin
$1^1/_2$ teaspoons kosher salt
$1^1/_2$ teaspoons ground black pepper
1 serrano chile pepper, seeded and finely chopped

Heat the oil in a sauté pan over medium heat and cook the onions until translucent, about 3 minutes. Remove the onions from the pan and chill in the refrigerator. Mix the lamb, pork, paprika, cumin, kosher salt, black pepper, and the chile pepper in a bowl and add the chilled onions. Form the sausage into 4-ounce patties and grill until cooked through, about 3 minutes each side.

Chapter Five **THE GARDEN**

*W*hen we moved here in the late 1980s and opened Arrows, we started our garden out of necessity. Like the farmers raising meat and poultry there were also local vegetable farmers and people selling herbs, but there wasn't enough. It wasn't what we necessarily wanted to cook or they couldn't get it to us that day. Now, of course, we have our own garden right outside our doorstep and have complete control over what we grow, with three full-time gardeners in season, making it the most vibrant food possible. The lettuce still has the dew on it when it comes through the kitchen door, the radishes have clods of dirt, and both are on the plate hours after being harvested.

We didn't know anything about gardening when we started, and certainly not on the East Coast. We didn't know about zones or raised beds or greenhouses, about which lettuce would thrive, which would wither. We learned about gardening in Maine through trial and error. That lovely meadow outside looked like a great place to start, but it turned out to be a leach field—a draining field for a septic system. In our first year we also learned the garden we'd finally create was woefully inadequate for a restaurant of our size. In our travels to Southeast Asia and Europe, we brought back new flavors so we tried to grow lemongrass, chiles, even okra. The okra didn't work, but we learned how to grow the things we wanted to use in our cooking and offer to our guests. Back then, there weren't many restaurants with their own gardens, but we really wanted to make ours the backbone of the restaurant and we did what we set out to do. Our garden is now a great source for us, but it's also a soothing spot on a hectic day. A five minute walk through the garden is a balm for the soul.

You don't need to have three gardeners and a big plot of land to have fresh vegetables on the table—we didn't at first—but the vibrancy of our food comes from fresh produce. Even if you don't have a garden, you can have a few pots of herbs growing on a windowsill or go to the local farmers' market. Don't go with a list, just go there and see what's good. Go with three meals in mind and then shop like you garden. See what's out there at the local market and come back and look in this book. We're sure you'll find a dish or two that will take advantage of what you've found. You don't have to slavishly follow the recipe, be adventurous and if you can't find something don't be afraid to substitute. A wander through your own garden or sneaking into your neighbor's garden or a bustling farmers' market will show you the possibilities.

NAPA CABBAGE *with* CARAMELIZED GARLIC *and* APPLE CIDER VINEGAR

NAPA OR CHINESE CABBAGE GROWS INCREDIBLY WELL IN OUR GARDEN SO WE'VE *come up with some clever ways to use it. Serve this cabbage as a side dish with roasted or grilled meats, especially pork and ham.*

YIELD: 6 SERVINGS

6 garlic cloves
$^1/_3$ cup canola oil
$^1/_4$ cup cider vinegar
$^1/_4$ cup malt vinegar
1 tablespoon kosher salt
$^1/_4$ teaspoon freshly ground black pepper
2 pounds Napa cabbage leaves

In a large, nonreactive pot, sauté the garlic cloves in the canola oil until soft and caramelized, about 10 minutes. Remove the garlic and save the oil.

In a bowl, make the dressing by mixing the cider vinegar, malt vinegar, salt, and pepper.

Remove the tough outer leaves of the cabbage, cut in half lengthwise and remove the core. Separate the leaves, chop, and add the leaves to the pot. Sauté the leaves in the reserved garlic oil. Toss in the dressing and serve with the garlic.

CELERY ROOT SALAD
with Sour Cream and Herbs

TWENTY YEARS AGO NO ONE AROUND HERE ATE CELERY ROOT, AN UGLY GNARLED *root usually encrusted with dirt. Now chefs all over are taking a cue from Eastern European cooking and using it as an alternative vegetable. It grows here in New England. However, it takes a long time from planting to harvest to get it by late summer, but it's worth waiting for. When you get to the inside of the root, its flavor is delicate and celery like. It's an old-world classic to use mustard and mayo with celery root, but we make it a little lighter by using sour cream and garden herbs.*

YIELD: 6 SERVINGS

1 (2-pound) celery root bulb
$^1/_2$ gallon water
$^1/_2$ Spanish onion, julienned (about 1 cup)
$^1/_2$ lemon, juiced (about 1 tablespoon)
2 teaspoons chopped fresh chives
$^1/_2$ tablespoon chopped fresh tarragon
1 tablespoon chopped fresh basil
$^2/_3$ cup sour cream
$^1/_2$ teaspoon kosher salt

Peel and julienne the celery root bulb. In a large nonreactive pot, boil the water and add the celery root and onion and blanch for 1 minute. Drain the celery root through a colander. Toss the celery root and onion with the lemon juice, chives, tarragon, basil, sour cream, and salt in a bowl. Serve chilled.

WARM RED CABBAGE SALAD

THIS SALAD HAS BEEN ON THE MENU AT ALL OF OUR RESTAURANTS AT ONE POINT *or another and it hearkens back to Mark's childhood. He grew up in a German-American family with dinners of roast pork served with his uncle's sauerkraut or braised cabbage. We eventually went on to cook several varieties of red cabbage salads when we worked with Jeremiah Tower at Stars, but we always go back to cooking this favorite. A lot of people never really think of cabbage as a good vegetable side dish, but it can be so delicious and inexpensive. The way this salad is prepared, the cabbage remains crisp and doesn't turn too soft. We like it as an appetizer, but it's also good as a side dish with roasted meats and you can even serve it with a sturdy fish like salmon.*

YIELD: 6 SERVINGS

$^1/_2$ cup olive oil

2 slices bacon, chopped

1 large head red cabbage, halved, cored, and thinly sliced

$^1/_2$ cup red wine vinegar

1 teaspoon kosher salt

$^1/_4$ teaspoon freshly ground black pepper

Warm the olive oil in a large sauté pan over medium-high heat. Cook the bacon in the pan until crisp. Toss the cabbage with the vinegar in a large bowl and sprinkle with the salt and pepper. Add the cabbage to the bacon in the pan and cook, stirring constantly, until the cabbage is hot and slightly wilted, about 5 minutes. Divide among six plates and serve.

BOK CHOY *with* SHIITAKE MUSHROOMS

WE GROW BOK CHOY YEAR-ROUND, OUTSIDE IN COLD WEATHER COVERED, IN THE *greenhouse, and in the summer time, it grows really well right in the garden. Shiitakes are a natural pairing, the light bok choy complements the earthy mushrooms. Because it does have a lot of moisture, cook it like the Chinese do, very fast at high heat using a low smoking oil, such as canola. Use just a dash of stock. Bok choy is best when it's about 4 inches tall. This dish is great with our Pan Fried Trout (page 128) and with the Crab Fritters (page 51) for a lighter dinner.*

YIELD: 6 SERVINGS

6 small heads baby bok choy
3 tablespoons canola oil
1 tablespoon peeled and sliced garlic
10 ounces of shiitake mushrooms, stemmed and sliced
1 teaspoon kosher salt
$^1/_4$ cup chicken stock

Separate the bok choy leaves. Heat the canola oil in a large sauté pan and sauté the garlic for 1 minute at medium heat, but do not brown. Add the mushrooms and the salt and sauté for 1 minute. Increase the heat to high, add the bok choy and stir. Add the chicken stock and cook until the bok choy is tender but not mushy, about 2 minutes.

FRIED GREEN TOMATOES

WE LOVE FRIED GREEN TOMATOES. THE UNRIPE, CRISP, UNFORMED FLAVOR OF *the green tomatoes and the corn flavor of the coating are a perfect match. If you do have a lot of tomatoes and you think the frost might be coming, it's a good way to make the best of what might become a bad situation—too many tomatoes and not enough time to use them up. We've served them with grilled tuna and aïoli, and they're also great with white fish or just a simple steak or grilled chicken. Of course you can just eat them by themselves.*

YIELD: 6 SERVINGS

3 medium, firm green tomatoes
$1/2$ teaspoon kosher salt
$1/4$ teaspoon freshly ground black pepper
1 cup cornmeal
$1/4$ cup olive oil

Cut the unpeeled tomatoes into $1/2$-inch slices. Sprinkle the slices with the salt and pepper. Dredge the tomato slices in the cornmeal. Heat the olive oil in a large sauté pan on medium heat. In the sauté pan fry half of the coated tomato slices at a time until brown, 2 to 3 minutes on each side. Cook the rest of the tomatoes, adding more oil if needed. Serve at once.

TEN ESSENTIAL HERBS

EVEN IF YOUR GARDEN IS JUST A WINDOW BOX HANGING OUT-side of your apartment, or a series of small pots on the sill, if you have these ten herbs on hand, your cooking will be more versatile, vibrant, and flavorful.

BASIL. Many of us have pesto in the fridge, the first resort when basil takes over your garden. Sweet and strong, basil stands up to many hearty dishes, including your favorite tomato sauce, and it's terrific eaten fresh as we do with our heirloom tomatoes with a splash of olive oil and balsamic vinegar. Add basil at the end of cooking to add a bright earthiness.

CHERVIL. A delicate herb with a mild anise flavor, chervil should be used just at the end of cooking or right on top of a salad. You'll find it alongside tarragon in traditional French cooking, but cooking often removes the flavor so when you can use it fresh and "raw," it's always best.

CILANTRO. You might know this herb from Mexican cooking, but it's used in many cuisines, including Thai and Vietnamese. It's the leafy part of the coriander plant, and its delicate flavor is a bit deceptive—it's distinctive with a hint of peppery licorice. It's probably in your salsa but be sure to put it in your chili, chowder, chicken dishes, and fish stew.

CHIVES. Chives not only add a touch of color to dishes but also a mild flavor when you want just a hint of onion but not the harshness. Toss snipped chive into sauces, dips, salads, and soups—and, of course, on your baked potato with sour cream. If nothing else, have a little pot of chives growing on your windowsill to snip off and throw into any dish you like.

ITALIAN PARSLEY. Don't throw away that parsley garnish; it's a wonderful versatile herb that adds a fresh, subtle bite to mild dishes and color and texture to anything. Add it to sauces, mashed potatoes, soups, and pasta for a brighter flavor. It also goes well with other herbs like dill, chives, oregano, and thyme. Use Italian parsley for its hearty flavor.

MINT. There are so many varieties of mint, each one could have its own section. We know it's great in ice cream and with chocolate, sometimes with both together, but it jazzes up many a savory dish. You'll see it in tabouli and, of course, with lamb at the Easter dinner table, but it's also terrific with fish and scallops, shrimp and lobster, adding a playful touch to anything that uses lemon.

OREGANO. Found in the cooking of Greece and Italy as well as many other Mediterranean cuisines, oregano is actually a member of the mint family. It stands up to hearty meats, especially lamb and pork, but toss a salmon fillet with chopped oregano and olive oil and throw it on the grill for an instant crowd pleaser. Add it to pasta sauce, clams, and scallops, as well as any salad dressing with a vinegar and oil base.

ROSEMARY. Rosemary can stand up to the heartiest of meats. Popular in Italian and other Mediterranean cuisine, it's great for roasts and stews with lamb or beef, but also with roasted potatoes and mushrooms sautéed with red wine. Be sure to chop very finely since the leaves can be quite tough. You can even blanch rosemary ahead of time to soften it.

TARRAGON. It's no secret that tarragon is our favorite herb. The flavor is a bit like licorice or anise, but that flavor is subtle so it won't overwhelm such dishes as poached fish, scallops, or chicken. It's the essential ingredient in another favorite, béarnaise sauce. Use it to infuse vinegar or just chop it up in your scrambled eggs. It stars in Mark's Mustard Vinaigrette (page 218).

THYME. A bit of mint melded into a touch of lemon, the flavor of thyme adds pizzazz to soups, roasted fish, and chowders. Add thyme early when cooking as the flavors will take some time to infuse your dish.

BROCCOLI CASSEROLE

THIS IS A HOME-SWEET-HOME SIDE DISH. ONE OF THE THINGS THAT CLARK *loved the most about getting to know Mark was getting to know Mark's mother, which meant getting to know her bountiful cooking. Mark's mother always had a huge table laden with German-American food. You could never lift a finger in her house because she wouldn't allow it. She wanted to spoil all her boys. Dishes like this one were sure to appear among the many offerings on the table. It's good with chicken, steaks, meat, poultry, and our Cider Poached Salmon with Apples (page 124).*

YIELD: 6 SERVINGS

8 tablespoons (1 stick) unsalted butter, divided

1 pound broccoli florets

2$\frac{1}{2}$ teaspoons kosher salt, divided

1 cup finely chopped Spanish onions

$\frac{1}{4}$ cup all-purpose flour

1 cup heavy cream

2 cups milk

1 cup stemmed and sliced raw shiitake mushrooms

1 cup Monterey Jack or Cheddar cheese

$\frac{1}{4}$ teaspoon freshly ground black pepper

$\frac{1}{2}$ cup chopped fresh chives

1 cup panko breadcrumbs

2 tablespoons olive oil

Preheat the oven to 375°F. Grease a 2-quart casserole dish with 1 tablespoon of the butter. In a pot, blanch the broccoli for 1 minute in boiling water with 2 teaspoons of the salt. Remove immediately and chill in an ice bath. In a saucepan over medium heat, sauté the onions in 6 tablespoons of the butter. Whisk in the flour and cook but do not let it brown. In another saucepan over medium low, heat the cream and milk, and then whisk it into the onion mixture. Cook on low heat for 5 minutes. Melt the remaining tablespoon of the butter in a separate sauté pan over medium heat. Sauté the mushrooms in the butter. Mix the mushrooms into the flour and milk mixture along with the broccoli and the cheese. Season with the black pepper and the remaining $\frac{1}{2}$ teaspoon of salt. Add the chives. Place the mixture into the prepared casserole dish. Mix the breadcrumbs with the olive oil and spoon over the top of the broccoli mixture. Bake for 15 minutes.

WARM DANDELION GREENS SALAD

DANDELION GREENS ARE NOT ALWAYS FOR SALE IN THE SUPERMARKET BUT *you'll frequently see them in season or at the farmers' market. They do seem a bit intimidating because they're in these big, unwieldy, long bunches, but just chop them up to get a real treat. They have a unique flavor not unlike Belgian endive or radicchio. We think this is a great technique for preparing any kind of warm salad. Serve as a start to dinner or with dishes such as Scallops with Corn Pudding (page 102) or Cod Cakes with Tartar Sauce (page 127).*

YIELD: 6 SERVINGS

$1/3$ cup finely chopped onion

1 teaspoon finely chopped garlic cloves

1 teaspoon finely chopped fresh rosemary

$1/2$ teaspoon chili flakes

1 tablespoon sugar

$1/3$ cup dried currants

$1/2$ cup white vinegar

$1/4$ cup canola oil

$1/3$ cup pine nuts

$1/4$ cup olive oil

10 cups (about 3 ounces) dandelion greens, washed and chopped

Kosher salt and freshly ground black pepper

In a nonreactive saucepan, make the vinaigrette by mixing the onion, garlic, rosemary, chili flakes, sugar, currants, vinegar, and canola oil. Heat the vinaigrette over medium heat until just hot. Toast the pine nuts in a sauté pan over medium heat until just lightly brown. Heat the olive oil in a sauté pan and toss in the dandelion greens to warm, about 2 minutes. Toss the greens in the vinaigrette and top with the pine nuts. Serve at once.

"EVERYTHING IN THE GARDEN" SALAD

A TYPICAL GARDEN SALAD IN RESTAURANTS ACROSS THE COUNTRY HAS REALLY *very little to do with a garden, and more to do with agribusiness and whatever is in the walk-in refrigerator. But in Maine where so many houses have a little hidden vegetable garden and the roads are dotted with roadside stands filled with produce, one can easily create a salad from, well, anything in the garden. It doesn't have to be lettuce, tomatoes, and cucumbers; use soft herbs like parsley, basil and tarragon to enliven your salad and yellow and green squash, nutty carrots, and even beets. Flowers give a salad a riot of color and have a distinctive flavor, so try citrus marigolds, which add a lemony flavor, and roses, which really do add a mellow, floral hint.*

YIELD: 6 SERVINGS

1 tablespoon cumin
1 tablespoon caraway
1 tablespoon dill seed
1 tablespoon coriander
1 tablespoon fennel seed
Pinch of saffron
2 cups sherry vinegar, divided
$^1/_2$ cup honey
$1^1/_2$ cups olive oil
12 cups assorted greens and vegetables

Toast the dry spices over low heat in a sauté pan. In a nonreactive saucepan, heat $1^1/_2$ cups of the sherry vinegar and the honey and cook to reduce the liquid by one-half, about 10 minutes. Add the spices to the vinegar liquid. Reduce the mixture for another 10 minutes. Take the mixture off the heat and place in a bowl. Whisk in the olive oil and the remaining $^1/_2$ cup of the sherry vinegar. Chill the vinaigrette and then toss the greens and vegetables with the vinaigrette.

GRILLED HEARTS *of* ROMAINE SALAD

FRESH GARDEN GREENS HAVE A GREAT FLAVOR. TOSSING THEM WITH OIL AND *giving them a quick grilling adds a nice smoky flavor. It turns a piece of undressed lettuce into a really tasty vegetable. Serve these warm, still-crisp lettuce hearts as a salad or as a side dish with our Duck Roasted with Garlic and Thyme (page 158).*

YIELD: 6 SERVINGS

1 cup white wine vinegar
4 tablespoons sugar
$^1/_4$ teaspoon chili flakes
2 garlic cloves, finely chopped
$^1/_2$ shallot, peeled and finely chopped
$^3/_4$ cup olive oil, divided
6 large heads Romaine lettuce, each cut in half
$^1/_2$ teaspoon kosher salt
$^1/_4$ teaspoon freshly ground black pepper
$^1/_2$ cup grated Parmesan cheese

Heat the grill as hot as it will go. Combine the vinegar, sugar, and chili flakes in a nonreactive saucepan over medium-high heat Boil for 5 minutes. Add the garlic and shallot, remove from the heat, and slowly whisk in $^1/_4$ cup of the olive oil. Peel off the outer leaves of the lettuce heads and toss with the remaining $^1/_2$ cup of the olive oil. Sprinkle with the salt and pepper. Grill the lettuce until lightly brown. Drizzle with the dressing and sprinkle with the Parmesan cheese. Serve at once.

COLESLAW *with* CARAWAY SEEDS

CARAWAY IS AN UNUSUAL, UNEXPECTED FLAVOR TO FIND SOMEWHERE OTHER *than bread. This coleslaw can add a real zip to your lunch, and an exotic flavor that's not just for rye bread anymore. Try this slaw with our lobster roll and it will change your life, or at least your lunch.*

YIELD: 6 SERVINGS

1 tablespoon caraway seeds

1 (1-pound) green cabbage head, finely sliced

2 teaspoons kosher salt

2 teaspoons sugar

$^1/_3$ cup mayonnaise (see Herb
Mayonnaise, page 49, but omit the herbs)

3 tablespoons cider vinegar

Toast the caraway seeds in a dry sauté pan on low heat for 5 minutes. Set aside. In a bowl, toss the cabbage with the salt and sugar. Place the cabbage in a colander and press it down with a weight over a bowl for 1 hour. Remove the cabbage from the colander and mix the cabbage with the mayonnaise, caraway seeds, and cider vinegar. Chill and serve.

TEN ESSENTIAL VEGETABLES
(Ok, two are fruits)

LL OF THE VEGETABLES LISTED HERE ARE AVAILABLE IN THE farmers' markets in season. Some enhance and flavor your cooking right from the beginning, and others will make an easy side dish for a quick meal.

CABBAGE. You can't make coleslaw without cabbage. The versatility of cabbage is amazing. Eat it raw, pickled as in sauerkraut, cooked in your boiled dinner, or wrapped around a mixture of rice and beef in stuffed cabbage.

CARROTS. Sweet and nutty, the carrot is usually best just chomped down raw, but they can add color shredded into your salad as well. The carrot is an essential first step to stock and they can go with many different herbs. Steam slices with dill, mint, tarragon, ginger, even horseradish, and you've got five different dishes right there.

CELERY. We use celery in so many ways, as the base to a soup or sauce or to add crunch to our lobster salad, but we think celery is underappreciated as a vegetable side dish. Try it braised with a Russian dressing and you've got a dish that is extremely tasty and healthy too.

GARLIC. Sharp and pungent when raw, mellow and nutty when roasted, garlic can be a flavor enhancer or a condiment for just about every dish we make. Use garlic on breads, in olive oils, sauces, and chopped in salads.

LEMON. This tangy fruit is essential to a great fish or shellfish dish—who can resist a squeeze or two on shrimp cocktail or a steaming lobster tail—but adding a squeeze at the end of cooking a stew or a light sauce will add a brightness and complexity to the dish that will astound.

LETTUCE. Like many things we grow in our garden, lettuces come in so many varieties that it's almost like they're not even a part of the same species. From peppery arugula to bitter radicchio to soft and delicate butter lettuce, there is one for every purpose whether it's tossed in a salad or adding the crunch to your BLT.

POTATOES. Our Maine potatoes are legendary, but there are many varieties of potatoes for different purposes. Our large potatoes are great for baking, but fingerlings can be roasted or boiled with herbs for an easy side dish. Try new potatoes tossed with fresh parsley or Yukon Golds boiled and simply "smashed" with plenty of butter. Use potatoes as a thickener in sauces, and in Maine, you cannot and will not be allowed to make a clam chowder without diced potato.

SHALLOTS. We love to use the mild shallot, a member of the onion family that looks like something between garlic and onions, but sweeter and more delicate than either. We're more likely to just slice these and use them raw or use them "melted" in butter in a sauce.

SPANISH ONIONS. Onions are the start of just about every great stew, soup, and many sauces. You'll see many recipes here begin with finely chopped onions sautéed in a bit of butter, sending an aroma through the house that says, "dinner is coming." This first step caramelizes the onions, which spreads flavor to whatever comes next.

TOMATOES. We could live on the tomatoes from our garden, and there are so many varieties with brilliant colors and flavors they can complement meats and fish alike. Or just slice them and toss with a bit of sea salt for a lunch or snack. If you have tomatoes and basil, you have marinara sauce. Just a plate of sliced tomatoes is a salad. Chopped with garlic, it's something like a relish. All you need is a little salt and it's practically a meal.

RADISHES *in* VINAIGRETTE

ONE OF THE FUN CHALLENGES FOR A CHEF IS TO CHANGE SOMEONE'S OPINION *about what you like or dislike and we've met many people who are now radish converts thanks to this simple dish, where the common radish becomes a jewel. Normally the radish is the last vegetable on the crudite tray, but if you use the radishes you get right from the garden instead of those from the plastic bag, they'll be the first to go. Look for radishes that still have the top attached and that are not dried or cracked. When served with this refreshing vinaigrette we think it will change your mind about the once "lowly" radish.*

YIELD: 6 SERVINGS

$1^1/_2$ pounds radishes
$^1/_4$ cup sliced ginger
$^1/_2$ cup sugar
$^1/_4$ cup Champagne vinegar
$^1/_4$ teaspoon kosher salt
$^1/_4$ teaspoon black pepper

Cut the radishes in half and slice them into half moons. Place the rest of the ingredients in a heavy saucepan and bring to a boil. Let the mixture cool to room temperature. Place the radishes on a flat pan and pour the vinaigrette on top of the radishes. Toss to coat.

FLAVORED VINEGAR

HERE ARE TWO INTENSE FLAVORFUL HERBS THAT TAKE YOUR ORDINARY STORE- *bought vinegar to a different level. Using these infused vinegars you can really be creative with your vinaigrettes. When you have these in your culinary arsenal, you're already halfway to making a rosemary vinaigrette or Mark's Mustard Herb Vinaigrette (page 218). It's also a great way to preserve herbs from your garden and have summer flavors in the dead of winter.*

Rosemary Vinegar

YIELD: 1 1/2 CUPS

2 cups distilled white vinegar
6 sprigs rosemary

Bring the vinegar to a boil in a nonreactive saucepan. Add the rosemary to the vinegar and let cool. Place in a nonreactive container to keep.

Tarragon–Shallot Vinegar

YIELD: 2 1/2 CUPS

2 cups distilled white vinegar
1 cup finely chopped shallots
6 sprigs tarragon

Bring the vinegar and shallots to a boil in a nonreactive saucepan. Add the tarragon to the vinegar and let cool. Place in a nonreactive container to keep.

MARK'S MUSTARD HERB VINAIGRETTE

THIS IS SO GOOD ON JUST ABOUT ANYTHING. IT GOES BEYOND A VINAIGRETTE *and becomes a great sauce when used on grilled Romaine and artichokes. It's one of the sauces we make at home and since it doesn't involve butter or eggs, it balances our rich dishes. It also goes well with grilled meats and poultry.*

YIELD: 1¹⁄₂ CUPS

¹⁄₂ cup olive oil

¹⁄₄ cup Champagne vinegar

2 shallots, peeled

¹⁄₄ cup fresh tarragon, picked

¹⁄₄ cup parsley, picked

1 tablespoon whole-grain mustard

1 tablespoon Dijon mustard

1 teaspoon kosher salt

¹⁄₄ teaspoon whole black peppercorns

¹⁄₂ cup extra virgin olive oil

Combine the olive oil, vinegar, shallot, tarragon, parsley, both mustards, salt, and peppercorns in a blender and purée. Gradually add the extra virgin olive oil and blend until smooth.

TEN THINGS WE'VE LEARNED
ABOUT GARDENING

START EARLY, SO YOU CAN GO LONG. We start seedlings in February under grow lights in the basement and then transfer them to the greenhouse. They then go to raised beds and row covers so that by the time our restaurant opens we can at least start with the lettuces and herbs. In this way, we always have things from our garden.

NOT EVERYTHING GROWS. In Maine, we say, "If you don't like the weather, just wait five minutes." We have droughts, forty days of rain, snow in spring—you just never know. One crop is great and then something just doesn't come up. Some years it's too hot and sunny and the lettuce will bolt but there will be wonderful tomatoes. Don't get all hung up on it. That's Mother Nature and you'll learn what works and what doesn't.

BE VIGILANT. This is especially true with tomatoes. You have to stake properly and cover just right. Be on the constant lookout for discoloration and pests.

KEEP IT CLEAN. Weed and get the junk out of the garden. If you don't have time to keep it clean, make your garden smaller because a clean garden keeps the pests away and keeps the moisture from attacking the crops.

KNOW YOUR SEEDS. Don't use any seeds if you don't know where they came from. Use only tested seeds from reputable sources or you'll wind up with some mongrel vegetable on your land.

PICK THE RIGHT SPOT. Figure out what will grow in the sun, what in the shade, and where the sun will be in various months and seasons.

KEEP THE SOIL CLEAN. Know the source of your soil to keep from bringing disease into your garden. If that happens, it will take years to get rid of it.

GET RID OF PESTS. Set up a program for insecticides or maintenance for an organic garden. It's essential that you do preventative maintenance.

WATER. Drip irrigation is wonderful because it prevents water waste and it's far more efficient than other methods. You don't get the plants wet, which can be a haven for pests.

TAKE A WALK IN YOUR GARDEN EACH EVENING. Relax with your favorite beverage and stroll through the garden. The garden is all about enjoyment.

Chapter Six **THE DAIRY**

*I*t's always a treat to pile into the car and go out for ice cream and in Maine, the landscape is dotted with small dairy farms and creameries, providing a place to stop, relax, and dig into an ice cream cone made from milk from cows wandering around in pastures right within reach. While our locally owned dairy farms have been dwindling as they have all over New England, we're seeing a resurgence in artisan cheese-making from places like Silvery Moon Creamery in Westbrook and Seal Cove Farm in Lamoine, butter-making from award-winning Kate's Butter in Old Orchard Beach, which is even bringing back buttermilk, and dairy cooperatives joining together to offer organic milk from small family farms where cows are allowed room to graze and thrive. And, of course, let's not forget the ice cream. Gifford's has been around for more than one hundred years and honors Maine with a crowd favorite—Moose Tracks with vanilla ice cream, fudge, and peanut butter.

While there are many great cheese-makers now in Maine, we learned to make our own goat cheese, farmer's cheese, mozzarella, queso fresco, and even butter. At Arrows we like to offer different kinds of butter, both our own house-made varieties and others from our region. Cheese-making is something you can do at home and it's a great fun project for the family. It keeps us in touch with the feeling of where food comes from to be able to make it ourselves. We have many farms around the restaurant, and when you visit one there's an immediate sense of belonging to the land.

Local people are on these farms raising sheep, goats, and cows with no antibiotics, no hormones, and room for the animals to roam free. And what we get from that is pure and simple—delicious milk, cheese, butter and, of course that sweet, rich ice cream.

One of Clark's earliest childhood memories was sitting at a school desk at Baskin Robbins and enjoying mint chocolate chip ice cream. For Mark, it was going for ice cream at least once a week, taking a drive out into the countryside. In keeping with Maine's "Vacationland" motto, on summer nights you'll see long lines of folks waiting to get their cones and plenty of sunburned kids fresh from the beach. There's really no end to the kinds of ice cream you can make, but these are some of our favorites.

MINT CHOCOLATE CHIP ICE CREAM

YIELD: 1^1/$_2$ PINTS

1 cup heavy cream
1 cup whole milk milk
^{1}/$_4$ cup finely chopped fresh mint
Kosher salt
4 egg yolks
^{1}/$_2$ cup sugar
^{1}/$_8$ teaspoon vanilla extract
^{1}/$_2$ cup chocolate chips

Bring the cream, milk, mint, and a pinch of salt to a boil in a heavy saucepan. Turn the heat off when it comes to a boil and allow the mint to steep for 30 minutes. Mix the egg yolks, sugar, and vanilla together in a bowl. Bring the milk and the cream back to a boil over medium-high heat. Add ^{1}/$_4$ cup of the dairy mixture to the egg mixture to heat and then add the rest of the dairy mixture. Allow to cool. Strain the mint from the mixture. Place the liquid in an ice cream machine. Process until done, according to the machine's instructions. After removing the ice cream from the machine, mix in the chocolate chips. Freeze until ready to use. Serve at once for soft ice cream or freeze for 2 hours for harder ice cream.

PUMPKIN ICE CREAM

YIELD: 2 PINTS

1 cup heavy cream
1 cup whole milk
Kosher salt
4 egg yolks
^{1}/$_2$ cup sugar
^{1}/$_8$ teaspoon vanilla extract
1 (12-ounce) can pumpkin purée

Bring the cream, milk, and a pinch of salt to a boil in a heavy saucepan. Turn off the heat when it comes to a boil. Mix the egg yolks, sugar, and vanilla together in a bowl. Bring the milk and the cream back to a boil over medium-high heat. Add ^{1}/$_4$ cup of the dairy mixture to the egg mixture to heat. Add the rest of the dairy mixture to the egg and add the pumpkin purée. Allow to cool. Place the mixture in an ice cream machine. Process until done, according to the machine's instructions. Freeze until ready to use. Serve at once for soft ice cream or freeze for 2 hours for harder ice cream.

BLUEBERRY CRÈME FRÂICHE ICE CREAM

YIELD: 1$^1/_2$ PINTS

$^1/_2$ cup heavy cream
1$^1/_2$ cups whole milk
Kosher salt
4 egg yolks
$^1/_2$ cup sugar
$^1/_8$ teaspoon vanilla extract
$^1/_2$ cup crème frâiche
$^1/_2$ cup blueberries

Bring the cream, milk, and a pinch of salt to a boil in a heavy saucepan. Turn off the heat when it comes to a boil. Mix the egg yolks, sugar, and vanilla together in a bowl. Bring the milk and the cream back to the boil over medium-high heat. Add $^1/_4$ cup of the dairy mixture to the egg mixture to heat. Add the rest of the dairy mixture to the eggs. Whisk the dairy mixture into the crème frâiche and blueberries. Allow to cool. Place the mixture in an ice cream machine and process according to machine's instructions. Freeze until ready to use. Serve at once for soft ice cream or freeze for 2 hours for harder ice cream.

HONEY-THYME ICE CREAM

YIELD: 1$^1/_2$ PINTS

1 cup heavy cream
1 cup whole milk
2 teaspoons fresh thyme
Kosher salt
4 egg yolks
$^1/_2$ cup sugar
$^1/_4$ cup honey

Bring the cream, milk, thyme, and a pinch of salt to a boil in a heavy saucepan. Turn off the heat when it comes to a boil and allow the thyme to steep for 30 minutes. Mix the egg yolks, sugar, and honey together in a bowl. Bring the milk and the cream back to a boil over medium-high heat. Add $^1/_4$ cup of the dairy mixture to the egg mixture to heat. Add the rest of the dairy mixture to the eggs. Allow to cool. Strain the thyme from the mixture. Place the mixture in an ice cream machine and process according to the machine's instructions. Freeze until ready to use. Serve at once for soft ice cream or freeze for 2 hours for harder ice cream.

ICE CREAM MAKING

THERE'S REALLY NOTHING MORE AMERICAN THAN ICE CREAM. WE have ice cream stands all over the state and ice cream cones topped with as many flavors as there are ideas. In August, when it's hot and sultry outside, the only thing that will cool us off is a dish of ice cream.

From the earliest days at Arrows, we always had some ice cream-making apparatus, and over the years, as our equipment has gotten more sophisticated, our technique has improved as well. We experiment with ingredients from the garden, even exotic things like lemongrass, spices, even tomatoes. We're always ready, spoon in hand to make sure quality is maintained.

There are many ice cream-makers to choose from and you can get by with a small countertop ice cream maker that doesn't need huge amounts of ice and rock salt and still gets great tasting, buttery ice cream. You just need to freeze the bowl, pour the ice cream mixture in, and hit the switch. Place the special bowl or canister in the freezer and wait.

Using an electric or hand-cranked machine makes the ice cream smoother because these machines help break up the hard ice crystals more efficiently, but there are also ways to make ice cream without electricity including "still freezing" in which you make the ice cream mixture, place it in the freezer in the bowl and periodically take it out to mix.

For you McGyver fans out there, fill a one-pound cleaned coffee can with your mixture, seal well, and place that inside a three-pound coffee can. Place rock salt and ice between the cans and then seal the large can. Roll it on the floor back and forth for fifteen minutes. Take the smaller can out and wipe off the salt and water and stir the contents. Reseal and do it all over again.

Don't be afraid to experiment with flavors and ingredients. Anything in the garden is fair game in many combinations. Lemongrass and ginger, tomato and basil, raspberry and orange liquor, we've even had bacon ice cream. Peanut butter and jelly, anyone?

CHOCOLATE-BASIL POT DE CRÈME

THE COMBINATION OF BASIL AND CHOCOLATE MIGHT SEEM ODD BUT BASIL IS *really a member of the mint family so we're really not as crazy as we seem! Once you try it you'll find it's a natural combination. Pot de Crème is a real return to old ways when cream was pure, flavorful, and unadulterated. Once you know how to make this, you can use other flavors, such as peppermint, vanilla, orange, even bacon. Well, maybe not bacon. It's all about your imagination.*

YIELD: 6 SERVINGS

1 cup whole milk

1 cup heavy cream

$^1/_2$ cup fresh basil

3 egg yolks

1 large egg

$^3/_4$ cup sugar

1 teaspoon vanilla

1 cup bittersweet chocolate chips

Preheat the oven to 350°F. In a large saucepan heat the milk and the cream and bring to a boil. Turn off the heat and add the basil. Allow the basil to steep for 30 minutes. Mix the egg yolks and the egg with the sugar in a bowl. Add the vanilla. Bring the milk and cream back to a boil and add the chocolate chips. Add one-fourth of the dairy mixture to the egg and sugar mixture to heat slightly. Add the rest of the dairy mixture. Mix then strain out the basil.

Place ovenproof pot-de-crème cups in a baking pan with sides and divide the mixture among the cups with a measuring cup or ladle. Cover the pan with foil, leaving one side slightly open. Add hot water to the baking pan so it's halfway up the sides of the cups. Close the open side of the pan. Reduce the oven temperature to 325°F and bake for 25 to 30 minutes, or until set, when the custard moves slightly when nudged. If you don't have pot-de-crème dishes, use coffee cups or small ramekins.

MAPLE WHIPPED CREAM

WHIPPED CREAM IS JUST ABOUT THE EASIEST THING TO MAKE IN THE WORLD SO *it's hard to believe many of us grew up with whipped cream out of a can. When cane sugar was an expensive luxury, maple and honey were natural sweeteners. You can use our delicious Maine maple syrup as a sweetener for many things, including in your coffee. We could just eat this out of the bowl before it makes it to any cake, pie, or ice cream, but it's great with our Pumpkin Ice Cream (page 224) and the Bailey's Island Blueberry Tart (page 253).*

YIELD: 6 TO 8 SERVINGS

1 cup heavy cream
3 tablespoons maple syrup

Pour the chilled cream into a chilled metal mixing bowl. Whisk the cream until bubbles start to form. Add the maple syrup. Whisk the mixture until soft peaks form. Leave it at this stage or if you like a stiffer cream continue to whisk. You do not want to overwhisk, however, or your whipped cream will turn to butter.

FRESH BERRY FRAPPE

WHEN WE FIRST CAME TO MAINE, MARK ORDERED A BERRY MILKSHAKE. HE *thought he was going to get the thick berry milkshake he grew up with, but instead it was just berry flavored frothy milk. He asked a woman in the pharmacy why it was so thin and where the ice cream went and she told him. "De-ah," she said. "If you want ice cream, you should order a frappe." Obviously, he was from "away."*

YIELD: 6 SERVINGS

1 cup blueberries

1 cup raspberries

1 cup strawberries

$^3/_4$ cup orange juice

6 tablespoons sugar

3 teaspoons vanilla

3 cups vanilla ice cream

Purée all of the ingredients in a blender. Pour into tall glasses.

YOGURTY MELON SMOOTHIE

HEALTHY, EASY, AND GREAT ON HOT SUMMER DAYS, THIS SMOOTHIE BRINGS *nutritious and delicious together.*

YIELD: 6 SIX-OUNCE SERVINGS

1 cup chopped cantaloupe

1 cup chopped honeydew

1 cup chopped watermelon

1 cup plain yogurt

1 teaspoon sugar

$^3/_4$ cup orange juice

Place all of the ingredients in a blender and purée until smooth.

THE CURDS OF MAINE

ISCONSIN AND VERMONT ARE KNOWN FOR THEIR CHEDDAR cheese, but Maine's artisan cheese-makers are busting out some fantastic Cheddars along with Camembert, chèvre, tomme, quark, and feta made with sheep, cow, and goat's milk. In 2009 Maine cheeses won seventeen awards at the American Cheese Society in Chicago, and there were fewer Maine entries in 2010, but the state still brought home seven awards.

Raw milk is easier than ever to find and home cheese- makers are coming up with delicious recipes for quark, ricotta, simple farmstead cheeses, and those cheese curds to put on top of crisp french fries with gravy in that classic French Canadian dish, poutine. Given how simple and rustic a farm can be, it's quite surprising to see where some of these artisan cheeses and butters are made. The basic techniques are old, but the equipment is cutting edge. It's grueling work standing in a steamy cheese-making room in tall rubber boots, mixing and cutting over and over, but the result is worth it and more local farms are starting their own cheese-making programs to keep up with our demand. The after-dinner cheese plate has never had it so good.

THE CHEESEMAKER

WHILE MANY TEENAGERS WORRY ABOUT THE NEXT CONCERT or football game, Jennifer Betancourt had more on her mind during her teen years. She started making cheese in 1993 at age sixteen, and from then on her skills and the cheese culture in Maine grew. Starting at the Squire Tarbox Inn Westport Island, she learned to make cheese from then-owner Karen Mitman, using their goats to make soft, simple cheeses. When they asked if she was interested in continuing to make cheese, she agreed, going on to produce other varieties like the harder Caerfilly cheese. She later went on to study animal science at Cornell University with the intention of becoming a farmer, raising her own animals for the cheese.

By the time the Maine Cheese Guild was formed in 2003, a group of which she is a board member of, Jennifer was making cheese at Silvery Moon Creamery at Smiling Hill Farm in Westbrook. Back then there were only four licensed cheese-makers in Maine, but now there are over twenty. While at Silvery Moon, Jennifer was able to start an artisan cheese operation from scratch, beginning with four gallons at a time in her apartment and working up to batches of 250 gallons in a separate creamery. She developed more than a dozen unique varieties of cheese, five of which have received national awards from the American Cheese Society. With accolades in *Food and Wine Magazine* and *O Magazine*, Silvery Moon's Cheddars, Camemberts, and mellow white cheese became a household staple for many cheese lovers. She was able to make blooming rind cheeses, tweaking the recipe until she got it just right. Jennifer was also able to spread the word about Maine cheese. As the creamery grew, she got plenty of help from the close Maine cheese-making community who shared a passion for local sustainable food.

Mystique Farm, Seal Cove, York Hill, and Appleton Creamery have all made wonderful goat cheese since the guild was formed. The tight-knit community is making a name for Maine cheese. Now, Jennifer says that even larger scale cheese-making operations are very involved with the smaller farms, sharing ideas and working closely together.

Jennifer has now left Silvery Moon, but she's continuing to create cheese, through some product development, experimenting with new varieties, including a blue cheese and one using local seaweed. She's using a small "dug" cheese cave in a hill at her grandparent's homestead near the Sheepscot River to age some of her creations and says that while there is really not one or two varieties of cheese that define Maine cheese, it is certainly known for its quality. She points out that a dozen cheese-makers can use the same recipe for Tomme for example and because it's made with milk from different farms, aged in different spots in Maine, the result can be vastly different. Here, says Jennifer, cheese-making is about crafts people trying to create a cheese that is their own, unique to them and to their farm.

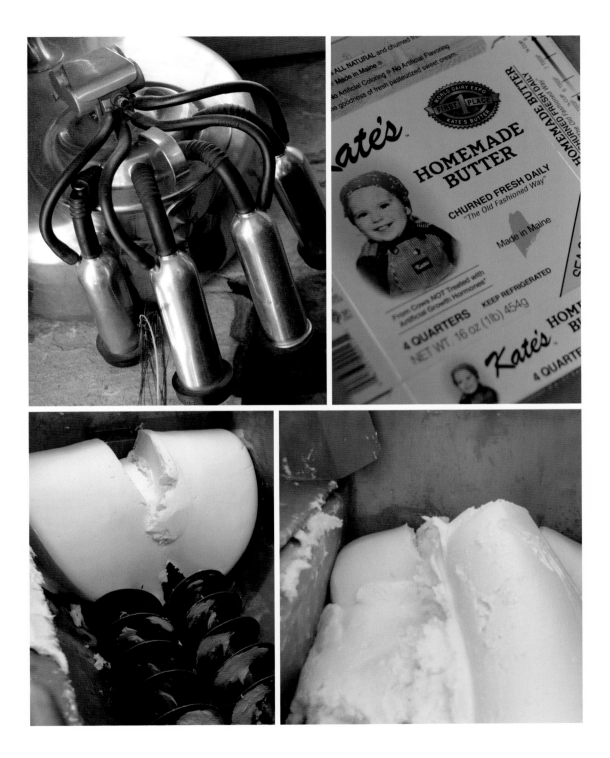

Chapter Seven **THE BAKERY**

W e've always made our own bread at Arrows. Maine's artisanal bakeries are rising in number now, but it hasn't always been easy to get people to warm up to the small local bakeries. In America, your Starbucks coffee is always the same, and that burger at the fast-food joint is always the same as well. As Americans we tend to feel comfortable when we know just what we're going to get and expect it to be that way every single time. Not us. Twenty-five years ago when a few strong-hearted souls said *gee, I want to have a bakery like I experienced in France*, the banker ran in the other direction. Now, it has caught on and through pure Yankee self-reliance we have dozens of artisan bakers, such as Matt James and Alison Pray, owners of The Standard Baking Company in Portland. Their baguettes, boules, and brioche are legendary, along with their chocolate croissants and their famous "morning buns." Along with bakeries like Beach Pea, Notre Dame, and When Pig's Fly, they've been a part of ensuring that the bread we eat on our home table or in a restaurant is fresh, wholesome, and delicious every time, even if it doesn't always look the same. While there are small bakeries all around now, we had to make our own breads, a legacy from back in a time when the only bread we could get here was massed produced and we had no choice. One of the most alluring things about arriving at Arrows is the smell of freshly baked bread, right along with the scents of the smoker roasting up some oysters.

Of course, desserts come from the baker's oven as well, and Maine desserts are so simple, you don't have to be a master pastry chef to make an apple crisp or a blueberry pie. Mainers just used what was around the farm to make sweet concoctions, such as hasty pudding, pumpkin pie, fritters, and those sweet treats from European history—plum pudding, gap and swallow (a pudding with maple syrup), and flummery. There were legacy desserts from Britain in custards and puddings, and the simplest and most "Yankee" of all desserts, Indian pudding made with cornmeal, molasses, and cold whole milk, invented when getting enough to eat meant using whatever was plentiful or stored in the cellar. In those days, sugar was scarce so maple syrup, honey, and molasses were the sweeteners. Now, we don't have those constraints because ingredients are cheap and easy to find, but the simplicity of this tradition still resonates for good cooks.

CRANBERRY UPSIDE-DOWN CAKE

WE'VE BEEN TRAINED TO THINK THAT CERTAIN VERY LARGE COMPANIES ARE THE *only cranberry producers around, but we have bogs all over backyards here in Maine, including some right near Arrows. We tend to think of cranberries as only for Thanksgiving or as juice, but when used in this cake, they're terrific. Upside-down cakes are fun because they're an easy way to make a tart Tatin without all of the effort and caramelizing. Bake it in a pan and when you flip it out, you have all this great caramelized fruit that becomes almost a fruit sauce for the fluffy cake. It's a perfect way to use our local ingredients.*

MAKES 1 10-INCH CAKE

$1/2$ pound (2 sticks) plus 1 tablespoon unsalted butter, divided

1 cup firmly packed brown sugar, divided

1 pound cranberries

$1/2$ cup granulated sugar

5 large eggs

$2^1/4$ cups all-purpose flour

1 teaspoon ground cinnamon

1 teaspoon baking soda

$1/2$ teaspoon baking powder

1 cup buttermilk

2 teaspoons orange zest

Preheat the oven to 350°F. Use 1 tablespoon of the butter to grease a 10-inch round, 1-inch-deep cake pan and line the bottom with a circle of parchment paper. Butter the parchment. Melt 4 tablespoons of the butter and pour it into the cake pan. Sprinkle $1/2$ cup of the brown sugar evenly on top. Place the cranberries on top of the brown sugar. In a large bowl, beat the remaining 12 tablespoons butter until smooth, about 4 minutes. Add the granulated sugar and the remaining $1/2$ cup of brown sugar and beat until light and fluffy. Beat in the eggs, one at a time, scraping the bowl as needed. Sift together the flour, cinnamon, baking soda, and baking powder. Add the dry ingredients and the buttermilk to the butter mixture, mixing in gradually until combined. Do not overmix. Fold in the orange zest. Gently spread the batter over the cranberries. Bake the cake for about 45 minutes, or until a toothpick inserted in the center comes out clean. Cool the cake in the pan on a rack for 10 minutes. Loosen the cake from the pan by running a thin knife around the edge and invert it onto the cooling rack. Peel off the parchment and let the cake cool completely.

SHORTCAKE *with* BERRIES

NOTHING SCREAMS SUMMER LIKE SHORTCAKE WITH BERRIES. MOST GO RIGHT FOR *the classic strawberry shortcake but in a state where blueberries, blackberries, and raspberries grow right by the side of the road, why not take advantage of what's outside the door? Just take a look at what's in season and offer this treat with our Maple Whipped Cream (page 229).*

YIELD: 6 TWO-CAKE SERVINGS

$1^1/_2$ cups all-purpose flour

$1^1/_2$ teaspoons baking powder

$^1/_2$ teaspoon baking soda

$^1/_2$ teaspoon salt

2 tablespoons sugar, divided

12 tablespoons ($1^1/_2$ sticks) cold butter, cubed

$^3/_4$ cup buttermilk

$^1/_4$ cup heavy cream

1 cup raspberries

1 cup blueberries

1 cup blackberries

2 cups whipped cream

Preheat the oven to 325°F. Combine the flour, baking powder, baking soda, salt, and 1 tablespoon of the sugar in a bowl. Cut the butter into the dry ingredients. Add the buttermilk, a bit at a time until a soft dough is formed. Roll the dough out to $^1/_2$-inch thickness and cut with 3-inch round cookie cutters. Place the cakes on a cookie sheet and brush with cream. Bake until lightly brown, about 15 minutes.

Toss the berries with the remaining 1 tablespoon of the sugar. Split each short cake in half horizontally. Place two halves on the plate and then top with berries. Top with the remaining halves to create a sandwich. Add a dollop of whipped cream on top of each sandwich.

PEACH COFFEE CAKE

PEOPLE DON'T THINK OF MAINE AS A PLACE WHERE STONE FRUIT GROWS, BUT *there are actually very good peaches here and they are perfect with this coffee cake. Have it at breakfast or brunch, but try it for dessert with our Blueberry Crème Frâiche Ice Cream too (page 226).*

YIELD: 6 SERVINGS

4 cups all-purpose flour

2 cups granulated sugar

2 teaspoons baking powder

1 teaspoon kosher salt

$^{1}/_{2}$ cup shortening

2 cups buttermilk

1 teaspoon baking soda

Six peaches, peeled and thinly sliced

$^{1}/_{4}$ cup ($^{1}/_{2}$ stick) unsalted butter

1 cup firmly packed brown sugar

Preheat the oven to 350°F. Sift together the flour, granulated sugar, baking powder, and salt in a large bowl. Blend in the shortening. Remove $^{1}/_{2}$ cup of this mixture and save for the topping. Blend the buttermilk and baking soda in a bowl and add to the dry ingredients. Layer the peaches at the bottom of a 9-inch pan. Pour the batter over the peaches. Melt the butter and drizzle on top. Add the $^{1}/_{2}$ cup of reserved topping mixture to the brown sugar. Mix and sprinkle over the cake. Bake about 30 minutes, or until a toothpick placed in the center of the cake comes out clean. Allow to cool for 15 minutes before serving.

DOWN-EAST SIZZLERS

MANY SUMMER VISITORS ASSOCIATE MAINE WITH FRIED SEAFOOD, BUT ACTUALLY *some of the earliest known fried dishes and foods weren't fried clams but such confections as these sizzlers, much like a dumpling. One thing that's very important about frying sweet things is to start with clean oil no matter what. You don't want your lovely sweet sizzlers tasting like fried clams.*

YIELD: 12 SERVINGS

1 cup sifted all-purpose flour
$^1/_4$ cup sugar
1 teaspoon kosher salt
$1^1/_2$ teaspoons baking powder
2 tablespoons unsalted butter
$^1/_3$ cup milk
1 egg
1 cup finely chopped apple
1 cup canola oil
$^1/_2$ cup warm maple syrup

Sift together the flour, sugar, salt, and baking powder in a bowl. Cut in the butter until it looks like coarse cornmeal. Add the milk and egg. Stir until it forms a dough. On a floured board, roll the dough until thin, about $^1/_4$ inch thick. Cut into 4-inch circles. Place a heaping teaspoon of apple in the middle of each circle. Moisten the edges with water and fold in half, pinching closed. Heat the oil in a deep-fat fryer or a heavy-bottomed pot to 325°F. The oil should be about 1 inch deep. Drop the sizzlers into the hot oil, working in batches, and fry until browned, 2 to 3 minutes.

    Drain well on paper towels and then serve with warm maple syrup.

OUR INDIAN PUDDING

WE COULD WRITE A WHOLE BOOK ABOUT INDIAN PUDDING AND ITS NEW ENGLAND *roots. Most Yankee cooks agree it's a staple, although there are variations. In Rhode Island you'll see white corn meal and elsewhere tapioca. Some use sweet apples and pears, others raisins, all of which float to the top and create a sweet juice. Every recipe has the basics—molasses, cornmeal, and milk. Every school child knows that Native Americans taught the early settlers to raise corn and that molasses came from the Caribbean following the great Triangle Trade. All of this history makes Indian or "injun" pudding one of the oldest recipes in New England cookery. There are many variations even within Maine, but we think our version measures up with the best.*

YIELD: 8 SERVINGS

3 cups milk
$^1/_2$ cup yellow cornmeal
$^1/_4$ cup dark molasses
2 tablespoons sugar
2 tablespoons unsalted butter
$^1/_4$ teaspoon salt
$^1/_8$ teaspoon baking powder
1 egg

Preheat the oven to 300°F. Combine the milk and cornmeal in a saucepan over medium heat and bring to a simmer. Combine the rest of the ingredients in a bowl and whip in the cornmeal mixture. Pour the mixture into a 2-quart baking dish. Cover with foil and bake slowly for about 2 hours until the pudding is set. Serve warm.

OGUNQUIT BEACH S'MORES

DON'T DROP THESE IN THE SAND! OUR TOWN HAS ONE OF THE MOST PRISTINE *fine-grained white sand beaches in New England, but you don't want these covered in it. There's something very romantic about sitting around the fire on the beach on a late summer night telling stories and making s'mores. With all that gooey marshmallow and chocolate, they are truly easy squeezy but don't squeeze too hard. What else do you make where it's ok to be messy? For our s'mores we go all out and make our own graham crackers and marshmallow, and you can, too, or just buy good-quality graham crackers and marshmallows at the store and get to the beach faster.*

YIELD: 6 SERVINGS

GRAHAM CRACKERS

$1^{1}/_{4}$ cups all-purpose flour

1 cup whole wheat flour

1 teaspoon ground cinnamon

$^{1}/_{2}$ teaspoon ground ginger

$^{1}/_{2}$ teaspoon baking soda

$^{1}/_{2}$ teaspoon kosher salt

$^{3}/_{4}$ cup unsalted butter, slightly softened

$^{1}/_{3}$ cup firmly packed brown sugar

3 tablespoons granulated sugar

2 tablespoons honey

1 large egg

1 teaspoon vanilla

MARSHMALLOW

4 (1-ounce) packages powdered gelatin

$^{1}/_{3}$ cup water

$1^{1}/_{4}$ cups granulated sugar

$^{1}/_{4}$ cup light corn syrup

6 large eggs, separated

$^{3}/_{4}$ cups confectioners' sugar

$^{3}/_{4}$ cup cornstarch

S'MORES

12 ounces quality dark chocolate

Marshmallow

12 graham crackers

FOR THE GRAHAM CRACKERS: Whisk together the flour, whole wheat flour, cinnamon, ginger, baking soda, and salt in a large bowl. Mix the butter on medium speed with an electric mixer until softened and then mix in the sugars. Stir in the honey, egg, and vanilla. Scrape down the sides of the bowl as needed. Add the dry ingredients in three parts, mixing well after each addition until blended. Divide the dough in half. Wrap in plastic wrap and chill for 2 hours.

Preheat the oven to 350°F. Line two cookie sheets with parchment paper. Lightly flour a work surface. Working with one piece of dough at a time, roll it into an 8-inch square, about $^{1}/_{4}$ inch thick. Using a knife, trim the sides of the dough to leave a 7-inch square.

Reserve the scraps. Divide the dough into 9 even squares and place them about 1½ inches apart on the cookie sheets. Re-roll the trimmings and make 3 more squares, to total 12. Bake the crackers until lightly browned around the edges, about 10 minutes. Let rest on the cookie sheets for 5 minutes and then transfer them to wire racks to cool.

FOR THE MARSHMALLOW: Sprinkle the gelatin into 6 ounces cold water. Let stand 1 minute. In a heavy saucepan, bring ⅓ cup water, the granulated sugar, and corn syrup to 240°F. In a large bowl whip the egg whites to stiff peaks, about 5 minutes. (Freeze the left-over egg yolks for use in sauces or other recipes.) Pour the cooked sugar down the side of the bowl into the egg whites. Dissolve the gelatin in a hot pan and add to the sugar and egg mixture. Whip until stiff and fluffy, about 7 minutes.

Spray the bottom and sides of a parchment-covered baking sheet with vegetable cooking spray and spread the marshmallow mixture evenly, but do it gently so the marshmallow doesn't deflate.

Combine the confectioners' sugar and the cornstarch. Using a fine mesh sieve, sprinkle some of the mixture over the top of the marshmallow. Reserve the remaining mixture for additional sprinklings. Let stand for 2 to 4 hours to dry. Add more of the sugar and starch mixture to the top and invert the marshmallow. Remove the parchment paper and dust the bottom with the sugar and starch mixture. Cut into squares. Gently toss the cut pieces in the sugar and cornstarch mixture to coat completely.

FOR THE S'MORES: Place a square of chocolate on one graham cracker. Heat the marshmallow over a fire or put under a broiler. Place the marshmallow on the chocolate and then top with another piece of graham cracker. Squeeze.

THE WAY WE SHOP

IF YOU HAVE IT IN YOUR MIND THAT YOU'RE CRAVING CHICKEN, just leave it at that. With that one idea in mind, go to the grocery store or farmers' market and see what's fresh and in season. Wing it! Whatever is in season will go well together whether it's an herb, a green, or a vegetable. Find what catches your fancy instead of bringing a list. If you must have a list or are trying a new recipe, write an outline just like you did in sixth grade for your first paper so you can adapt. If the recipe calls for leeks and they look horrible or are too expensive because they're not in season, get some spring onions. Don't be afraid to explore your options.

Buy in season. Don't buy raspberries in January, they can't be from here. Just think about where things are coming from and when. Corn is the summertime, carrots are coming in long into the winter in some areas, including in Maine. The seasonal foods will taste better, and buying seasonally means buying economically. How many times have you dropped your jaw in shock when you looked at the price tag on strawberries in December?

Now, if you're really using this book, you will have raspberries in February because you bought them in season and froze them or you have potatoes and onions in the root cellar along with those pickles you made from the summer cucumbers and beans.

Don't be afraid to ask the butcher or fishmonger for advice. Tell them what you want to do and they can tell you which meats would be best and steer you toward meats and fish that are from local sources as well as fresh and tasty. Once you've developed a relationship with your butcher, he'll go out of his way to let you know when there is something special to build a meal on.

APPLE-RHUBARB CRISP

CRISPS AND GRUNTS, COBBLERS AND SLUMPS—ALL NAMES FOR ONE-DISH BAKED *desserts, usually involving fruit. They might be simple, but they're so delicious. Rhubarb is actually one of the first crops to come up in the Maine garden each season, and it grows like a tropical plant. You can't eat the leaves, but the long stalks are sweet and tangy. These sorts of dishes are great for when the garden takes over and you have too much of one fruit. Freeze your berries and rhubarb and use them all year long.*

YIELD: 6 SERVINGS

FRUIT MIXTURE
6 apples, peeled, cored, and diced
6 cups chopped rhubarb
1 cup sugar
1 teaspoon ground ginger
4 tablespoons unsalted butter
1 teaspoon cornstarch
$^1/_2$ cup hot water
1 teaspoon lemon juice

TOPPING
$^3/_4$ cup all-purpose flour
$^1/_2$ cup sugar
$^1/_2$ teaspoon kosher salt
$^1/_2$ teaspoon cinnamon
$^1/_4$ teaspoon ground nutmeg
$^1/_4$ cup firmly packed brown sugar
8 tablespoons (1 stick) unsalted butter

FOR THE FRUIT MIXTURE: Preheat the oven to 350°F. Mix the fruit mixture ingredients in a large bowl and then place in a buttered 12 x 9-inch baking dish.

FOR THE TOPPING: Combine the ingredients in a bowl and then work in the butter until it resembles coarse meal. Top the fruit mixture with the topping and bake for 30 to 40 minutes, or until golden on top.

BAILEY'S ISLAND BLUEBERRY TART

THERE IS A FAMOUS BRIDGE CONNECTING ORR'S ISLAND TO BAILEY'S ISLAND, *in fact it's the only cribstone bridge in the world. The bridge design allows the large tides to flow freely through it so that boats have an easier time getting through the channel opening. We just think it's beautiful and when we first started going to that area, just an hour or so away from Ogunquit, we loved it because we felt like we were truly "Down East." We used to go to a restaurant called the Log Cabin, and they had the best blueberry pies made by one of the waitresses who worked there. We took friends up there all the time. On one trip we hit a blizzard halfway up but kept going anyway. When we came out we were in a full blown Nor'easter and had to skid home. In the Bailey's Island Pie, the crust was light and flaky and not overdone, and there weren't many spices either, allowing the blueberries to shine. In our rendition we tried to duplicate these textures and flavors and by making it into a tarlet is to make it just a little more elegant.*

YIELD: 6 SERVINGS

CRUST
1¹/₂ cups all-purpose flour
¹/₂ teaspoon kosher salt
2 tablespoons sugar
4 tablespoons unsalted butter
4 tablespoons shortening
1 large egg

FILLING
1 pound blueberries
¹/₂ cup sugar
¹/₂ teaspoon ground cinnamon
1 teaspoon ground ginger
1 teaspoon vanilla
1 tablespoon lemon juice
2 tablespoons cornstarch
2 tablespoons cold water

CRUMBLED TOPPING
8 tablespoons (1 stick) unsalted butter
¹/₂ cup sugar
1 teaspoon vanilla extract
¹/₂ cup all-purpose flour

FOR THE CRUST: Preheat the oven to 425°F. In a food processor, place the flour, salt, and sugar and process until combined. Add the butter and shortening and process until the mixture resembles coarse meal, about 20 seconds. In a small bowl, whisk the egg. Gradually pour the egg into the dough and process for 15 seconds or until the pastry holds together. Add water, if necessary. Do not process more than about 30 seconds. On a floured work surface, roll the dough to fill a 10-inch tart pan and press into the pan at both the bottom and the sides.

FOR THE FILLING: Place the blueberries, sugar, cinnamon, ginger, vanilla, and lemon juice in a saucepan and bring to a boil. Mix the cornstarch with the cold water. Add to the blueberry mixture. Boil again and then remove from the heat.

FOR THE TOPPING: Beat the butter and sugar together in a bowl. Add the vanilla and then the flour. Pour the blueberry mixture into the tart shell and top with the topping. Bake for 30 minutes, or until the crust is lightly brown. Let cool until just warm to the touch.

WILD FOR BLUEBERRIES

MAINERS WILL MAKE ANYTHING WITH OUR SWEET LITTLE WILD Maine blueberries from pie, crisps, and cobblers to jams, ice cream, and even vodka. Our sixty thousand acres of wild blueberries have adapted to our harsh winters and grow without much tending all over the state, ready for harvest in August, when blueberry festivals abound.

Rich with antioxidants, the blueberries were used extensively by the Native Americans for nutrition, healing, and flavor. It was likely they who guided the settlers into harvesting the blueberries using a technique of burning the fields in alternate years to cut back the crop and promote growth. You'll still see flaming fields now but also farmers pruning the bushes to an inch high. The blueberries are indeed wild in the sense that they are not usually manually planted, but they do need a little help from farmers, who prune, fertilize, and protect the barrens from pests.

And the flavor is fantastic, delicate and tart, often sweet and crunchy. These gems are full of nutrients. It's no wonder Mainers will find many ways to make use of them, including just eating them right off of the bush.

WHOOPIE PIES

HOW THE WHOOPIE PIE BECAME A STATE TREASURE IS A MYSTERY TO US. ONE *theory holds that whoopie pies were brought north during the Depression by way of the "Yummy Book," a recipe pamphlet first published in 1930 by Durkee-Mower, the Massachusetts company that makes Marshmallow Fluff. But they might have come to us from the Amish. According to another theory, the recipe might have come to us from one of the many local radio programs aimed at housewives during the 1930s. No matter how they arrived, they've been a favorite in Maine for about eighty years, and today you'll find them stacked next to cash registers in stores all over the state. So you see, we couldn't have a book about Maine without these decadent treats.*

YIELD: 9 SERVINGS

CAKE

1 tablespoon canola oil

$^{1}/_{2}$ cup vegetable shortening

1 cup firmly packed brown sugar

1 egg

$^{1}/_{4}$ cup unsweetened cocoa powder

2 cups all-purpose flour

1 teaspoon baking powder

1 teaspoon baking soda

1 teaspoon kosher salt

1 cup milk

1 teaspoon vanilla extract

FILLING

1 cup solid vegetable shortening

$1^{1}/_{2}$ cups confectioners' sugar

2 cups marshmallow crème

$1^{1}/_{2}$ teaspoons vanilla extract

FOR THE CAKE: Preheat the oven to 350°F. Grease two baking sheets with canola oil. Cream the shortening, brown sugar, and egg in a large bowl. In a separate bowl, mix the cocoa, flour, baking powder, baking soda, and salt. In another bowl, mix the milk and vanilla. Add the dry mix to the shortening. Mix a little at a time and alternate adding the milk mixture. Beat until smooth.

Drop the batter in $^{1}/_{4}$ cup increments onto the cookie sheets, making 18 cakes. Spread out the batter into 4-inch circles with a spoon. Leave about 2 inches between each circle. Bake the cake until firm when touched, about 15 minutes. Remove from the oven and let cool.

FOR THE FILLING: Beat together the shortening, confectioners' sugar, marshmallow crème, and vanilla. When the cakes are cool, spread the filling on one cake and then top with another. Repeat to make eight more whoopie pies.

RED, WHITE, *and* BLUE ANGEL FOOD CAKE

ANGEL FOOD CAKE IS THE ONLY TRUE AMERICAN PASTRY RECIPE, MADE WITHOUT *French technique. It's probably even more American than apple pie. It likely originated with the Pennsylvania Dutch who made and first named angel food. We see references in our early New England cookbooks to this all-American original as well. We decided to make it even more American and dress this cake up in red, white, and blue, something we came up with for the Fourth of July. The egg whites might seem daunting, but the results are worth it.*

YIELD: 6 SERVINGS

$1^1/_2$ cups superfine sugar, divided

$3^1/_2$ ounces cake flour, sifted

$^1/_4$ teaspoon kosher salt

16 eggs, separated

2 teaspoons vanilla extract

2 teaspoons cream of tartar

3 cups heavy cream

$^1/_3$ cup raspberry purée

$^1/_3$ cup blueberry purée

Preheat the oven to 325°F. Sift half of the sugar with the flour and the salt. Set the remaining sugar aside. In a large bowl, whip the egg whites with a mixer to thoroughly combine them. Add the vanilla extract and the cream of tartar. Slowly add the reserved sugar into the mixture, beating continuously at medium speed. When soft peaks begin to form, sift half of the flour mixture in so that it dusts the top. Fold the remaining flour in very gently. Continue until all of the flour mixture is incorporated.

Carefully spoon the batter into a tall ungreased tube pan. Bake for 35 minutes. Check for doneness with a wooden skewer. It should come out dry. Cool upside down on a cooling rack for 1 hour before removing the cake from the pan.

Whip the cream with a mixer until stiff. Divide into three parts. Add the blueberry purée to one part, raspberry purée to the next, and leave one as is. Cut the cake into three horizontal parts with a long serrated knife. Place the red cream on the bottom layer and top with the next cake layer. Place white cream on top of the second layer and then top with another cake layer. Finish with the blue cream.

BUTTERNUT SQUASH DONUTS
with MAPLE SYRUP

MOST OF US WOULD THINK NOTHING ABOUT PUMPKIN IN A DONUT OR CAKE, BUT *somehow using squash seems a bit odd. It's really not. Squash can be wintered in the root cellar, and it's been traditional in Maine to use them in baking instead of pumpkin. If you like to garden you'll need a lot of space because squash grow like plants in the Amazon with curling tendrils and blossoms. It's great to have butternut squash not only in the height of the summer but also long after the first frost comes. These donuts are a fun dessert that the kids will enjoy.*

YIELD: 24 DONUTS

2 eggs

1^1/$_4$ cups sugar

1 cup peeled, cooked, pureed butternut
  squash

^{1}/$_2$ cup milk

2 tablespoons unsalted butter, softened

2 teaspoons vanilla extract

3^1/$_2$ cups all-purpose flour

1^1/$_2$ teaspoons baking soda

1^1/$_4$ teaspoons ground nutmeg

1 teaspoon baking powder

1 teaspoon cream of tartar

^{1}/$_2$ teaspoon kosher salt

^{1}/$_4$ teaspoon ground ginger

Oil, for deep-fat frying

2 cups hot maple syrup

Combine the eggs, sugar, squash, milk, butter, and vanilla in a bowl. In a separate bowl, combine the flour, baking soda, nutmeg, baking powder, cream of tartar, salt, and ginger. Add the dry ingredients to the squash mixture. Mix well, cover, and refrigerate for 1^1/$_2$ hours.

Place the dough onto a floured board and roll it out to a half-inch thickness. Cut with a 3-inch donut cutter. Heat 1 inch of oil in a heavy pan to 375°F. Fry a few at a time, until golden on both sides. Drain on paper towels and serve drizzled with maple syrup.

MARK'S BOSTON BROWN BREAD

BOSTON BROWN BREAD IS MADE WITH ONE OF THE CLASSIC NEW ENGLAND *ingredients—molasses—and it's one of New England's oldest recipes, a popular dish traditionally baked with a crust so tough it wasn't even eaten, but softened with water the next day and used to create the next batch. You won't break your teeth with this recipe, but it's still great to chew on. Brown bread was baked in tins long ago and still can be. The molasses gives it color and a rich, deep flavor. We like to use it in stuffing. It gives the turkey dinner a real Maine touch and it's also great with the Warm Dandelion Greens Salad (page 209) and the Clam Chowder with Thyme (page 42).*

YIELD: 1 3-POUND BREAD

1 cup wheat flour
1 cup rye flour
1 cup cornmeal
1 teaspoon kosher salt
1 teaspoon baking soda
1 cup raisins
$^2/_3$ cup dark molasses
2 tablespoons unsalted butter
2 cups milk

Preheat the oven to 350°F. Mix the flours, cornmeal, salt, and baking soda. Add the raisins, molasses, butter, and milk, mixing well. Put the dough into a 3-pound cleaned coffee can or a bread pan and bake until the dough springs back when poked with a finger, about 2 hours.

SLOWER THAN MOLASSES

THE WORLD IS NOW JOINED TOGETHER BY PLANE, TRAIN, AUTO-mobile, and the information super highway, but even before these modern conveniences, the economics of food has always been interrelated. This is certainly true of molasses, one of the commodities used in the Triangle Trade. New England made rum from the sugar and molasses that came in from the Caribbean and shipped it to Africa to buy slaves, which were, in turn, sold in the Caribbean. Whether or not New England was a part of the full triangle is unclear, but molasses was certainly used as a commodity as well as a sweetener later and before the arrival of refined white sugar.

We do know that molasses, a word derived from the Portuguese, *melaco*, which itself is from the Latin *mel*, for honey, was exported to the U.S. from the West Indies to make rum. Molasses was taxed by the British after 1733, but as stubborn New Englanders, we ignored the tax and it was reduced. Molasses was popular until the 1880s or so, but after World War I, white sugar became cheaper and overcame molasses in use and popularity.

One story we find so interesting is about the Great Molasses Flood in Boston. In 1919 a vat of molasses at the Purity Distilling Company in the North End exploded, killing 21 people and sending two million gallons of molasses rushing through the streets at 35 miles per hour. Residents today claim that they can still smell the molasses on hot muggy days.

Molasses is making a bit of a nostalgic comeback, and we use it in our stuffing, with pork, and in chewy gingerbread cookies. There are a few grades of molasses, including Gold Star or Fancy, used in baking because of its light sweetness: light molasses, with 40 percent less sugar and used in breads and cooking molasses, and a darker variety, which is great in ginger cookies. Less used in cooking is the dark and bitter blackstrap, which some use when cooking meats or more robust dishes. We think it adds a bit of history and a lot of flavor to dishes when used just right.

PARKER HOUSE ROLLS

THE PARKER HOUSE IS A REAL HOTEL IN BOSTON WHERE ALL THE FAMOUS LITERARY *people gathered. Although Portland is Maine's biggest city and closer to us than Boston, when people say, "I'm going to the city," they often mean Boston. These rolls were made famous at the Parker House and their light, buttery flavor makes them great with virtually anything. They've made quite a comeback in recent years and they're a good alternative when you're tired of those crunchy breads laden with nuts and fruit. Watch these soak up the melting butter and you won't resist them.*

YIELD: 20 ROLLS

3 tablespoons warm water

3 tablespoons sugar, divided

1 (0.25-ounce) package active dry yeast (2$\frac{1}{2}$ teaspoons)

10 tablespoons (1 stick, plus 2 tablespoons) unsalted butter, divided

1 cup whole milk

2 cups bread flour

1$\frac{1}{2}$ teaspoons kosher salt

1$\frac{1}{2}$ to 2 cups all-purpose flour

Stir together the warm water, 1 tablespoon of the sugar, and the yeast in a small bowl. Let stand until foamy, about 5 minutes. Melt 6 tablespoons of the butter in a small saucepan. Add the milk and heat to lukewarm. Stir together the yeast mixture, the remaining 2 tablespoons of the sugar, the butter and milk mixture, the bread flour, and salt in a bowl with a wooden spoon until combined. Stir in the all-purpose flour, a little at a time, until it makes a slightly sticky dough that forms a ball.

Butter a large bowl with 1 tablespoon of the butter. Knead the dough on a lightly floured surface, adding in a little more all-purpose flour if the dough is too sticky. Knead for about 10 minutes, or until smooth and elastic but still slightly sticky. Form the dough into a ball and place in the buttered bowl. Turn the dough to coat with butter, cover with plastic wrap, and let the dough rise in the bowl in a warm place until it doubles in size, about 1 hour.

Butter a 13 x 9-inch baking pan with 1 tablespoon of the butter. Divide the dough into 20 equal pieces and roll into balls. Arrange evenly in 4 rows of 5 in the pan and loosely cover with a light kitchen or tea towel. Let the dough rise until doubled in size, about 45 minutes. Make a crease in the center of each roll using a floured chopstick. Let the rolls rise again, for about 15 minutes.

Preheat the oven to 375°F. Melt the remaining 2 tablespoons of butter in a small saucepan. Brush the tops of the rolls with the butter and bake in the middle of the oven until golden, 20 to 25 minutes. Let the rolls cool in the pan on a rack for 5 minutes. Remove the rolls from the pan and serve.

BREAD STICKS

AT ARROWS WE START THE MEAL BY SERVING OUR GUESTS A LIGHT, SALTY BREAD *stick. They're perfect with cocktails or an ice cold flute of Champagne while gazing at the garden. Bread sticks are great right out of the oven as we serve them but also for snacks and hors d'oeuvres.*

YIELD: 6 THREE-STICK SERVINGS

$1^1/_2$ ounces yeast
1 quart warm water
$3^1/_2$ pounds bread flour
2 tablespoons kosher salt
2 tablespoons unsalted butter

Mix the yeast and the warm water in a large bowl and let sit for 10 minutes. Add the flour and salt to the yeast mixture and mix until a dough forms. Using a dough hook on an electric mixer, continue to mix for 3 minutes, until the dough is silky, smooth, and elastic. Place the dough in a buttered bowl covered with plastic wrap until it doubles in size, about 1 hour. Punch down the dough and refrigerate for 1 hour.

Preheat the oven to 350°F. Roll out the dough until it is as thin as pizza dough. With a pizza cutter, cut the dough into $^1/_4$-inch-wide strips. Lay the strips on a lightly buttered cookie sheet. Bake until crisp, 10 to 15 minutes. Remove from the oven and let cool.

CARAWAY BREAD

MAINE COOKS HAVE TRADITIONALLY LOVED CARAWAY SO MUCH SO THAT THEY *tend to get quite romantic about it. Get a load of this quote about caraway cookies from the* Yankee Cookbook*: "Full of the flavor of June fields, starred with daises and washed with golden sunshine, they cling to a man's memory all the days of his life." We don't swoon quite so much, but it's still a wonderful spice. Make the starter the day before. You won't use all of it so keep it in the refrigerator for your next baking day.*

YIELD: 1 LARGE OR 2 SMALL LOAVES

STARTER
18 ounces bread flour
18 ounces yeast
18 ounces water

BREAD
1¹⁄₂ tablespoons yeast

3 cups warm water
4 ounces starter
1 pound, 10 ounces bread flour
1 tablespoon kosher salt
3 tablespoons caraway seeds
1 tablespoon unsalted butter

FOR THE STARTER: Blend the ingredients in a bowl and keep covered overnight.

FOR THE BREAD: Dissolve the yeast in the warm water for 10 minutes in a large bowl. Add the starter, bread flour, and salt and mix at low speed with a dough hook attachment on an electric mixer until combined. Mix for 2 more minutes and then add the caraway seeds. Mix for 2 more minutes.

Turn the dough out onto a floured surface and allow to rest for 4 minutes. If the dough is sticky, add more flour. Knead for 10 minutes. Butter a large bowl. Place the dough in the buttered bowl. Cover tightly with plastic wrap and place in a warm area until it doubles in size, about 1¹⁄₂ hours.

Punch the dough down in the bowl then turn it out onto the work surface. Shape into a loaf or divide into two small loaves. Cover the loaves with a light towel and leave at room temperature until the dough doubles in size, about 2 hours.

Preheat the oven to 425 °F. Uncover the loaves and brush the tops with water. Place the loaves on a baking sheet in the middle rack of the oven. Bake until browned and hollow sounding when tapped on the bottom, about 40 minutes. Remove from the oven and cool on a rack.

BLUEBERRY-THYME MUFFINS

IN MAINE IT'S HARD TO RUN OUT OF THINGS TO PUT BLUEBERRIES INTO AND THE *flavor of thyme goes so perfectly with the sweet, earthy blueberry. Everyone seems to enjoy a good muffin and in addition to the great flavor one of the things that makes a superior muffin is using old-fashioned ingredients. That means no oil, just good, fresh creamery butter.*

YIELD: 24 MUFFINS

$2^1/_2$ cups all-purpose flour

$1^1/_4$ cups sugar

2 teaspoons kosher salt

1 tablespoon baking powder

3 tablespoons unsalted butter

4 eggs

$1^1/_2$ cups milk

1 tablespoon vanilla

1 teaspoon finely chopped fresh thyme

1 cup whole blueberries

Preheat the oven to 400°F. Mix the flour, sugar, baking powder, and salt in a large bowl. Melt the butter. Mix the butter and the eggs in a bowl. Add the butter and egg mixture to the dry ingredients. Add the milk and the vanilla. Mix in the thyme and the blueberries. Portion the batter into buttered muffin tins. Bake until a toothpick comes out clean when inserted in the middle, 20 to 25 minutes.

THE BAKERS

A SMALL SPACE, OFF THE BEATEN PATH, IN AN ALLEY IN PORTLAND offering just a few kinds of breads and pastries in 1995 was the "starter" bakery that gave rise to what is now Standard Baking Company, a bustling enterprise housed in a former warehouse on Portland's waterfront. It's still a "neighborhood" bakery, even if that neighborhood has expanded with trendy restaurants and tourist activities. Alison Pray and Matt James strive to keep the feel and flavors coming from Standard. It's all about comfort and craft.

Back in 1995 and still in 1999 when they moved to the larger space, their breads were European in style, but most people who came in had never heard of foccacia or were unfamiliar with the crusty style of baguettes the couple was selling. Their sourdough was in the French style, a *pain de levain*, but it was so alien to their customers they were reluctant to call it by the French name. It seemed like they were selling some sort of unrecognizable object that only a few customers remembered or appreciated.

It took time to get Portlanders used to the "new" old-world way of baking. Alison started at Clear Flour in Boston, one of few artisan bakeries in the country along with Acme in Berkeley, California; La Brea in Southern California; and Zabar's in New York. The couple wanted to get back to Portland—they had lived there before—so they moved from Boston and launched Standard. In 1993 they were part of forming the Bread Baker's Guild of America and later Alison was able to learn more about European style bread and pastry baking from two Frenchmen, Didier Rosada and Phillipe LeCorre, who were brought to the U.S. by the guild to teach the French techniques at the National Baking Center in Minneapolis. Those two men influenced not only her baking but also her teachings, which still resonate through many baking "generations."

Back in 1995, many ingredients were hard to come by. The only wheat available was spring wheat, which didn't give the bread the texture they wanted. Finally after the influence of the guild, bakers were able to get more of the winter wheat with the lower protein content needed to create just the right textures. Getting chocolate meant either settling for whatever inferior variety their supplier had or spending much more to get quality chocolate shipped to Maine.

In addition to making sure the texture is right, Alison and Matt have learned over the years that baking is a slow and gentle process and a tricky ratio. The foundation of good baking is the handling of the dough, and it's important not to overhandle as is often done in industrial baking, where additives make the texture "feel" like handmade bread. Alison says that the only way to handle bread properly is to learn through experience and from being responsible for making judgments about the dough each and every day. Every day is different because there are variations in humidity, quality of the flour, and heat.

Alison also studied pastry under Le Corre, forty hours alone on "laminated" or layered doughs like the croissant or puff pastry. Alison and Matt started by offering their famous "morning bun," and people were surprised that they were eating sweets because they were so used to the usual corn syrup-saturated, frosting-topped breakfast fare. Now, customers flock to Standard just for the flaky morning bun, a cup of coffee, and a baguette for the evening's supper.

Alison and Matt say that they still see themselves as a neighborhood bakery, even though that neighborhood is evolving. There are now neighborhood bakeries all over Portland and the state and the "eat local" movement has made it easier for bakers to get the fresh quality ingredients they need. No longer do they have to get such ingredients as artisan chocolate, organic dairy, or special grains shipped in. They are being produced and crafted nearby, and the couple says locals now understand the craft of their baking as well. The couple says they feel like they've stepped back in time, to when people were living the "old ways," and Alison and Matt feel they help to revive this good and healthier way of life.

MONDAY
Sesame Semolina
Pain De Mie
Whole Rye

TUESDAY
Light Rye w/ Caraway
Organic Whole Wheat
Pain De Mie

WEDNESDAY
100% Whole Wheat Pain Au Lait

Chapter Eight **THE ROOT CELLAR**

*F*or our forbearers, preserving food was an essential part of life. They didn't have refrigeration, freezers, or Tupperware. With all of our conveniences it's hard for us to connect to what their lives were like. Today we have a high-speed infrastructure that brings food from around the globe. The ice man and the milk man were necessities for our grandparents, but now they're just fodder for quaint stories. Reconnecting with some of these old traditions is one of the great pleasures of cooking. Like gardening, foraging, and making your own cheese, preserving is one of those things that reminds us of what's really important in life. It's spiritually fulfilling, and once you get in the swing of things, it's a lot of fun. It's also a great help in your everyday cooking.

If you're going to start canning, you don't have to make it a big deal. As a weekend retreat, we'd go pick fruits and then make jams, a refreshing change from the expensive trappings of modern life. And you don't need a garden or an orchard to do it, just go to the farmers' market and get cucumbers for your sweet and sour pickles, berries for your preserves, ripe red apples for apple sauce, and fresh from the garden tomatoes for marinara. Your grandmother didn't have a master's degree in chemistry to learn how to can, and with a little bit of research you can start simply and advance quickly. Rely on your local college or university extension adult classes, they'll often have a course on canning and there is usually a demo going on at the local farmers' market a few times a week. Once you get started with canning, you'll find there's really nothing as satisfying as thinking, "I have those blueberries put aside to have for dessert and I don't have to go to the supermarket to make a nice hot cobbler." As you delve further in the garden, you'll get used to preserving even more vegetables and fruits, and on some dreary February afternoon when there's no green to be seen, you'll just go to your basement and pick out that tomatillo salsa you made in August. You have your vibrant garden throughout the year.

ROOT CELLAR GRATIN

YAM AND POTATO GRATIN IS DECEPTIVELY SIMPLE TO MAKE, AND THE RESULTS *are both delicious and impressive to look at. This particular gratin is always a favorite at Arrows because of the rich and mellow flavors that work well with both meat and fish. It can also be the centerpiece for a vegetarian dinner and it's great for pot lucks.*

YIELD: 6 SERVINGS

6 yams, peeled and sliced very thinly
   (no more than $1/8$-inch thick)
6 white potatoes peeled and sliced very thinly
   (no more than $1/8$-inch thick)
Kosher salt
Freshly ground black pepper
2 cups heavy cream

Preheat the oven to 350°F. Butter an 8 x 8-inch, 2-quart casserole. Place a layer of yams slightly overlapping each other in the bottom of the casserole. Follow with a layer of potato. Sprinkle with salt and pepper. Repeat the process, finishing with the yams. Pour the heavy cream over the yams and potatoes. Cover the casserole with foil. Bake for 1 hour. Remove the foil from the casserole and bake until the yams are golden brown, about 20 more minutes. Remove from the oven and let sit for 10 minutes. Cut the gratin into squares and remove the squares from the casserole with a metal spatula. Serve immediately.

ROASTED TURNIP PURÉE

EVERYONE LOVES MASHED POTATOES, BUT OCCASIONALLY IT'S FUN TO GO CRAZY *and stray with these two purées. Carrots and parsnips are great together, but turnips can be a little bitter. By roasting a turnip, you bring out the sweet flavor. It's one of the nicest ways to cook turnips and very easy. Serve these at your Thanksgiving dinner and more traditional fall dinners or with our ham dishes. It's also nice to make several of these purées as a part of a vegetarian dinner.*

YIELD: 6 SERVINGS

6 turnips (about 2 pounds), peeled
   and chopped into 1-inch pieces
4 tablespoons extra virgin olive oil
$1/2$ teaspoon kosher salt
Pinch of freshly ground black pepper
4 tablespoons unsalted butter

Preheat the oven to 400°F. Toss the turnips with the olive oil, salt, and pepper to coat. Cover and bake in a baking dish for 1 hour. Melt the butter in a sauté pan and cook until lightly brown. Add the turnips and the butter to a food processor and purée until smooth. Serve at once.

CARROT AND PARSNIP PURÉE

YIELD: 6 SERVINGS

1 pound carrots, peeled and sliced
1 pound parsnips, peeled and sliced
4 tablespoons extra virgin olive oil
$^1/_4$ cup heavy cream
4 tablespoons unsalted butter
Kosher salt and freshly ground black pepper

Preheat the oven to 400°F. Toss the carrots and parsnips in the olive oil and bake, covered, in a baking dish until soft, about 45 minutes. In a saucepan, bring the cream to a boil. Place the carrots and parsnips into a food processor and add the cream and butter. Purée until smooth. Add salt and pepper to taste. Serve.

SETTING UP YOUR ROOT CELLAR

THERE'S NOTHING AT ALL MYSTERIOUS ABOUT A ROOT CELLAR, IT'S really just a cool dry place that the animals can't get to. Your garage can be a root cellar or your basement can hold those potatoes, carrots, and onions you want to keep all year long. It simply has to be a place where vegetables can't freeze. A few shelves or hanging metal baskets are perfect places to store onions, shallots, parsnips, turnips and potatoes or you can get more elaborate and build shelves with wire mesh over them to keep away the critters.

The two things you need to control in the root cellar are temperature and humidity. It's best if you have at least one underground wall in your basement and invest in a thermometer and a hygrometer to make sure the humidity is above 80 percent to prevent withering and wrinkling of your vegetables.

Don't wash the root vegetables before storing and for vegetables such as beets, leave the stems. Cut the tops of other vegetables close to the vegetable itself. You'll need to cover the vegetables with about one-half inch of insulation, such as sawdust, and in about 34 degrees Fahrenheit or above with that high humidity. Keep them raised off of the floor and you can use a simple cardboard box for storage. Place a layer of sawdust in the box and add a layer of root vegetables. Keep layering the saw dust and vegetables finishing with about two inches of sawdust on top.

Even a lined trash can will work for storage. Keep checking your root vegetables for blemishes. One bad "apple" will rot the rest. Every time you go downstairs to get a few parsnips for your stew, you'll be glad you went to all the trouble.

VINEGAR- *and* HERB-BRAISED ONIONS

WE LOVE TO BRAISE ONIONS BECAUSE IT BRINGS OUT THE RICH FLAVOR OF THE *onion. It's also fun to experiment cooking with different wines, herbs, and vinegars. Once you've tried these out, try some other wine vinegar or even wine like ports and sherries, or liquors like bourbon and scotch—the technique remains the same. Make this dish ahead of time and simply slowly reheat when you're ready to serve. This is another terrific addition to any vegetarian dinner and lovely with grilled steaks, roasts, and hams. You don't have to cook them in the oven either; cook them wrapped in foil nestled among the coals of a barbecue the old-fashioned way to give them a smoky flavor.*

YIELD: 8 SERVINGS

4 cups pearl onions, peeled

1 sprig rosemary

2 sprigs thyme

2 teaspoons kosher salt

1 teaspoon freshly ground black pepper

$^1/_4$ cup sugar

$^3/_4$ cup red wine vinegar

Simmer all of the ingredients on low heat in a nonreactive saucepan until the onions are fully cooked, 10 to 15 minutes. Serve.

CHIVE MASHED POTATOES

WE LOVE MASHED POTATOES THE WAY MOM USED TO MAKE THEM, CLEAN AND *uncluttered. Chefs often make forays into messing with Mom's perfection—wasabi mashed, anyone? Yuck. But just adding chive brings a clean, bright flavor to mashed potatoes that we find pleasant. Try them with the Salmon Grilled with Green Beans and Corn (page 123) or any of the grilled scallop recipes (pages 92–96).*

YIELD: 6 SERVINGS

3 pounds large Maine potatoes, peeled and cubed
2 tablespoons kosher salt
$^1/_4$ cup unsalted butter, softened
1 cup milk
$^1/_4$ cup finely chopped chives

In a large pot, cover the potatoes with cold water. Add the salt and cook until very soft. Drain the potatoes and transfer to a mixing bowl. Using a mixer with a whip attachment or a simple hand masher, whip or mash the potatoes, gradually adding the butter, milk, and then the chives. Season to taste. Mashed potatoes can be kept warm in a pan for about 1 hour.

TWICE-BAKED POTATOES

ONE OF THE FEW REALLY GREAT STANDBYS OF THE RESTAURANT SCENE IN AMERICA *in the 50s and 60s and then stumbling into the 70s was the twice-baked potato. When done well it's worth rescuing from the disco era and with just a little more work, it takes the plain baked potato to a new level. Friends and family will love you. We've even served them as a centerpiece in a vegetarian dinner. Match it with some of our other vegetable selections and you'll have a sumptuous feast. For the carnivores in the crowd, it's terrific with steamed lobster, the Striped Sea Bass Sautéed with Bacon and Onions (page 131), or the Double Lamb Chops with Mint Relish (page 189).*

YIELD: 6 SERVINGS

1 tablespoon canola oil
6 large Maine baking potatoes
1 tablespoon kosher salt
1 cup shredded Cheddar cheese
1 cup sour cream
3 eggs, separated and yolks beaten
Kosher salt and freshly ground black pepper
2 tablespoons chopped chives

Preheat the oven to 350°F. Brush the potatoes with canola oil and sprinkle with the 1 tablespoon of salt. Place on a cookie sheet and bake for 1^1/$_2$ hours. Remove from the oven and let cool until the potatoes are warm to the touch. Slice in half. Scoop out the inside of the potato, leaving the skin intact. Mash the potato by hand with a ricer or masher in a bowl. Mix in the cheese, sour cream, and beaten egg yolks. Season with salt and pepper. Fill the potato skins with the mixture. Place the filled skins on a cookie sheet and bake until lightly browned, about 30 minutes. Garnish with chives.

YES, YOU CAN, CAN

CANNING BRINGS THE SUMMER BACK THROUGHOUT OUR LONG winters. It's another one of those practices born out of necessity. We need to eat all year-round, but when there's no refrigeration, preserving is key. Now, those old ways are coming back and we're glad they are. Canning not only saves money, it gives us fresh tasting foods all year long.

In late summer we have a plethora of vegetables even we just can't use up, so out come the Ball jars, lids, racks, and canning pots and it's a party. We pickle tomatoes in Maine when the frost is coming so fast we need to get them off the vine. We have a passion for pickles. We both grew up in families that canned, and Clark remembers going to Gizditch Farm in Castroville, California, on Sundays for olallieberries, a mix of blackberries and raspberries. He and his family would pick the berries, can, and talk and either keep them for themselves or give them away as gifts.

There are a few important things to remember about canning to keep yourself and anyone eating your great canned goods safe. Canning is basically heating foods in jars until they're at a temperature that destroys the micro-organisms that spoil food. Air is removed from the jar and a vacuum is created in the jar as it cools so no air or contamination will enter.

The two methods of canning are water bath and pressure canning and each has its own uses. Use the boiling water bath for tomatoes, fruits, jams, jellies, pickles, and other preserves. The submerged filled jars are heated to boiling and cooked for a set amount of time. Use pressure canning for vegetables, seafood, and meats, basically low acidic foods. In this method the jars are placed in water in a pressure cooker heated to 240°F or above.

We've gone over the basic principles but to learn proper canning methods, get a book, such as *The Joy of Cooking: All About Canning and Preserving,* or take a lesson at a local University Extension program. They'll be able to give you the ins and outs of canning, and after that, your pantry will be filled for the entire year.

SAVING THE SUMMER
(ROOT CELLAR PRESERVES)

Cranberry-Orange Compote

CRANBERRY AND ORANGE IS A CLASSIC *New England combination. You just can't go wrong with this easy and fun-to-make compote. It's not just for turkey anymore. Serve with roast chicken or lamb or just eat it with a spoon.*

YIELD: 6 SERVINGS

1 (12-ounce) bag cranberries, rinsed

Zest from 3 oranges

1 cup orange juice

1 tablespoon peeled and finely chopped ginger

$^1/_2$ cup maple syrup

Pinch of kosher salt

Place the cranberries and orange zest into a heavy nonreactive saucepan. Add the orange juice, ginger, maple syrup, and salt. Cook at medium low heat until the cranberries pop, about 10 minutes. Let cool and serve.

Blueberry Sauce with Cinnamon

THIS IS ANOTHER CLASSIC COMBINATION, *like apple pie and vanilla ice cream, but it's important that the cinnamon doesn't overwhelm the blueberry, similar to the fact that more than a dash of anchovy in your Caesar dressing can ruin it all. Keep this sauce canned or in the fridge and use it whenever you have a craving for a scoop of vanilla ice cream but also as a savory sauce with duck.*

YIELD: 6 SERVINGS

2 cups blueberries, cleaned

1 tablespoon peeled and chopped ginger

1 teaspoon ground cinnamon

$^1/_4$ cup Chianti or other light spicy red wine

$^1/_4$ cup firmly packed light brown sugar

Place the blueberries, ginger, cinnamon, wine, and sugar in a nonreactive heavy saucepan. Cook on medium heat until the berries are soft, about 5 minutes. Let cool to warm and purée in a blender.

Sweet Pickles

WE HAVE A CONFESSION TO MAKE. AT *least one shelf in our pantry is filled to the brink with pickles. When Clark used to visit Mark's family, Mark's mom would run to the store to get the largest jar she could find. Clark's mother said she couldn't afford his pickle habit and showed him the more economic way to do it—going to the farmers' market to get the ingredients and making his own. It's easy and satisfying. The ones you make at home are always better than those you get in the jar so put them out at your next dinner party and impress your friends.*

YIELD: 6 SERVINGS

6 large cucumbers (about 3 pounds), washed
1 large Spanish onion
$^1/_4$ cup coriander seeds
$^1/_2$ cup chopped cilantro
1 cup sugar
4 cups rice wine vinegar
1 teaspoon kosher salt

Cut the cucumbers into $^1/_4$-inch slices. Peel and slice the onion. Toast the coriander seeds in a dry sauté pan until lightly browned, about 2 minutes. Combine the coriander, cilantro, sugar, vinegar, and salt in a large nonreactive saucepan. Bring the mixture to a boil and then add the cucumbers and onions and turn off the heat. Let steep until cool. Serve when cool or chill further.

Sour Pickles

YIELD: 6 SERVINGS

6 large cucumbers (about 3 pounds)
4 cups cider vinegar
$^1/_2$ cup water
2 teaspoons kosher salt
$^1/_8$ cup sugar
$^1/_8$ cup mustard seed

Wash the cucumbers and slice into $^1/_4$-inch-thick slices. Mix the vinegar, water, salt, sugar, and mustard seed in a heavy nonreactive saucepan. Bring the mixture to a boil; then add the cucumbers and turn off the heat. Let steep until cool. Serve when cool or chill further.

PRESERVING AND SMOKING FISH

FROM THE EARLIEST DAYS, MAINERS HAVE ALWAYS PRESERVED FISH, such as cod, a staple of New England life. Cod and haddock were salted and then literally "hung out to dry" on barn doors all over the state. Many of us are intimidated by the concept of preserving fish and even more freaked out by the concept of smoking, but it's easy. All you need is sugar and salt to activate the process, the rest is merely flavoring and patience. The simplest thing to do is to buy a fillet of fish, sprinkle it with sugar, and then cover the fish with salt, like a bed of snow. Press it for three days under a weight or a bunch of large cans of tomatoes and you've got a preserved fish that's far better than anything you can get in your local deli. Add dill or other herbs and experiment with different sugars.

One of our favorite projects during our first year at Arrows and now is to make smoked fish. Clark's father Vance made his smoked fish in his simple Weber barbecue grill, and the results were the finest we've had. All you need is a hot plate with soaked hickory or other hardwood chips and a kettle grill. Marinate the fish in salt and sugar the night before and smoke the next day. It can be a fun family activity, and the fun is in making it again and again, becoming a better artisanal home cook the more you do it.

PICKLED ONION *with* STAR ANISE

STAR ANISE MAY SEEM LIKE A RATHER EXOTIC SPICE, BUT AS YOU GET TO KNOW *it, you'll find many uses for it's mellow flavor. It's actually easy to find and has a great burnt orange and honey flavor that gives many things a completely different and unexpected taste, one that's bold enough to infuse even something as strong as an onion. We like to serve it with some of our Asian dishes, like the Pan-Fried Trout (page 128), Bok Choy with Shiitake (page 203), and the Cider-Poached Salmon with Apples (page 124).*

YIELD: 6 SERVINGS

$^3/_4$ pound pearl onions, peeled

$^1/_2$ cup firmly packed brown sugar

4 star anise pods

1 tablespoon pink peppercorns

$^1/_2$ teaspoon peeled and finely chopped ginger

$1^1/_2$ cup cider or malt vinegar

Place all of the ingredients into a large nonreactive saucepan on low heat. Cook until the onions are just tender, about 30 minutes. Turn off the heat and let the onions steep. Serve when cool or chill in the refrigerator.

SPICY CABBAGE

WHEN CLARK WAS A YOUNG STUDENT IN BEIJING, HE ENCOUNTERED A STRANGE *happening in the fall. Everywhere he went, cabbages started piling up in balconies, doorways, halls— the entire city looked like one big mound of cabbage. He was soon to learn the reason why. For the entire winter, all there was for vegetables was cabbage. He learned to love it because the Chinese are miracle workers with cabbage and turning the simplest ingredients into something delicious is easy for them. They even serve cabbage for breakfast. We prefer to serve it as a condiment with sandwiches or with our Crab Fritters (page 51) and as a side dish for any of our fish dishes.*

YIELD: 6 SERVINGS

$2^1/_2$ pounds green cabbage, cored and finely sliced

5 tablespoons sugar, divided

2 tablespoons kosher salt

2 tablespoons peeled and finely chopped ginger

2 tablespooons sambal oelek chili paste

1 cup sherry vinegar

Place the cabbage in a colander and sprinkle with 3 tablespoons of the sugar and the salt. Place a plate over the cabbage and place a weight on top (a large can of tomatoes will do). Then place the colander in a bowl for at least 1 hour or overnight. Drain the cabbage and toss with the ginger, sambal oelek, vinegar, and the remaining 2 tablespoons of sugar. This cabbage can be kept in a sealed container refrigerated for a week.

BLUEBERRY JAM

MAINE MEANS BLUEBERRIES AND ANYONE WHO'S SPENT ANY TIME IN MAINE *has grown to appreciate the beauty of the blueberry. We've never known a kid who doesn't love walking through our high bush blueberries and sneaking a few before dinner at Arrows. Blueberry jam is probably one of the biggest sellers of any small food producer in Maine, and jars are tucked into corners of suitcases going across the world. There's no need to risk the explosion in the suitcase, just make ours and the results are satisfying and delicious.*

YIELD: 6 SERVINGS

$4^1/_2$ cups blueberries, cleaned
1 lemon
1 cup sugar

Crush the berries with a fork in a bowl. Juice the lemon and save the rind. Slice the rind. Add the lemon juice, rind, and sugar to the blueberries. Place in a heavy non–reactive saucepan and bring to a boil. Boil for 2 minutes. Reduce the heat to simmer and cook until thick, 30 to 45 minutes. Skim any froth and stir for 5 minutes. Let cool to room temperature. The jam can be kept in a nonreactive container.

APPLESAUCE

AT ARROWS WE HAVE MANY APPLE TREES AROUND OUR GARDEN AND WE'RE FRE-
quently asked what kind of apples they are. We have to admit that we just don't know, but we do know they are delicious. Use a variety of apples, mixing tart with sweet. Old-fashioned apples might shock you a bit because the flavors are so different and they also vary wildly from what you usually get at the store. This sauce is perfect with our ham dishes and the Grilled Venison with Huckleberry Sauce (page 146).

YIELD: 6 SERVINGS

3 pounds apples, peeled, cored and cut into quarters
1 tablespoon lemon juice
$^{1}/_{4}$ cup sugar
$^{1}/_{2}$ cup water
1 tablespoon dark rum (optional)

Place the apples, lemon juice, sugar, and water in a nonreactive saucepan. Cover and cook over medium-low heat until the apples are completely soft and falling apart. Remove from the heat and cool until just warm to the touch. Add the rum if using. Place the apple mixture in a food processor or food mill and process until smooth. The applesauce can be kept in a sealed container in the refrigerator for three days.

PEAR CHUTNEY

EVEN THE NAME "CHUTNEY" SOUNDS EXOTIC AND DIFFICULT TO MAKE BUT IN
reality chutneys are quite easy. Many of the famous Indian chutneys are cooked for a very long period of time until they reach a marmalade consistency, but we like to cook ours for shorter periods, which results in a lighter, fresher tasting chutney. Although it may have originated in India and Indonesian cooking, chutney found its way to Maine. No doubt many a ship's captain became hooked on these delicious creations.

YIELD: 6 SERVINGS

1 teaspoon unsalted butter
2 tablespoons peeled and chopped ginger
2 cups peeled and diced pears
$^1/_4$ cup firmly packed brown sugar
$^1/_4$ cup rice wine vinegar
1 serrano chili, whole
1 tablespoon finely chopped mint

Melt the butter in a heavy nonreactive saucepan and sauté the ginger until soft, about 1 minute. Add the remaining ingredients and cook, stirring occasionally, until the pears are tender, about 20 minutes. Let the chutney cool to room temperature and remove the chili. The chutney can be kept in a sealed container for three days.

GREEN BELL PEPPER RELISH

AT ARROWS NONE OF US USED TO LIKE GREEN PEPPERS, AND WHEN FACED WITH *the oncoming early frost, which would rob us of the more mature peppers, eventually red and yellow ones, we gathered the still-green peppers and made a relish. It cured us of our green bell pepper aversion. We serve it with our Grilled Oysters (page 26) and at cooking demos and competitions it's a huge hit. We bring back very few dishes on the Arrows menu, but this one frequently returns. Just put it on crackers or grilled bread if you don't like oysters.*

YIELD: 6 SERVINGS

4 large green bell peppers

1 cup sherry vinegar

$1/2$ cup firmly packed brown sugar

$1/2$ cup peeled and finely chopped shallots

$1/4$ teaspoon red pepper chili flakes

1 teaspoon chopped fresh thyme

$1/2$ teaspoon kosher salt

Grill the peppers over a stove burner or on your outdoor grill until lightly charred on the outside. Place them in a bowl and cover tightly with plastic wrap to steam for about 10 minutes. Uncover the bowl and remove the pepper stems and skins, reserving the pepper juice. In a large nonreactive saucepan, heat the sherry vinegar and brown sugar. Reduce the liquid until it forms a heavy syrup, about 10 minutes. Add the shallot, chili flakes, thyme, and salt into the syrup and combine. Add the reserved juice to the syrup. Chop the peppers and add them to the liquid. Cook for 5 minutes. Turn off the heat and chill. The relish can be kept in a sealed container for up to three days.

GREEN TOMATO PICKLES

ANY GARDENER—PROFESSIONAL OR AMATEUR ALIKE— KNOWS THERE'S ALWAYS *a crop that has produced more than you can use. That's when canning and preserving comes in handy. In Maine, tomatoes come in at the end of the warm season, and they might not get a chance to mature before the first frost. When nature gives you tomatoes, pickling is one thing you can do to keep the summer "crisp" throughout the winter. Serve with anything you usually enjoy with your cucumber pickles.*

YIELD: 6 SERVINGS

$^3/_4$ cup Champagne vinegar

4 bay leaves

5 whole cloves

$^1/_8$ cup peeled and sliced horseradish root

$^1/_4$ teaspoon freshly ground black pepper

1 teaspoon kosher salt

$^1/_2$ cup sugar

$^1/_4$ cup water

3 green tomatoes, sliced

Heat all of the ingredients except for the tomatoes in a nonreactive saucepan. Boil the mixture and then pour over the tomatoes in a shallow pan. Let cool to room temperature. The pickles can be kept in a sealed container for up to three days.

DILLY BEANS

FORGET CHIPS, THIS IS MAINE'S FAVORITE SNACK AND IT'S MUCH HEALTHIER FOR *you. Munch on them the same way you would potato chips, even with onion dip. In this case, we're not reinventing the wheel, just adding some improvements to a true Maine classic.*

YIELD: 6 SERVINGS

1 cup white vinegar
2 teaspoons sugar
1 teaspoon kosher salt
1 pound green beans, trimmed
3 tablespoons fresh dill

Boil the vinegar, sugar, and salt in a nonreactive heavy saucepan. Add the green beans and dill and cook until the beans are just tender, about 4 minutes. The beans can be stored in a sealed container in the refrigerator for up to three days.

HARVARD BEETS

ALTHOUGH EVERYONE KNOWS THE BEST COLLEGES—COLBY AND BOWDOIN— *are in Maine, a short drive south is one of New England's better colleges, Harvard, where these beets allegedly originated.*

YIELD: 6 SERVINGS

12 beets, washed
$^1/_2$ cup sugar
$^1/_2$ teaspoon cornstarch
$^1/_2$ cup white vinegar

Cook the beets in boiling salted water in a saucepan until soft, about 15 minutes. Remove the skins and cut into thin slices. Mix the sugar and cornstarch in a nonreactive saucepan. Add the vinegar and boil slowly for 5 minutes. Remove from the heat. Add the beets and let sit at room temperature for 30 minutes. The beets can be stored in a sealed container for up to three days.

Chapter Nine

THE BASICS AND THE PANTRY

WE'RE HERE TO TELL YOU THAT YOU DO NOT NEED MUCH IN YOUR KITCHEN TO make great meals. As you read this book, you'll notice that we use just a few kinds of pots and pans, a blender or food processor, some sharp knives, and beyond that, not much else in the way of bells and whistles. Okay, sometimes we'll use a bell to get guests to come to the dinner table. We recommend stocking the pantry with just these basics in food and equipment.

EQUIPMENT

BAKING DISHES. There are number of baking dish sizes. The 13 x 9-inch is most versatile, but it would be good to have a smaller one on hand too, such as an 8 x 8-inch square dish.

BOX GRATER. You need a good box grater with multiple blades.

CUTTING BOARDS. A big wooden cutting board that won't slip on your counter is great. Having two is helpful: one for cutting meat and one for vegetables.

GRINDER. A pepper grinder or coffee grinder comes in handy. Keep in mind you will need separate grinders for herbs and coffee.

KITCHEN TOWELS. A few of these on hand come in great for grabbing hot things—you don't even need oven mitts. Just don't use your decorated towels for grabbing a messy skillet.

KNIVES. A few good knives are essential. Get a paring knife, a chef's knife, and a knife sharpener.

LADLES. Having a selection of ladles is good in case one gets dirty.

MANDOLIN. A simple flat mandolin slicer. The plastic ones available at Asian markets work just as well as the expensive ones.

MIXING SPOONS. A selection of wooden and metal spoons is important.

SAUCEPANS. It is important to have a few saucepans. They come in various sizes. You'll need a small, medium, and large one. Look for ones with heavy bottoms.

SAUTÉ PANS. Three sizes of sauté pans and two nonstick pans are needed.

SPATULA. A high-heat rubber spatula is best.

STOCK POT. A 10- to 12-quart pot is necessary for pasta, popcorn, soups, and stocks.

PIE DISHES. It is good to have a 9- and 10-inch pie dish as recipes vary.

VEGETABLE PEELER. You don't need to spend a lot of money on this. Buy the cheapest plastic vegetable peeler you can find.

WHISK. At least one whisk is needed in the kitchen.

APPLIANCES

EVERYONE HAS A SHELF OR CABINET FILLED WITH APPLIANCES THEY don't need. Remember that juicer Aunt Mim gave you that left no space on the counter? Just get a hand juicer and throw it in a drawer. If you must have something to plug in, here are our recommendations.

Think about how versatile each individual appliance is. Can you only use it for one thing? Can you make your pancakes on a griddle or do you really need that electric skillet? A food processor and a blender are both handy. If you're going to do a lot of baking, you might invest in a big mixer for bread-making and pasta-making with all the attachments. It will make your life a lot easier. A toaster oven is awfully handy as well, and microwaves are great for defrosting and reheating coffee but other than that, we really don't like to cook with them.

IN THE PANTRY

NOW, FOR PANTRY ITEMS, THESE ARE THE ITEMS TO ALWAYS HAVE ON HAND: Chicken stock, flour, sugar, canola oil, vinegars of various types (see opposite page), pasta in various shapes, canned tomatoes, olive oil, garlic, kosher salt, beans, rice, panko breadcrumbs, chiles, and black peppercorns. We also like to have Sriracha chili sauce. It's good to have lemons on hand to add brightness to your dishes, aïoli, mayonnaise, and a few mustards, but at least Dijon and whole grain.

Versatile Vinegar

WE LIKE TO USE MANY DIFFERENT KINDS OF VINEGARS FOR VARIOUS purposes. All add balance and brightness to a dish and bring out flavors.

BALSAMIC VINEGAR has been all the rage in the U.S. for many years now. Originally from Modena, the heartland of great Italian cooking, true balsamic is passed down through generations as a dowry. A few drops can change the flavor of a recipe. Most are commercially made, and although full flavored, won't have that intense smoothness. Use for red meats, lamb, and bitter lettuces like radicchio.

BASIC DISTILLED WHITE VINEGAR is terrific for marinating vegetables, canning, pickling, and brining volume foods.

BERRY VINEGARS, such as raspberry and blueberry, are good for summer salads, prosciutto, and anything you are using fruit in like pears with roasted meats or oranges with bitter greens. The fruit balances bitterness.

CHAMPAGNE VINEGAR is the king of white wine vinegars. It's light and elegant just like a good glass of Champagne without the bubbles. It's perfect for lighter greens like butterhead lettuce and in cooking when you want the flavor of vinegar without the intrusion of stronger flavors.

CIDER VINEGAR goes with apple dishes, roasted fruit, pears, citrus salads, and pickling.

HERB VINEGAR is great if you have lots of extra herbs and you want to use them up before they go bad. Throw them in some white vinegar. It's the first step in a tasty vinaigrette.

MALT VINEGAR is great in Chinese cooking because it's very robust. Use it with fried food and with Chinese and northern Asian cooking.

RED WINE VINEGAR is intense and strong flavored for use in marinades, with meats, and with more intensely flavored vegetables.

RICE WINE VINEGAR is light and sweet, appropriate for Japanese and Southeast Asian cooking. Its sweetness makes it great for vegetables, salads, dipping sauces with herbs, and anything you want a sweet flavor for.

SHERRY VINEGAR has a rich, smooth, elegant, full-bodied flavor and is great for more intensely flavored salad greens like frisee and Belgian endive. It's also a good choice for Asian cooking.

WHITE WINE VINEGAR is great for basic cooking. Use better quality wine vinegar and you'll get better flavor. It's just like choosing a wine, you get less harsh flavors if you pay more.

Oils

FOR COOKING, USE CANOLA OIL. YOU CAN GET IT REALLY HOT AND IT'S GOT A clean, light flavor. We always say there are no olive trees in Asia so why cook with it when making Asian cuisine? The same is true in Maine.

Nut oils like hazelnut are a great accompaniment to bitter greens like Belgian endive and field greens but also with fowl as an added flavor. You can't sauté with it because it has a low burn point but you can get fancy nut oils like pumpkin oil, pistachio, and really any nut or seed you like the flavor of. Make it yourself with canola or olive oil and infuse the nut flavor by simmering the nut in the oil over low heat. Add caraway, pink peppercorns, and herbs and make marinades or oils for grilling.

We like the intensity of extra virgin olive oil and drizzle it on sliced prosciutto and risotto. Extra virgin has an intense olive flavor since it's the first press of olives and has an emerald green look to it, but sometimes you want to cut that with regular olive oil, which will still give you a robust flavor without overwhelming your dish.

We steer way from "deadly" oils like palm and cottonseed oils, coconut, and peanut oils because many are allergic to them and studies show that they lead to heart disease and high cholesterol.

RESOURCES and INFORMATION

CONTACT INFORMATION FOR BUSINESSES AND ORGANIZATIONS MENTIONED IN this cookbook or for more information.

Our Restaurants

ARROWS RESTAURANT
Berwick Road
Box 803
Ogunquit, ME 03907
(207) 361-1100

MC PERKINS COVE
11 Perkins Cove Road
Ogunquit, ME 03907
(207) 646-MCME (6263)

SUMMER WINTER
Marriott Hotel
1 Mall Road
Burlington, MA 01803
(781) 221-6643
**www.markandclark
restaurants.com**

The Shore

**PEMAQUID OYSTER
COMPANY**
Christopher V. Davis, Ph.D.
1957 Friendship Road
P.O. Box 302
Waldoboro, ME 04572
(207) 832-6067

**GLIDDEN POINT OYSTER
COMPANY**
707 River Road
Edgecomb, ME 04556
(207) 633-3599
www.oysterfarm.com

**SPINNEY CREEK
SHELLFISH, INC.**
27 Howell Drive
P.O. Box 310
Eliot, ME 03903
(207) 439-2719
www.spinneycreek.com

PEARL OYSTER BAR
18 Cornelia Street
New York, NY 10014-4138
(212) 691-8211
www.pearloysterbar.com

**MAINE AQUACULTURE
AND INNOVATION
CENTER**
5717 Corbett Hall,
Room 436
Orono, ME 04469-5717
(207) 581-2263
www.maineaquaculture.org

The Sea

**BROWNE TRADING
COMPANY**
Merrill's Whark
260 Commercial Street
Portland, ME 04101
1-800-944-7848
www.brownetrading.com

MONTERERY BAY
AQUARIUM
FOUNDATION

886 Cannery Row
Monterey, CA 93940
(831) 648-4800
www.montereybay

aquarium.org

MAINE LOBSTERMEN'S
ASSOCIATION

21 Western Ave., Suite 1
Kennebunk, ME 04043
(207) 967-4555
www.mainelobstermen.org

LOBSTER INSTITUTE

210 Rogers Hall,
University of Maine
Orono, ME 04469-5763
www.lobster.um.maine.edu

MAINE LOBSTER
COUNCIL

45 Memorial Circle,
Suite 102
Augusta, ME 04330
(207) 287-5140
www.lobsterfrommaine.com

MAINE SEA SALT
COMPANY

11 Church Lane
Marshfield, ME 04654
(207) 255-3310
www.maineseasalt.com

The Forest

To find more information
about Maine mushrooms
visit
www.mushroomcollecting.com

WILD BLUEBERRY
COMMISSION OF MAINE

University of Maine
5784 York Complex,
Suite 52
Orono, ME 04469-5784
(207) 581-1475
www.wildblueberries
.maine.edu

The Farm

BREEZY HILL FARM

69 Bennett Lot Road
S. Berwick, ME 03908
(207) 384-2937

GET REAL MAINE

28 State House Station
Augusta, ME
04333-0028
(207) 287-3491
www.getrealmaine.com

The Garden

MAINE ORGANIC
FARMERS AND GAR-
DENER ASSOCIATION

294 Crosby Brook Rd
Unity, ME 04988
(207) 568-4142
www.mofga.org

GOLDEN HARVEST
PRODUCE MARKET

47 State Road
Kittery, ME 03904-1566
(207) 439-2113

CROWN OF MAINE
ORGANIC COOPERATIVE

www.crownofmainecoop.com

MAINE SEAWEED
COMPANY

P.O. Box 57
Steuben, ME 04680
(207) 546-2875
www.alcasoft.com/
seaweed/index.html

The Dairy

MAINE CHEESE GUILD

www.mainecheeseguild.org

KATE'S HOMEMADE BUTTER

P.O. Box 79
Old Orchard Beach, ME 04064
(207) 934-5134
www.kateshomemadebutter.com

SMILING HILL FARM (HOME OF SILVERY MOON CHEESE)

781 County Road
Westbrook, ME 04092
(207) 775-4818
www.smilinghill.com
www.silverymooncheese.com

SEAL COVE FARM

202 Partridge Cove Road
Lamoine, ME 04605
(207) 667-7127
www.mainegoatcheese.com

GIFFORD'S ICE CREAM

25 Hathaway Street
Skowhegan, ME 04976
1-800-950-2604
(207) 474-6120
www.giffordsicecream.com

The Bakery

STANDARD BAKING COMPANY

75 Commercial St.
Portland, ME 04101
(207) 773-2112

THE BAKERY AT NOTRE DAME

7 George Road
Alfred, Maine 04002
(207) 324-8811

WHEN PIGS FLY BAKERY

447 U.S. 1
Kittery, ME 03904-5513
(207) 439-3114
www.sendbread.com

BEACH PEA BAKING COMPANY

53 State Road
Kittery, ME 03904-1772
(207) 439-3555
www.beachpeabaking.com

The Root Cellar

COLD RIVER VODKA

Maine Distilleries, LLC
437 US Route One
Freeport, ME 04032
(207) 865-4828
www.coldrivervodka.com

INDEX